THE
KING
IS
COMING

H. L. WILLMINGTON

Tyndale House
Publishers, Inc.
Wheaton, Illinois

This revised and expanded version is dedicated to five
of my most faithful associates here at Thomas Road:

Ken Chapman
Lindsay Howan
Jerry Edwards
Roy Newman
Rick Lawrenson

Cover photo copyright © 1991 S. Feld/H. Armstrong Roberts

Library of Congress Catalog Card Number 91-65355
ISBN 0-8423-2078-4, paper
Copyright © 1973, 1981, 1991 by
Tyndale House Publishers, Inc., Wheaton, Illinois
Printed in the United States of America

97 96 95 94 93 92 91
 7   6   5   4   3   2   1

CONTENTS

FOREWORD

Harold Willmington, outstanding Bible teacher, is greatly loved by the students of Lynchburg Baptist College and the Thomas Road Bible Institute, of which he is the dean. I, too, have benefited much from his written and spoken ministry of God's Word, and many of my radio programs are supported by information compiled at my request by this capable and devoted scholar.

If Mr. Willmington has one talent which stands out above the many others, it is his remarkable ability to take profound truths from Scripture and simplify them so that every listener fully understands. This textbook is a prime example of this ability, for here we have a succinct yet detailed summary of what the Bible teaches about the events of "the last days"— what the Word of God calls the blessed hope of the return of the Lord Jesus Christ.

The doctrinal position of this book is that the rapture of the Church will be premillenial and pretribulational. No doctrine in the Word provides a greater incentive for witnessing and soul-winning than that of the imminent return of Christ, as it is outlined in *The King Is Coming*. May we who "love his appearing" be inspired and stimulated to wait, watch, and work as never before.

Jerry Falwell, *Pastor*
Thomas Road Baptist Church

ONE
THE RAPTURE OF THE CHURCH

THE MEANING OF THE RAPTURE

The next great event in prophecy is often referred to as the rapture. Some time ago I received a letter from a very upset viewer of the "Old Time Gospel Hour" TV program. In essence, the letter read:

"You people down there in Virginia bother me. Your choir sings songs about an event called the rapture. The TV preacher preaches sermons on the rapture. And you—you've actually written a book on the rapture. Now my concern is this: You folks are singing, preaching, and writing about a word that's not even found in the Bible!"

In answering this letter I agreed that he was indeed correct, inasmuch as the word rapture is nowhere to be found among the 774,747 words in the King James Version of the Bible. But I then pointed out that neither are the words Trinity, demon, Bible, or grandfather mentioned in that version of the Word of God. But there is a Trinity, there are demons, grandfathers do exist, and the rapture is a reality!

Actually, the word rapture is from *rapere*, found in the expression "caught up" in the Latin translation of 1 Thessalonians 4:17. However, if one so desires, the rapture could be scripturally referred to as the *harpazo*, which is the Greek word translated "caught up" in 1 Thessalonians 4:17. The identical phrase is found in Acts 8:39, where Philip was caught away by the Holy Spirit, and in 2 Corinthians 12:2, 4, when Paul was caught up into the third heaven. Or, if you'd rather, the rapture could be known as the *allasso*, from the Greek translated "changed" in 1 Corinthians 15:51, 52. *Allasso* is also used in describing the final renewal and transformation of the heavens and the earth. (See Heb. 1:12.) So then, use whatever name suits your fancy. Of course, the important thing is not what you name it, but rather, can you *claim it*? That is, will you participate in it?

Thus, the next scheduled event predicted in the Word of God will take place when the Savior himself appears in the air to catch up his own!

AN ILLUSTRATION OF THE RAPTURE

Let us consider an illustration of the *harpazo-allasso* or rapture: A man is cleaning out his garage and discovers a small box filled with a mixture of tiny iron nails, wooden splinters, sawdust, and pieces of paper. Suppose he desires to save the nails. How could he quickly separate them from the wooden splinters? If a magnet was available, the task would be quite simple. He would simply position the magnet over the box. Immediately all those objects possessing the same physical nature would be caught up to meet the magnet in the air.

If his wife were watching all this, spotting a particular object in the box, she might say: "Look at the sharp point on that! I bet the magnet will zap that up!" But unknown to her, that tiny item might be a sharp sliver of wood which would not be taken up. Or, she might conclude: "That fragment over there is a piece of wood for sure." However, in reality it could be a "backslidden" nail with some rust on it. But in both cases the magnet would quickly and accurately discern the character of the piece and act accordingly.

When Christ appears, he will *not* come especially for black or white people, for Catholics or Protestants, for Jews or Gentiles, but *only* for those individuals who possess the same nature as himself. One of the most thrilling things God does for each repenting sinner is to give him or her the very mind of Christ and a brand new creation! (See 1 Cor. 2:16; 2 Cor. 5:17; Eph. 4:24; 2 Pet. 1:4.)

FIRST MENTION OF THE RAPTURE

The first mention of the rapture in the Bible is found in John 14:1–3.

Let not your heart be troubled: ye believe in God, believe also in me. In my Father's house are many mansions: if it were not so, I would have told you. I go to prepare a place for you. And if I go and prepare a place for you, I will come again, and receive you unto myself; that where I am, there ye may be also.

While the Old Testament prophets spoke in glowing terms of the Messiah's eventual return to earth and the establishment of his perfect kingdom upon the earth (Isa. 2:2–5; 9:6, 7; 11:1–16; 32:1; 35:1–10; etc.), they knew absolutely nothing of that event whereby God himself would (for a brief period of time) remove his people from *off* the earth. For whom will Jesus come? It is the view of this theological summary that Christ will come again for his church, which is composed of all saved people from Pentecost up to the rapture itself. (Other passages that speak of the rapture are 1 Cor. 1:7; Phil. 3:20; Titus 2:13; Heb. 9:28.)

TWO DESCRIPTIONS OF THE RAPTURE

However, the two most important passages describing the rapture are found in 1 Thessalonians 4 and 1 Corinthians 15. Let us briefly examine these two passages.

A. 1 Thessalonians 4:13–17:

But we do not want you to be uninformed, brethren, about those who are asleep, that you may not grieve, as do the rest who have no hope. For if we believe that Jesus died and rose again, even so God will bring with Him those who have fallen asleep in Jesus. For this we say to you by the word of the Lord, that we who are alive, and remain until the coming of the Lord, shall not precede those who have fallen asleep. For the Lord Himself will descend from heaven with a shout, with the voice of the archangel, and with the trumpet of God; and the dead in Christ shall rise first. Then we who are alive and remain shall be caught up together with them in the clouds to meet the Lord (1 Thess. 4:13–17, NASB).

In this great passage Paul answers a question that had bothered the Thessalonians. When he was among them (Acts 17) they had doubtless learned many precious truths about the glorious return of Christ to earth someday and the establishing of his kingdom. In fact, to some this all seemed to be just around the corner. But since the apostle's departure, a number of believers had died. They obviously then would not be on earth at the time of Christ's return. Did this mean they would miss everything? This then is the background to the great rapture passage before us here in chapter 4. These six verses thus present for us:

1. A realization: "But I would not have you to be ignorant, brethren, concerning them which are asleep, that ye sorrow not, even as others which have no hope" (4:13). This is but one of four key areas that Paul would not have us to be ignorant. The other three are:
   a. The events in the Old Testament (1 Cor. 10:1).
   b. The restoration of Israel (Rom. 11:25).
   c. The manifestation of spiritual gifts (1 Cor. 12:1).
2. A repose: "For if we believe that Jesus died and rose again, even so them also which sleep in Jesus will God bring with him" (4:14). The death of a believer is looked upon as a peaceful sleep. (See Mt. 27:52; Jn. 11:11; Acts 7:60; 13:36; 1 Cor. 15:6; 18, 20, 51; 2 Pet. 3:4.) However, it should be quickly stated that this verse in no way teaches soul sleep. That unscriptural doctrine is refuted by Matthew 17:3 and Revelation 6:9–11.
3. A revelation: "For this we say unto you by the word of the Lord, that we which are alive and remain unto the coming of the Lord shall not prevent [precede] them which are asleep" (4:15). Note Paul's usage of the pronoun "we." The apostle apparently hoped at this time to be here when Christ came. He would later know otherwise. (See 2 Tim. 4:6.)
4. A return: "For the Lord himself shall descend from heaven with a shout, with the voice of the archangel, and with the trump of God" (4:16). It is often supposed that Michael will be this archangel on the basis of Daniel 12:1, 2. However, it is not unreasonable to suggest that Gabriel will be the angel involved at this time because of the vital part he played in those events surrounding the first coming of Christ. (See Lk. 1:19, 26; Mt. 1:20; 2:13.)

Note the little phrase, "With a shout." This is the final of three instances in which Christ shouted. On each occasion a resurrection took place!

a. The shout at Bethany.

And when he thus had spoken, he cried with a loud voice, Lazarus, come forth. And he that was dead came forth, bound hand and foot with graveclothes: and his face was bound about with a napkin. Jesus saith unto them, Loose him, and let him go (Jn. 11:43, 44).

b. The shout at Calvary.

Jesus, when he had cried again with a loud voice, yielded up the ghost. And, behold, the veil of the temple was rent in twain from the top to the bottom; and the earth did quake, and the rocks rent; and the graves were opened; and many bodies of the saints which slept arose, and came out of the graves after his resurrection, and went into the holy city, and appeared unto many (Mt. 27:50–53).

5. A resurrection: ". . . and the dead in Christ shall rise first" (4:16).

6. A rapture: "Then we which are alive and remain shall be caught up together with them in the clouds. . . ."

7. A reunion: ". . . to meet the Lord in the air: and so shall we ever be with the Lord" (4:17).

8. A reassurance: "Wherefore comfort one another with these words" (4:18).

B. 1 Corinthians 15:51–53:

Behold, I shew you a mystery; We shall not all sleep, but we shall all be changed, in a moment, in the twinkling of an eye, at the last trump: for the trumpet shall sound, and the dead shall be raised incorruptible, and we shall be changed. For this corruptible must put on incorruption, and this mortal must put on immortality.

Dr. John Walvoord writes:

"One of the two main passages on the doctrine of the rapture in the New Testament is found in 1 Corinthians 15:51–58. In many respects, this passage complements the other major passage in 1 Thessalonians 4:13–18. In 1 Thessalonians 4, the question was whether those who had died in Christ would have the same benefits and experience as those who were

11

translated. In 1 Corinthians 15, the question is whether those who are translated will have the same experience and benefits as those who have died and who are resurrected."

Observe some phrases from 1 Corinthians 15:51, 53:
1. "I shew you a mystery."
     What is this mystery or secret concerning the rapture? Let us suppose you began reading the Bible in Genesis chapter 1, and read through 1 Corinthians chapter 14. If you stopped your reading there, you would already have learned about many important facts, such as creation, man's sin, the flood, Bethlehem, Calvary, the resurrection, and the existence of heaven and hell.
     But you would be forced to conclude that a Christian could get to heaven only after physically dying. You would of course note the two exceptions of Enoch (Gen. 5:24) and Elijah (2 Ki. 2:11), but apart from these it would be clear that believers have to travel the path of the grave to reach the goal of glory.
     But now the secret is out, and here it is: Millions of Christians will someday reach heaven without dying! "Behold, I show you a mystery; we shall not all sleep, but we shall all be changed" (1 Cor. 15:51). This, then, is the mystery of the rapture!
2. "We shall all be changed . . . in the twinkling of an eye." Does anything have to happen before the rapture can take place and this glorious change be effected? The surprising answer seems to be yes! One final event must transpire and that event is the adding of the last repenting sinner into the body of Christ by the Holy Spirit. Thus, when the body is complete, the Head will appear, or, to use another scriptural analogy, the Bridegroom will come for his beloved bride. The entire book of Ephesians seems to suggest this. See especially 1:10, 22, 23; 2:21; 4:4, 13, 16; 5:22-33.
     A very practical truth may be seen here. According to Acts 2, the first convert was added to the body of Christ at Pentecost. What an occasion that must have been, with 3,000 answering Peter's "altar call." And God had provided 120 "personal workers" to deal with them

(Acts 1:15; 2:1). We know that God himself keeps all records. Perhaps someday at the judgment seat of Christ one of these 120 will hear the Master say: "Well done, thou good and faithful servant. You led the first individual into that spiritual body!" If this be true, and if Christ's coming is at hand, it is entirely possible that a soul-winner reading these very words might one day hear similar words from Jesus: "Well done, thou good and faithful servant. You led the *last* individual into that spiritual body!" At any rate, someday a soul-winner will point some seeking sinner to the Savior and it will all be over!

3. "For the trumpet shall sound."

In at least three biblical passages concerning the rapture a trumpet is mentioned (1 Cor. 15:52; 1 Thess. 4:16; Rev. 4:1). How are we to understand this? Dr. J. Dwight Pentecost writes, "The phrase 'the trump of God' is significant, for in the Old Testament the trumpet was used for two things—to summon to battle and to summon to worship" (*Prophecy for Today*, Zondervan, p. 30).

Which of the two meanings, however, is involved at the rapture? Dr. Pentecost suggests that both meanings are in mind, one directed toward angels and the other to believers.

a. To angels the trumpet blast will mean "Prepare for battle!" According to various New Testament passages (Jn. 14:30; Eph. 6:12; 1 Jn. 5:19) this present world lies in the hands of the evil one, the devil, and the very atmosphere is filled with his wicked power and presence. Satan will obviously resist believers being caught up through his domain and becoming freed from his wicked worldly system. Therefore, the trumpet commands the angels, "Prepare for battle! Clear the way for the catching up of those resurrected bodies and those living believers!"

b. To all believers the trumpet blast will mean "Prepare to worship!" In Numbers 10:1-3 we read, "And the Lord spake unto Moses, saying, Make thee two trumpets of silver . . . that thou mayest use them for the calling of the assembly . . . and when they shall

13

blow with them, all the assembly shall assemble themselves to thee at the door of the tabernacle. . . .'

Regarding the rapture trumpet, Numbers 10:4 seems to be especially significant: "If they blow but with one trumpet, then the princes, which are heads of the thousands of Israel, shall gather themselves unto thee." At the rapture only one trumpet is sounded, suggesting that in God's sight all believers occupy a place of utmost importance! We are all "head princes" in the mind of God.

4. "For this corruptible must put on incorruption, and this mortal must put on immortality."
   a. Corruptible: that supernatural act whereby the bodies of departed believers will be resurrected.
   b. Mortal: that supernatural act whereby the bodies of living believers will be transformed.

SOME FALSE VIEWS OF THE RAPTURE

C. That the rapture and Second Coming are one and the same event. Although these two are inseparably linked together, they are not the same. In essence, the rapture introduces the great tribulation, while the Second Coming will conclude it. Other distinguishing features are:
   1. The rapture.
      a. Christ comes in the air (1 Thess. 4:16, 17).
      b. He comes for his saints (1 Thess. 4:16, 17).
      c. The rapture is a mystery, i.e., a truth unknown in Old Testament times (1 Cor. 15:51).
      d. Christ's coming for his saints is never said to be preceded by signs in the heavens.
      e. The rapture is identified with the day of Christ (1 Cor. 1:8; 2 Cor. 1:14; Phil. 1:6, 10).
      f. The rapture is presented as a time of blessing (1 Thess. 4:18).
      g. The rapture takes place in a moment, in the twinkling of an eye (1 Cor. 15:52). This strongly implies that it will not be witnessed by the world.
      h. The rapture seems to involve the church primarily (Jn.

14:1-4; 1 Cor. 15:51-58; 1 Thess. 4:13-18).
  i. Christ comes as the bright and morning star (Rev. 22:16).
  2. The Second Coming.
    a. He comes to the earth (Zech. 14:4).
    b. He comes with his saints (1 Thess. 3:13; Jude 14).
    c. The revelation is not a mystery; it is the subject of many Old Testament prophecies (Ps. 72; Isa. 11; Zech. 14).
    d. Christ's coming with his saints will be heralded by celestial portents (Mt. 24:29, 30).
    e. The revelation is identified with the day of the Lord (2 Thess. 2:1-12, ASV).
    f. The main emphasis of the revelation is on judgment (2 Thess. 2:8-12).
    g. The revelation will be visible worldwide (Mt. 24:27; Rev. 1:7).
    h. The revelation involves Israel primarily, then also the Gentile nations (Mt. 24:1; 25:46).
    i. Christ comes as the sun of righteousness with healing in his wings (Mal. 4:2).
  D. That the rapture will include only "spiritual" Christians, leaving carnal believers behind to endure a seven-year "Protestant purgatory" of some sort. Maybe this is what God should do, as it would serve most of us right—but it is not what he is going to do! The rapture is, in a sense, the proof of redemption, and both are based on grace and not human works. Dr. John Walvoord writes:

"Most of the scriptural basis for the partial rapture theory is found by its adherents in exhortations to watch or look for the coming of the Lord, coupled with the teaching that some who fail to watch will not be ready when He comes. Passages commonly used include Matthew 14:40-51; 25:13; Mark 13:33-37; Luke 20:34-36; 21:36; Philemon 3:10-12; 1 Thessalonians 5:6; 2 Timothy 4:8; Titus 2:13; Hebrews 9:24-28; Revelation 3:3; 12:1-6. In citing these passages, little distinction is observed between references to Israel and references to the church, and passages referring to the Second

Coming of Christ to establish the millennial kingdom are freely applied to the rapture" (*The Rapture Question,* Zondervan, p. 100).

Thus, the partial rapture theory is to be rejected for the following three reasons.

1. First, it confuses grace with rewards.
2. Second, it divides the bride of Christ. How can the marriage of the Lamb take place if part of the bride is left on earth?
3. Third, it ignores the clear scriptural teaching to the contrary. (See 1 Thess. 1:9, 10; 2:19; 4:14–16; 5:4–11; Rev. 22:12.) Perhaps the most conclusive evidence against the partial rapture theory is 1 Corinthians 15:51. This church was one of the most carnal in the history of Christianity, yet Paul declares in this verse that if the rapture occurred in their day, *all* of the saved in that church would be raptured.

E. That the rapture will not occur until the middle of the tribulation, thus forcing the entire church to go through the first three and a half years of God's wrath. This theory is called mid-tribulationism.

This position agrees to a seven-year tribulation period but distinguishes between the first three and a half years, which (adherents say) may be thought of as the "beginning of sorrows" in Matthew 24:8, as opposed to the "great distress" of 24:21, describing the last three and a half years. The mid-tribulation theory says the rapture will take place in Revelation 11 at the time when the two witnesses are resurrected. A common argument of the mid-trib position is: "It is egotistical for us to believe the church in our day will escape suffering and judgment. Where was the rapture for the multitudes of Chinese believers murdered by the Japanese during World War II, or the Russian Christians slaughtered by the godless Communists?" The shallowness of this argument should be immediately evident, for it confuses satanic wrath with divine wrath. Nowhere are we promised we will escape suffering or even martyrdom. But we are assured we will escape divine wrath, for this is the very essence of the great tribulation, when God will punish the world. (Compare Isa. 24:1; 63:3-6; Rev. 6:17 with 1 Thess. 1:20; 5:9.)

The New Testament pictures the church as the body and bride of Christ. If the mid-tribulation or post-tribulation view were correct, then a part of his body would suffer amputation, and a section of the bride would be left behind!
In addition to this, one would be forced to conclude that all bodies of carnal departed Christians would likewise be left in the grave. This simply is not the clear teaching of the Word of God.

The Bible teaches clearly that the rapture is pre-tribulational in nature and includes all believers. See 1 Thessalonians 1:10 and Romans 5:9. Perhaps the strongest proof of this statement is the fact that up to chapter 6 of Revelation the church is mentioned many times, but from chapter 6 to chapter 19 (the period of the tribulation) there is no mention whatsoever of the church on earth. In fact, the only godly group which Satan can find to persecute is the nation Israel. (See Rev. 12.)

In Revelation 4:1 John declares, "After this I looked, and, behold, a door was opened in heaven: and the first voice which I heard was as it were of a trumpet talking with me; which said, Come up hither. . . ." We are told that Christians are God's ambassadors on earth (2 Cor. 5:20) and that he will someday declare war on this earth. The first thing a king or president does after he declares war on another country is to call his ambassadors home. Thus we conclude that the church will escape the tribulation. In addition to this there are two serious problems connected with the mid-tribulation position.

First, it destroys the imminence of Christ's return, for, according to their view the Savior could not possibly come until at least three and a half years after the time of this writing.

Second, it creates a date-setting chronology, for if it is known when the tribulation begins (usually thought to occur when the antichrist makes his seven-year covenant with Israel) and if Christ appears during the middle of the seven years, then one can know the dates of both the rapture and Second Coming. But Jesus said this information would not be

17

revealed. (See Mt. 24:36.) Thus, it is best to conclude that the rapture will occur *prior* to the seven-year tribulation. Dr. John Walvoord has listed fifty arguments for this position. Some of these are as follows:

1. Pre-tribulationism is the only view that allows literal interpretation of all Old and New Testament passages on the great tribulation.

2. Pre-tribulationism distinguishes clearly between Israel and the church and their respective programs.

3. The great tribulation is properly interpreted by pre-tribulationists as a time of preparation for Israel's restoration (Deut. 4:29, 30; Jer. 30:4-11). It is not the purpose of the tribulation to prepare the church for glory.

4. None of the Old Testament passages on the tribulation mention the church (Deut. 4:29, 30; Jer. 30:4-11; Dan. 8:24-27; 12:1, 2).

5. None of the New Testament passages on the tribulation mention the church (Mt. 13:30, 39-42, 48-50; 24:15-31; 1 Thess. 1:9, 10; 5:4-9; 2 Thess. 2:1-11; Rev. 4-18).

6. In contrast to mid-tribulationism, the pre-tribulational view provides an adequate explanation for the beginning of the great tribulation in Revelation 6. Mid-tribulationism is refuted by the plain teaching of Scripture that the great tribulation begins long before the seventh trumpet of Revelation 11.

7. The proper distinction is maintained between the prophetic trumpets of Scripture by pre-tribulationism. There is no proper ground for the pivotal argument of mid-tribulationism that the seventh trumpet of Revelation is the last trumpet in that there is no established connection between the seventh trumpet of Revelation 11, the last trumpet of 1 Corinthians 15:52, and the trumpet of Matthew 24:31. They are three distinct events.

8. The unity of Daniel's seventieth week is maintained by pre-tribulationists. By contrast, post-tribulationists and mid-tribulationists destroy the unity of Daniel's seventieth

week and confuse Israel's program with that of the church.

9. The translation of the church is never mentioned in any passage dealing with the Second Coming of Christ after the tribulation.

10. The church is not appointed to wrath (Rom. 4:9; 1 Thess. 1:9, 10; 5:9). The church therefore cannot enter "the great day of their wrath" (Rev. 6:17).

11. The church will not be overtaken by the day of the Lord (1 Thess. 5:1-9), which includes the tribulation.

12. It is characteristic of divine dealing to deliver believers before a divine judgment is inflicted on the world as illustrated in the deliverance of Lot, etc. (2 Pet. 2:5-9).

13. At the time of the translation of the church, all believers go to the Father's house in heaven (Jn. 14:3) and do not immediately return to the earth after meeting Christ in the air as post-tribulationists teach.

14. Pre-tribulationism does not divide the body of Christ at the rapture on a works principle. The teaching of a partial rapture is based on the false doctrine that the translation of the church is a reward for good works. It is rather a climactic aspect of salvation by grace.

15. The Scriptures clearly teach that all, not part, of the church will be raptured at the coming of Christ for the church (1 Cor. 15:51, 52; 1 Thess. 4:17).

16. As opposed to the view of a partial rapture, pre-tribulationism is founded on the definite teaching of Scripture that the death of Christ frees from all condemnation.

17. Those of the godly remnant of the tribulation are pictured as Israelites, not members of the church, as maintained by the post-tribulationists.

18. The pre-tribulational interpretation teaches that the coming of Christ is actually imminent.

19. The exhortation to be comforted by the coming of the Lord (1 Thess. 4:18) is very significant in the pre-tribulational view and is especially contradicted by most post-tribulationists.

20. The exhortation to look for "the glorious appearing" of

Christ to his own (Titus 2:13) loses its significance if the tribulation must intervene first. Believers in that case should look for signs.

21. The Holy Spirit as the restrainer must be taken out of the world before "the lawless one," who dominates the tribulation period, can be revealed (2 Thess. 2:6-8).

22. According to 2 Corinthians 5:10, all believers of this age must appear before the judgment seat of Christ in heaven, an event never mentioned in the detailed accounts connected with the Second Coming of Christ to the earth.

23. The coming of Christ for his bride must take place before the Second Coming to the earth for the wedding feast (Rev. 19:7-10).

24. Tribulation saints are not translated at the Second Coming of Christ but carry on ordinary occupations such as farming and building houses, and they will bear children (Isa. 65:20-25). This would be impossible if all saints were translated at the Second Coming to the earth, as post-tribulationists teach (from *The Rapture Question*, Zondervan, 1978, pp. 270-274).

THE CHALLENGES OF THE RAPTURE

F. Because of this glorious coming event the child of God is instructed to do many things.

   1. He is to attend the services of the Lord regularly.
    . . . not forsaking the assembling of ourselves together, as the manner of some is; but exhorting one another; and so much the more, as ye see the day approaching (Heb. 10:25).

   2. He is to observe the Lord's Supper with the rapture in mind.
    For as often as ye eat this bread, and drink this cup, ye do show the Lord's death till he come (1 Cor. 11:26).

   3. He is to love believers and all men.
    And the Lord make you to increase and abound in love one toward another, and toward all men . . . to the end he may stablish your hearts . . . at the coming of our Lord Jesus Christ with all his saints (1 Thess. 3:12, 13).

4. He is to be patient.
   Be ye also patient; stablish your hearts; for the coming of the Lord draweth nigh (Jas. 5:8).
5. He is to live a separated life.
   ... we know that, when he shall appear, we shall be like him, for we shall see him as he is. And every man that hath this hope in him purifieth himself ... (1 Jn. 3:2, 3).

   ... denying ungodliness and worldly lusts, we should live soberly, righteously, and godly, in this present world; looking for that blessed hope, and the glorious appearing of the great God and our Saviour Jesus Christ (Titus 2:12, 13).

   And now, little children, abide in him, that, when he shall appear, we may have confidence, and not be ashamed before him at his coming (1 Jn. 2:28).
6. He is to refrain from judging others.
   Therefore judge nothing before the time, until the Lord come, who both will bring to light the hidden things of darkness, and will make manifest the counsels of the hearts: and then shall every man have praise of God (1 Cor. 4:5).
7. He is to preach the Word.
   I charge thee therefore before God, and the Lord Jesus Christ, who shall judge the quick and the dead at his appearing and his kingdom; preach the word ... (2 Tim. 4:1, 2).

   Feed the flock of God ... and when the chief Shepherd shall appear, ye shall receive a crown of glory that fadeth not away (1 Pet. 5:2, 4).
8. He is to comfort the bereaved.
   For the Lord himself shall descend from heaven ... wherefore comfort one another with these words (1 Thess. 4:16, 18).
9. He is to win souls.
   Keep yourselves in the love of God, looking for the mercy of our Lord Jesus Christ unto eternal life. And of some have compassion, making a difference: and others save with fear, pulling them out of the fire ... (Jude 21-23).
10. He is to be concerned with heaven.
    If ye then be risen with Christ, seek those things which are above, where Christ sitteth on the right hand of God. Set your affection on things above, not on things on the earth. For ye

21

are dead, and your life is hid with Christ in God. When Christ, who is our life, shall appear, then shall ye also appear with him in glory (Col. 3:1-4).

THE EFFECTS OF THE RAPTURE

What will be the reaction of a sin-sick society when millions of people suddenly disappear? In his well-known book *The Late Great Planet Earth*, Hal Lindsey suggests several possible conversations shortly after the rapture:

"There I was, driving down the freeway and all of a sudden the place went crazy . . . cars going in all directions . . . and not one of them had a driver. I mean it was wild! I think we've got an invasion from outer space!

It was the last quarter of the championship game and the other side was ahead. Our boys had the ball. We made a touchdown and tied it up. The crowd went crazy. Only one minute to go and they fumbled—our quarterback recovered—he was about a yard from the goal when—zap—no more quarterback—completely gone, just like that!

It was puzzling—very puzzling. I was teaching my course in the Philosophy of Religion when all of a sudden three of my students vanished. They simply vanished! They were quite argumentative—always trying to prove their point from the Bible. No great loss to the class. However, I do find this disappearance very difficult to explain."

Certainly the believers will be missed. It is evident from the Bible that the sudden disappearance of both Enoch and Elijah (two Old Testament types of the rapture) caused considerable confusion and alarm among their friends.
By faith Enoch was translated that he should not see death; and was not found, because God had translated him (Heb. 11:5).
Especially interesting are the words, "and was not found." Enoch was doubtless the object of a great manhunt!
The Scriptures describe the later translation of Elijah in even greater detail, as the citizens of Jericho ask Elisha about the disappearance of his master:

"Sir," they said, "just say the word and fifty of our best athletes will search the wilderness for your master; perhaps the Spirit of the Lord has left him on some mountain or in some ravine." "No," Elisha said, "don't bother." But they kept urging until he was embarrassed, and finally said, "All right, go ahead." Then fifty men searched for three days, but didn't find him (2 Ki. 2:16, 17, TLB).

How much more confusion and alarm will come from the sudden and mysterious disappearance of literally millions of men and women, boys and girls.

THE OLD TESTAMENT
FORESHADOWING OF THE RAPTURE

Seen in Enoch, who was taken from the world before the flood judgment (Gen. 5:24).

Seen in Lot, who was taken from Sodom before the fire judgment (Gen. 19:22–24).

In closing this section on the rapture, consider the words of German theologian Erich Sauer:

"The present age is Easter time. It begins with the resurrection of the Redeemer (Mt. 28), and ends with the resurrection of the redeemed (1 Thess. 4; 1 Cor. 15). Between lies the spiritual 'resurrection' of those called into life (Rom. 6:4–11; Col. 3:1). So we live between two Easters, as those who have been raised between two resurrections, as burning and shining lights. . . . And in the power of the First Easter we go to meet the Last Easter. The resurrection of the Head guarantees the resurrection of the members. The tree of life of the resurrection bears fully ripe fruit" (*The Triumph of the Crucified*, Eerdmans, 1955, p. 101).

There we have it, that wonderful coming event, the *harpazo-allasso* rapture! As has been previously noted, there are 774,747 words in the Bible. The greatest single word among these is the word *maranatha*, used but once in Scripture (1 Cor. 16:22). It literally means, "the Lord cometh." Keep this in mind as a World War II event is related.

The place is Nuremberg, Germany, where a gigantic Nazi

victory rally is being conducted. Nearly a quarter of a million party faithfuls have assembled to hear their great Fuhrer speak. The time is June, 1940.

German troops had defeated France only the week before, meaning that practically all of Europe lay at the feet of Hitler. The only feeble pocket of resistance was located on a tiny island, separated by a few miles of North Atlantic water from Hitler's mighty empire. At that time the entire world was absolutely certain that Great Britain (occupying that little island) would soon be invaded. The only question was when. This was the background as the German dictator approached the microphone.

He began: "I hear the British are asking, 'When is he coming, when is he coming?' Well, tonight I say to the British, be patient, for I AM COMING!"

Hitler screamed out the final phrase, "I am coming," no less than three times that warm June evening in Germany. According to witnesses, when he said it the first time there arose a growl from the throats of 250,000 people. The second time turned that growl into a mighty roar. But the results of the third time were as if a bomb had exploded, causing those thousands of Nazis to leap to their feet and scream out until many actually lost their voices: "SIEG HEIL, SIEG HEIL, SIEG HEIL!"

Nearly 2,000 years ago, Christ ascended to heaven (Acts 1). Since that time (apart from a few Bible apostles), no one has seen or heard from him. The sceptics and infidels sneeringly remind us of this, demanding to know, "When is he coming? When is he coming? He'll never come!" (See 2 Pet. 3:3, 4.) But if the believer listens carefully, he can hear that still, small voice witnessing to his heart, "I say to you, my child, be patient, for I AM COMING!"

When this great, and grand, and glorious truth becomes a reality to us, there should proceed from our spiritual throats a growl, then a roar, and finally that exhilaration causing us to jump to our feet and shout for all the world to hear: "MARANATHA! MARANATHA! MARANATHA!"

TWO
THE BEMA
JUDGMENT
SEAT OF CHRIST

As a boy I had a totally erroneous view concerning the subject of judgment. In my mind I pictured a celestial courtroom located somewhere beyond the stars where all the world's inhabitants would line up single file in front of a towering throne. An angel would then appear with a set of balancing scales. Each name would be solemnly called out: "John Jones, Chicago, Illinois, born 1910, died, 1970, step forward!"

As Jones stood there, all his recorded good works would be placed on one side of the scales and his bad deeds on the opposite side. If the good works outweighed the bad, then a much-relieved Jones would enter a door marked heaven; but if the reverse were true, poor Jones was designated to the door marked hell.

Of course nothing could be further from the truth. In reality, there are a number of biblical judgments, some already past, some going on at the present time, and others yet to occur.

A. Biblical judgments.
    1. Past judgments:
        a. The Garden of Eden judgment (Gen. 3:14–19; Rom. 5:12; 1 Cor. 15:22).
        b. The flood judgment (Gen. 6:5–7; 2 Pet. 3:1–6).
        c. The Calvary judgment (Mt. 27:33–37; Isa. 53:1–10; Ps. 22:1; Heb. 2:7; 1 Pet. 2:21–25; 3:18).
        d. The Israelite judgments.
            (1) At the hands of the Assyrians (2 Ki. 17).

      (2) At the hands of the Babylonians (2 Ki. 24–25).

      (3) At the hands of the Romans (Mt. 24:2; Lk. 19:41–44).

      (4) At the hands of Christ himself (Mt. 21:17–19, 33–46).

2. Present-day judgments:

  a. Upon local churches by the Savior (Rev. 2–3).

  b. Upon individual believers.

      (1) When the believer judges himself (1 Cor. 11:31; 1 Jn. 1:9).

      (2) When the Father has to step in and judge (1 Cor. 11:30; Heb. 12:3–13; 1 Pet. 4:17; 1 Jn. 5:16; Acts 5:1–11).

3. Future judgments:

  a. The judgment seat (*bema*) of Christ (Rom. 14:10; 1 Cor. 3:9–15; 2 Cor. 5:10; Rev. 22:12).

  b. The tribulational judgment (Rev. 6–19).

      (1) Upon man's religious systems (Rev. 17).

      (2) Upon man's economic and political systems (Rev. 18).

      (3) Upon man's military systems (Rev. 19:11–21).

      (4) Upon man himself (Rev. 6, 8, 9, 16).

  c. The lamp and talent judgment—this refers to Israel (Ezek. 20:33–38; Mt. 24:45–51; 25:1–30).

  d. The sheep and goat judgment—this refers to the Gentiles (Mt. 25:31–46).

  e. The judgment upon the antichrist and false prophet (Rev. 19:20).

  f. The judgment upon Satan.

      (1) In the bottomless pit for one thousand years (Rom. 16:20; Rev. 20:1–3).

      (2) In the lake of fire forever (Rev. 20:10).

  g. The fallen angel judgment (1 Pet. 2:4; Jude 1:6)

  h. The great white throne judgment (Rev. 20:11–15).

The two most important of these eight judgments are the great white throne judgment and the judgment seat of Christ. Every individual on earth today and the millions that have gone before will someday appear before one of these throne judgments. The decision is therefore not *whether* one is to be judged, but rather *where* this judgment will take place.

Details concerning the great white throne judgment (Rev. 20:11–15) will be discussed at a later place in this book. In passing, however, let it be said that only the unsaved will stand before this throne, the purpose and results being to determine degrees of punishment in hell. But what of the judgment seat of Christ?

B. The meaning of the *bema* judgment.
The Greek word *bema* (translated "judgment seat" in the KJV) was a familiar term to the people of Paul's day. Dr. Lehman Strauss writes:

"In the large olympic arenas, there was an elevated seat on which the judge of the contest sat. After the contests were over, the successful competitors would assemble before the *bema* to receive their rewards or crowns. The *bema* was not a judicial bench where someone was condemned; it was a reward seat. Likewise, the Judgment Seat of Christ is not a judicial bench . . . the Christian life is a race, and the divine umpire is watching every contestant. After the church has run her course, He will gather every member before the *bema* for the purpose of examining each one and giving the proper reward to each" (Lehman Strauss, *God's Plan for the Future*, Grand Rapids: Zondervan, p. 111. Used by permission).

The Apostle Paul seemed to have such an olympic arena in mind when he penned Hebrews 12:1:
Wherefore, seeing we also are compassed about with so great a cloud of witnesses, let us lay aside every weight, and the sin which doth so easily beset us, and let us run with patience the race that is set before us.
This amazing human being was many things. He was a missionary, a soul-winner, a pastor, a great theologian, a tentmaker, etc. But in his spare time he also seemed to be a sports lover. Often in his writings Paul uses sports as an analogy to get his point across. For example:
Wrestling. "For we wrestle not against flesh and blood, but against principalities, against powers, against the rulers of the darkness of this world, against spiritual wickedness in high places" (Eph. 6:12).

27

Boxing. "I have fought a good fight . . ." (2 Tim. 4:7). "So fight I, not as one that beateth the air" (1 Cor. 9:26).

Racing. "Know ye not that they which run in a race run all, but one receiveth the prize? So run that ye may obtain . . . I therefore so run . . ." (1 Cor. 9:24, 26).

Here in Hebrews 12 Paul chooses the third analogy—that of a footrace. This chapter may be titled God's Superbowl. J. Vernon McGee writes:

"The Christian life is likened to a Greek race. Along the way the Christian as a soldier is to stand, as a believer he is to walk, and as an athlete he is to run. One day he will fly— space travel to the New Jerusalem" (*Studies in Hebrews*, p. 240).

At the time Paul wrote, King Herod had built a thronelike seat in the theater at Caesarea (his headquarters) where he sat to view the games and make speeches to the people.

C. The fact of the *bema* judgment.

Many New Testament verses speak of this.

But why dost thou judge thy brother? Or why dost thou set at nought thy brother? For we shall all stand before the judgment seat of Christ. For it is written, As I live, saith the Lord, every knee shall bow to me, and every tongue shall confess to God. So then every one of us shall give account of himself to God (Rom. 14:10–12).

Every man's work shall be made manifest, for the day shall declare it . . . (1 Cor. 3:13).

For we must all appear before the judgment seat of Christ . . . (2 Cor. 5:10).

(To these passages could be added Gal. 6:7; Col. 3:24, 25; Heb. 10:30).

D. The purpose of the *bema* judgment.

　　1. Negative considerations.

　　　　a. The purpose of the *bema* judgment is not to determine whether a particular individual enters heaven or not, for every man's eternal destiny is already determined before he leaves this life.

　　　　b. The purpose of the *bema* judgment is not to punish believers for sins committed either before or after their salvation. The Scriptures are very clear that no child of God will have to answer for his sins after this life.

He hath not dealt with us after our sins; nor rewarded us according to our iniquities. For as the heaven is high above the earth, so great is his mercy toward them that fear him. As far as the east is from the west, so far hath he removed our transgressions from us (Ps. 103:10–12).

Thou hast in love to my soul delivered it from the pit of corruption: for thou hast cast all my sins behind thy back (Isa. 38:17).

I have blotted out . . . thy transgressions and . . . thy sins (Isa. 44:22).

Thou wilt cast all their sins into the depths of the sea (Micah 7:19).

For I will be merciful . . . and their sins and their iniquities will I remember no more (Heb. 8:12).

The blood of Jesus Christ his Son cleanseth us from all sin (1 Jn. 1:7).

2. Positive considerations.

What then is the purpose of the *bema* judgment? In 1 Corinthians 4:2 Paul says that all Christians should conduct themselves as faithful stewards of God: *Moreover it is required in stewards, that a man be found faithful.*

The Apostle Peter later writes in a similar way: "Minister . . . as good stewards of the manifold grace of God" (1 Pet. 4:10).

In the New Testament world, a steward was the manager of a large household or estate. He was appointed by the owner and was entrusted to keep the estate running smoothly. He had the power to hire and fire and to spend and save, being answerable to the owner alone. His only concern was that periodic meeting with his master, at which time he was required to account for the condition of the estate up to that point.

With this background in mind, it may be said that someday at the *bema* judgment all stewards will stand before their Lord and Master and be required to give an account of the way they have used their privileges and responsibilities from the moment of their conversion.

In conclusion, it can be seen that:
a. In the past, God dealt with us as sinners (Rom. 5:6-8; 1 Cor. 6:9-11; Eph. 2:1-3).
b. In the present, God deals with us as sons (Rom. 8:14; Heb. 12:5-11; 1 Jn. 3:1, 2).
c. In the future, God will deal with us (at the *bema*) as stewards.

E. The time of the *bema*.
J. Dwight Pentecost writes:

"The event herein described takes place immediately following the translation of the church out of this earth's sphere. There are several considerations that support this. (1) In the first place, according to Luke 14:14 reward is associated with the resurrection. Since, according to 1 Thessalonians 4:13-17, the resurrection is an integral part of the translation, reward must be a part of that program. (2) When the Lord returns to the earth with His bride to reign, the bride is seen to be already rewarded. This is observed in Revelation 19:8, where it must be observed that the 'righteousness of the saints' is plural and can not refer to the imputed righteousness of Christ, which is the believer's portion, but the righteousness which have survived examination and have become the basis of reward. (3) In 1 Corinthians 4:5; 2 Timothy 4:8; and Revelation 22:12 the reward is associated with 'that day,' that is, the day in which He comes for His own. Thus, it must be observed that the rewarding of the church must take place between the rapture and the return of Christ to the earth" (*Things to Come*, Findley, Ohio: Dunham Press, 1959, pp. 220, 221).

F. The materials to be tested at the *bema* judgment.
In 1 Corinthians 3:11 the Apostle Paul explains the glorious fact that at the moment of salvation a repenting sinner is firmly placed on the foundation of the death, burial, and resurrection of Christ himself! His continuing instruction after his salvation is to rise up and build upon this foundation.
Paul says, "But let every man take heed how he buildeth thereupon. . . . Now if any man build upon this foundation gold, silver, precious stones, wood, hay, stubble; every man's

work shall be made manifest: for the day shall declare it, because it shall be revealed by fire; and the fire shall try every man's work of what sort it is" (1 Cor. 3:10, 12, 13).

1. Negative considerations.

   It should be noted immediately that this passage does not teach the false doctrine known as purgatory, for it is the believer's works and not the believer himself that will be subjected to the fires.

2. Positive considerations.

   From these verses it is apparent that God classifies the works of believers into one of the following six areas: gold, silver, precious stones, wood, hay, stubble. There has been much speculation about the kinds of work down here that will constitute gold or silver up there. But it seems more appropriate to note that the six objects can be readily placed into two categories:

   a. Those indestructible and worthy objects which will survive and thrive in the fires. These are the gold, silver, and precious stones.

   b. Those destructible and worthless objects which will be totally consumed in the fires. These are the wood, hay, and stubble.

   Thus, what the fire cannot purify, it destroys, and what the fire cannot destroy, it purifies.

3. God's values.

   Though it is difficult to know just what goes to make up a "golden work" or a "stubble work," we are nevertheless informed of certain general areas in which God is particularly interested.

   a. How we treat other believers.

   For God is not unrighteous to forget your work and labour of love, which ye have showed toward his name, in that ye have ministered to the saints, and do minister (Heb. 6:10).

   He that receiveth a prophet in the name of a prophet shall receive a prophet's reward; and he that receiveth a righteous man in the name of a righteous man shall receive a righteous man's reward. And whosoever shall give to drink unto one of these little ones a cup of cold water only in the name of a disciple, verily I say unto you, he shall in no wise lose his reward (Mt. 10:41, 42).

It is tragic but all too factual that often the shabbiest treatment suffered by a believer comes from the hand of another believer.

b. How we exercise our authority over others.

Obey them that have the rule over you, and submit yourselves: for they watch for your souls, as they that must give account, that they may do it with joy, and not with grief . . . (Heb. 13:17).

Let not many of you become teachers, my brethren, knowing that as such we shall incur a stricter judgment (Jas. 3:1, NASB).

Almost every Christian at one time or another has had a measure of authority over another believer. This leadership role may have been that of a parent, pastor, teacher, employer, etc. It has been remarked that while some *grow* under authority, others simply *swell.*

c. How we employ our God-given abilities.

Now there are varieties of gifts, but the same Spirit. . . . But one and the same Spirit works all these things, distributing to each one individually just as He wills (1 Cor. 12:4, 11, NASB).

Wherefore I put thee in remembrance that thou stir up the gift of God which is in thee . . . (2 Tim. 1:6).

As each one has received a special gift, employ it in serving one another, as good stewards of the manifold grace of God (1 Pet. 4:10, NASB).

To these verses can be added the overall teaching of Jesus' parables of the ten pounds (Lk. 19:11–26) and the eight talents (Mt. 25:14–29). A spiritual gift is a supernatural ability to glorify God, given by the Holy Spirit to the believer at the moment of salvation. Each Christian has at least one gift (1 Cor. 7:7; 12:7, 11; Eph. 4:7; 1 Pet. 4:10). There are eighteen of these gifts (Rom. 12; 1 Cor. 12; Eph. 4). Thus, it is vital for every child of God to discover and employ his own gift, in light of the *bema.*

d. How we use our money.

Upon the first day of the week let every one of you lay by him in store, as God hath prospered him . . . (1 Cor. 16:2).

But this I say, He which soweth sparingly shall reap also sparingly; and he which soweth bountifully shall reap also bountifully. Every man according as he purposeth in his heart, so let him give; not grudgingly, or of necessity, for God loveth a cheerful giver (2 Cor. 9:6, 7).

Charge them that are rich in this world that they be not highminded, nor trust in uncertain riches, but in the living God, who giveth us richly all things to enjoy; that they do good, that they be rich in good works, ready to distribute, willing to communicate, laying up in store for themselves a good foundation against the time to come, that they may lay hold on eternal life (1 Tim. 6:17–19).

Perhaps the most accurate barometer to measure the spiritual condition of a Christian is to observe his or her relationship concerning money. Jesus himself often dealt with money matters, because money matters! In the New Testament there are some thirty-eight parables. Twelve of them are about money. How much of our money belongs to God? According to 1 Corinthians 6:19, 20 it *all* belongs to him, because we are his, purchased with an awesome price (1 Pet. 1:18, 19). What does all this mean? It means that if I gross $250 per week, I am not only responsible for the tithe ($25) but will, at the *bema*, be held accountable concerning the remaining $225!

e. How we spend our time.

So teach us to number our days, that we may apply our hearts unto wisdom (Ps. 90:12).

. . . redeeming the time, because the days are evil (Eph. 5:16).

Walk in wisdom . . . redeeming the time (Col. 4:5).

And if ye call on the Father, who without respect of persons judgeth according to every man's work, pass the time of your sojourning here in fear (1 Pet. 1:17).

Of course I have no way of knowing how much money each reader of this book earned last week, or what portion of that amount was saved. But I can accurately state (to the second) how much time you started out with, and what portion was saved. Each began with 168 hours and spent every single one of the 604,800 seconds involved! Someday at the *bema*, each of us will give an account just how we spent that time.

f. How much we suffer for Jesus.

Blessed are ye, when men shall revile you, and persecute you, and shall say all manner of evil against you falsely, for my sake. Rejoice, and be exceeding glad, for great is your reward in heaven . . . (Mt. 5:11, 12).

And Jesus answered and said, Verily I say unto you, there is no man that hath left house, or brethren, or sisters, or father, or mother, or wife, or children, or lands, for my sake, and the gospel's. But he shall receive an hundredfold now in this time, houses, and brethren, and sisters, and mothers, and children, and lands, with persecutions; and in the world to come eternal life (Mk. 10:29, 30).

For I reckon that the sufferings of this present time are not worthy to be compared with the glory which shall be revealed in us (Rom. 8:18).

For our light affliction, which is but for a moment, worketh for us a far more exceeding and eternal weight of glory (2 Cor. 4:17).

Beloved, think it not strange concerning the fiery trial which is to try you, as though some strange thing happened unto you; but rejoice, inasmuch as ye are partakers of Christ's sufferings, that, when his glory shall be revealed, ye may be glad also with exceeding joy (1 Pet. 4:12, 13).

I would like to insert a personal memory here. During my first semester at the Moody Bible Institute in 1952, I purchased a beautiful wall plaque which bore the imprint of Philippians 3:10: "That I may know him, and the power of his resurrection." I was so proud of and inspired by the words on this sign. It became the first object I looked at upon rising, and the last sight before retiring. In fact, I had decided to make this passage my life's verse. One day a friend came in my room, saw the plaque, admired it, but informed me that the entire verse was not printed upon it. Somewhat shocked, I hurriedly turned to look it up. Upon discovering the entire message, I suddenly became less sure I wanted this verse as my life's verse. What I read was:

That I may know him, and the power of his resurrection, and the fellowship of his sufferings, *being made conformable unto his death.*

You see, I had been tremendously inspired by the first part of the verse, but was definitely less excited about the second section. I wanted the power of the resurrection without the fellowship of the sufferings, but this is impossible! One simply cannot have the first apart from the second!

g. How we run that particular race which God has chosen for us.

Know ye not that they which run in a race run all, but one receiveth the prize? So run, that ye may obtain (1 Cor. 9:24).

. . . that I may rejoice in the day of Christ, that I have not run in vain . . . (Phil. 2:16).

Brethren, I count not myself to have apprehended; but this one thing I do, forgetting those things which are behind, and reaching forth unto those things which are before, I press toward the mark for the prize of the high calling of God in Christ Jesus (Phil. 3:13, 14).

Let us lay aside every weight, and the sin which doth so easily beset us, and let us run with patience the race that is set before us (Heb. 12:1).

Especially to be observed are the words found in Hebrews 12:1. Note the implications of this statement: Every believer has been entered in this race by God himself. It is not just for pastors and missionaries. Note: The usual word for race (*dromos*) is not used here, but rather the Greek word *agon*, from which we get our English word agony. This is a serious race. The pace of each runner is set by God.

The object of the race is to please God and win rewards. Its goal is not heaven. Every runner is expected to win.

"Looking unto Jesus" (12:2). The phrase here speaks of a steadfast, intent and continuous gaze. How easy it is to get our eyes off him and look to the left or right.

Perhaps to our left we see another runner behind us. Or it may be that there is a runner far ahead of us on the right. This can produce pride (as we view the left runner) and envy (as we see the runner on the right). Both are sin and cause us to slow down. Instead, we are to keep looking at Jesus. We are therefore to *run* down here in such a way that we might *rejoice* up there.

h. How effectively we control the old nature.

And every man that striveth for the mastery is temperate in all things. Now they do it to obtain a corruptible crown, but we an incorruptible. I therefore so run, not as uncertainly; so fight I, not as one that beateth the air. But I keep under my body, and bring it into subjection, lest that by any means when I have preached to others, I myself should be a castaway (1 Cor. 9:25-27).

The Greek word "castaway" here (*adokimos*) means disapproved. Without the *a* prefix it of course speaks of approval. A key passage where *dokimazo* is used can be seen in 1 Timothy 2:15:

Study to shew thyself approved unto God . . .

(See also 1 Cor. 16:3; Phil. 1:10; 1 Thess. 2:4; where the identical word is used.)

The point of the above is that Paul desired above all things to keep his old nature in check, lest he be disapproved of, rewardwise, at the *bema*.

i. How many souls we witness to and win to Christ.

The fruit of the righteous is a tree of life, and he that winneth souls is wise (Prov. 11:30).

And they that be wise shall shine as the brightness of the firmament, and they that turn many to righteousness as the stars for ever and ever (Dan. 12:3).

For what is our hope, or joy, or crown of rejoicing? Are not even ye in the presence of our Lord Jesus Christ at his coming? For ye are our glory and joy (1 Thess. 2:19, 20).

j. How we react to temptation.

My brethren, count it all joy when ye fall into divers temptations, knowing this, that the trying of your faith worketh patience (Jas. 1:2, 3).

Behold, the devil shall cast some of you into prison, that ye may be tried; and ye shall have tribulation ten days; be thou faithful unto death, and I will give thee a crown of life (Rev. 2:10).

k. How much the doctrine of the rapture means to us.

Henceforth there is laid up for me a crown of righteousness, which the Lord, the righteous judge, shall give me at that day; and not to me only, but unto all them also that love his appearing (2 Tim. 4:8).

l. How faithful we are to the Word of God and the flock of God.

Wherefore, I take you to record this day, that I am pure from the blood of all men. For I have not shunned to declare unto you all the counsel of God. Take heed therefore unto yourselves, and to all the flock over which the Holy Ghost hath made you overseers, to feed the church of God, which he hath purchased with his own blood (Acts 20:26–28).

I charge thee therefore before God and the Lord Jesus Christ, who shall judge the quick and the dead at his appearing and his kingdom, Preach the word . . . (2 Tim. 4:1, 2).

Feed the flock of God which is among you, taking the oversight thereof, not by constraint, but willingly; not for filthy lucre, but of a ready mind; neither as being lords over God's heritage, but being ensamples to the flock. And when the chief Shepherd shall appear, ye shall receive a crown of glory that fadeth not away (1 Pet. 5:2–4).

G. The results of the *bema* judgment seat of Christ.

1. Some will receive rewards.

If any man's work abide which he hath built thereupon, he shall receive a reward (1 Cor. 3:14).

The Bible mentions at least five rewards. These have already been described briefly under the last section. The rewards include:

a. The incorruptible crown—given to those who master the old nature (1 Cor. 9:25-27).

b. The crown of rejoicing—given to soul-winners (Prov. 11:30; Dan. 12:3; 1 Thess. 2:19, 20).

c. The crown of life—given to those who successfully endure temptation (Jas. 1:2, 3; Rev. 2:10).

d. The crown of righteousness—given to those who especially love the doctrine of the rapture (2 Tim. 4:8).

e. The crown of glory—given to faithful preachers and teachers (Acts 20:26-28; 2 Tim. 4:1, 2; 1 Pet. 5:2-4).

It has been suggested that these "crowns" will actually be talents and abilities with which to glorify Christ. Thus, the greater the reward, the greater the ability. Who down here has not longed to be able to sing like a George Beverly Shea or to preach like a Billy Graham? It may be that this blessing will be possible up there.

2. Some will suffer loss.

If any man's work shall be burned, he shall suffer loss . . . (1 Cor. 3:15).

This word for "suffer" is *zemioo* in the Greek New Testament, and is used again by Paul in Philippians 3, where he describes those things which were the greatest source of pride to him prior to salvation. He tells us, *For I went through the Jewish initiation ceremony when I was eight days old, having been born into a pureblooded Jewish home that was a branch of the old original Benjamin family. So I was a real Jew if there ever was one! What's more, I was a member of the Pharisees who demand the strictest obedience to every Jewish law and custom. And sincere? Yes, so much so that I greatly persecuted the church; and I tried to obey every Jewish rule and regulation right down to the very last point* (Phil. 3:5, 6, TLB).

But after his conversion, Paul writes, ". . . for whom I have suffered the loss of all things . . . that I may win Christ" (Phil. 3:8).

The point of all these teachings is simply this: At the *bema* judgment the carnal Christian will suffer the loss of many past achievements, even as Paul did, but with one important exception—Paul was richly compensated, since he suffered his loss to win Christ, while the carnal believer will receive nothing to replace his burned-up wood, hay, and stubble. Before leaving this section the question may be asked, "Is it possible for someone who has earned certain rewards down here to lose them somehow through carnality?" Some believe this to be tragically possible on the basis of the following verses:

Let no man beguile you of your reward . . . (Col. 2:18).

Look to yourselves, that we lose not those things which we have wrought, but that we receive a full reward (2 Jn. 1:8).

Behold, I come quickly; hold that fast which thou hast, that no man take thy crown (Rev. 3:11).

However, knowing the fairness and justice of God, it is far more probable that these verses refer to potential rewards, that is, rewards a believer *could have* earned, had he (or she) remained faithful.

Having now discussed the twelve main areas to be proved at the *bema*, it should be said that a major concern will center in not only the *action* performed, but that attitude which prompted it. In other words, God is vitally interested in both the *what* and *why* of my deeds.

Offering a personal—and painful—illustration, I am convinced that some of my sermons and teaching lessons which were theologically correct will nevertheless go up in flames as wood, hay, and stubble. Perhaps the Holy Spirit even used the sermon in question to convict sinners and exhort saints, for God always honors his word; but my attitude ruined any possible reward. My intent behind the sermon may have been to tickle the ears or impress the minds of those who heard.

H. The Old Testament foreshadowing of the *bema* judgment seat of Christ.

Although the church is nowhere mentioned in the Old Testament, there is nevertheless a passage which can very easily be applied to the *bema* judgment. This can be found in the words of Boaz (a foreshadowing of Christ) to Ruth (a foreshadowing of the church), when he says, "It hath fully been shewed me, all that thou hast done. . . . The Lord recompense thy work, and a full reward be given thee of the Lord God of Israel, under whose wings thou art come to trust" (Ruth 2:11, 12).

THREE
THE MARRIAGE OF
THE LAMB

A number of weddings are described in the Bible. The first wedding was performed by a very special guest minister. Whatever religious ceremony he may have chosen, it did not include those familiar words: "If any man can show just cause why these two should not be lawfully joined together, let him now speak, or else forever hold his peace." This phrase was unnecessary, for the minister was God himself, and the couple was Adam and Eve (Gen. 2:18–25).

Then there was a very unusual wedding in which the bridegroom found out the next morning, by light of day, that he had married the wrong girl (Gen. 29:21–25).

One of the most beautiful wedding stories began in a barley field outside the little town of Bethlehem (Ruth 2).

Perhaps the most tragic wedding was that between Ahab, King of Israel, and Jezebel, a godless Baal worshiper. This marriage would result in much sorrow and suffering for God's people (1 Ki. 16:29–31).

Finally, the Savior of men chose a wedding in the city of Cana to perform his first miracle (Jn. 2:1–11).

However, the most fantastic and wonderful wedding of all time is yet to take place.

A. The fact of this marriage.

    1. This marriage is described through the parables of Jesus.

The kingdom of heaven is like unto a certain king, which made a marriage for his son (Mt. 22:2).

Then shall the kingdom of heaven be likened unto ten virgins, which took their lamps, and went forth to meet the bridegroom (Mt. 25:1).

Let your loins be girded about, and your lights burning, and ye yourselves like unto men that wait for their Lord, when he will return from the wedding (Lk. 12:35, 36).

    2. This marriage is described through the vision of John.

Let us be glad and rejoice, and give honour to him; for the marriage of the Lamb is come, and his wife hath made herself ready (Rev. 19:7).

B. The Host of the marriage.

The New Testament very clearly presents the Father as the divine Host who gives this marriage. He is pictured as preparing it, then sending his servants out to invite the selected guests (Lk. 14:16–23).

C. The Bridegroom of the marriage.

The Father's beloved Son (Mt. 3:17; 17:5), the Lord Jesus Christ, is the bridegroom.

    1. As stated by John the Baptist.

John answered and said, A man can receive nothing except it be given him from heaven. Ye yourselves bear me witness that I said, I am not the Christ, but that I am sent before him. He that hath the bride is the bridegroom; but the friend of the bridegroom which standeth and heareth him, rejoiceth greatly because of the bridegroom's voice: this my joy therefore is fulfilled. He must increase, but I must decrease (Jn. 3:27–30).

    2. As stated by the Lord Jesus Christ.

I came not to call the righteous, but sinners to repentance. And they said unto him, Why do the disciples of John fast often, and make prayers . . . but thine eat and drink? And he said unto them, Can ye make the children of the bridechamber fast while the bridegroom is with them? But the days will come when the bridegroom shall be taken away from them, and then shall they fast in those days (Lk. 5:32–35).

D. The bride of the marriage.

In two key passages the Apostle Paul makes crystal clear the identity of the bride:

For I am jealous over you with godly jealousy, for I have espoused you to one husband, that I may present you as a chaste virgin to Christ (2 Cor. 11:2).

Wives, submit yourselves unto your own husbands, as unto the Lord. For the husband is the head of the wife, even as Christ is the head of the church; and he is the saviour of the body. Therefore, as the church is subject unto Christ, so let the wives be to their own husbands in everything. Husbands, love your wives, even as Christ also loved the church, and gave himself for it, that he might sanctify and cleanse it with the washing of water by the Word, that he might present it to himself a glorious church, not having spot, or wrinkle, or any such thing; but that it should be holy and without blemish. So ought men to love their wives as their own bodies. He that loveth his wife loveth himself. For no man ever yet hated his own flesh, but nourisheth and cherisheth it, even as the Lord the church. For we are members of his body, of his flesh, and of his bones. For this cause shall a man leave his father and mother, and shall be joined unto his wife, and they two shall be one flesh. This is a great mystery; but I speak concerning Christ and the church (Eph. 5:22–32).

E. The guests of the marriage.

And he saith unto me, Write, blessed are they which are called unto the marriage supper of the Lamb . . . (Rev. 19:9).

Who are these invited guests of the lamb's marriage to the church?

  1. In general.

A group which would include all believing Gentiles who were converted prior to Pentecost or after the rapture. This is so, for all those individuals saved between the day of Pentecost and the rapture make up the bride of Christ at this wedding.

  2. In particular.

A group which would include all saved Israelites everywhere. The ten virgins mentioned in Matthew 25 are Israelites. The five wise represent saved Israelites and the five foolish represent unsaved ones. They cannot represent the church, for the church is the bride, inside with the Bridegroom. The virgins are guests who have been invited to the wedding. Note that a bride is never

invited to her own wedding. If she refuses to come, there
is no wedding.
F. The service schedule of the marriage.
The marriage of Christ to the church will follow the Oriental
pattern of marriage as described for us in the New Testament.
It consisted of three separate stages:
  1. The betrothal stage.
  New Testament marriage contracts were often initiated
  when the couple was very young (sometimes even prior
  to birth) by the groom's father. He would sign a legal
  enactment before the proper judge, pledging his son to a
  chosen girl. The father would then offer the proper
  dowry payment. Thus, even though the bride had never
  seen the groom, she was nevertheless betrothed or
  espoused to him. A New Testament example of this first
  step is the marriage of Mary and Joseph.
  *Now the birth of Jesus Christ was on this wise: when as his
  mother Mary was espoused to Joseph, before they came
  together, she was found with child of the Holy Ghost* (Mt.
  1:18).
  Both Mary and Joseph had come from Bethlehem and
  had perhaps been betrothed, or promised to each other,
  since childhood. But now Mary was found to be with
  child before the marriage could be consummated, and of
  course Joseph could arrive at only one conclusion—she
  had been untrue to him! Then the angel of the Lord
  explained to Joseph the glories of the virgin birth.
  Thus the betrothal stage consisted of two steps: The
  selection of the bride and the payment of the dowry.
  With this in mind we can state that the marriage of
  the Lamb is still in its betrothal stage:
  a. The bride had been selected.
  *Blessed be the God and Father of our Lord Jesus Christ,
  who hath blessed us with all spiritual blessings in heavenly
  places in Christ, according as he hath chosen us in him
  before the foundation of the world, that we should be holy
  and without blame before him in love* (Eph. 1:3, 4).
  b. The dowry had been paid.
  What? Know ye not that your body is the temple of the

44

Holy Ghost which is in you, which ye have of God, and ye
are not your own? For ye are bought with a price.
Therefore, glorify God in your body and in your spirit,
which are God's (1 Cor. 6:19, 20).

  Forasmuch as ye know that ye were not redeemed with
corruptible things, as silver and gold . . . but with the
precious blood of Christ, as of a lamb without blemish and
without spot (1 Pet. 1:18, 19).

2. The presentation stage.

At the proper time the father would send to the house of
the bride servants carrying the proper legal contract. The
bride would then be led to the home of the groom's
father. When all was ready, the father of the bride would
place her hand in the hand of the groom's father. He
would then place her hand in that of his son. Applying
this background to the marriage of the Lamb, the church
still awaits this second phase, the presentation stage,
which we know as the rapture! The following verses
speak of this presentation stage:

. . . Christ also loved the church and gave himself for it . . .
that he might present it to himself a glorious church, not
having spot or wrinkle or any such thing, but that it should be
holy and without blemish (Eph. 5:25, 27).

  Now unto him that is able to keep you from falling, and to
present you faultless before the presence of his glory with
exceeding joy . . . (Jude 24).

  Let us be glad and rejoice, and give honour to him: for the
marriage of the Lamb is come, and his wife hath made herself
ready. And to her was granted that she should be arrayed in
fine linen, clean and white; for the fine linen is the right-
eousness of saints (Rev. 19:7, 8).

  Then follow the events which comprise the second
stage:

a. The Heavenly Father will send for the bride.

  After this I looked, and behold, a door was opened in
heaven; and the first voice which I heard was as it were of
a trumpet talking with me, which said, Come up hither
. . . (Rev. 4:1).

b. The proper legal papers of marriage will be shown.

*Nevertheless the foundation of God standeth sure, having
this seal, the Lord knoweth them that are his . . . (2 Tim.
2:19).*
  c. The bride will be taken to the Father's home.
    *In my Father's house are many mansions; if it were not so
    I would have told you. I go to prepare a place for you.
    And if I go and prepare a place for you, I will come again
    and receive you unto myself, that where I am, there ye may
    be also (Jn. 14:2, 3).*
  3. The celebration stage.
    After the private marriage service was completed, the
    public marriage supper would begin. Many guests would
    be invited to this celebration. It was during such a supper
    that our Lord performed his first miracle, that of
    changing water into wine (see Jn. 2:1–11). Jesus later
    made reference to this third step when he spoke the
    following words:
    *The kingdom of heaven is like unto a certain king, which
    made a marriage for his son, and sent forth his servants to
    call them that were bidden to the wedding . . . (Mt. 22:2, 3).*
      *Let your loins be girded about, and your lights burning; and
    ye yourselves like unto men that wait for their lord, when he
    will return from the wedding. . . . Blessed are those servants,
    whom the lord when he cometh shall find watching: verily I
    say unto you, that he shall gird himself, and make them to sit
    down to meat, and will come forth and serve them (Lk. 12:
    35–37).*
      *Then said he unto him, A certain man made a great supper
    and bade many, and sent his servant at supper time to say to
    them that were bidden, Come, for all things are now ready
    (Lk. 14:16, 17).*
G. The time of the marriage.
  When does the wedding transpire? In view of what has already been said, it would seem that the wedding service (the
  presentation stage) will be privately conducted in heaven,
  perhaps shortly after the *bema* judgment seat of Christ. The
  wedding supper (the celebration stage) will be publicly
  conducted on earth shortly after the Second Coming of
  Christ.
    It is no accident that the Bible describes the millennium as

occurring right after the celebration supper has begun. (The supper is described in Rev. 19 while the millennium is described in Rev. 20.) In New Testament times the length and cost of this supper was determined by the wealth of the father. Therefore, when his beloved Son is married, the Father of all grace (whose wealth is unlimited) will rise to the occasion by giving his Son and the bride a hallelujah celebration which will last for a thousand years!

H. The Old Testament foreshadowing of the marriage.
The forty-fifth Psalm, written by Korah, has often been referred to as "the Psalm of the Wedding of the King." It is reproduced here from *The Living Bible*:

My heart is overflowing with a beautiful thought!
I will write a lovely poem to the King, for I am
as full of words as the speediest writer pouring out
his story.

You are the fairest of all;
Your words are filled with grace;
God himself is blessing you forever.
Arm yourself, O Mighty One,
So glorious, so majestic!
And in your majesty
Go on to victory,
Defending truth, humility, and justice.
Go forth to awe-inspiring deeds!
Your arrows are sharp
In your enemies' hearts;
They fall before you.
Your throne, O God, endures forever.
Justice is your royal scepter.
You love what is good
And hate what is wrong.
Therefore God, your God,
Has given you more gladness
Than anyone else.

Your robes are perfumed with myrrh, aloes and cassia. In your inlaid palaces of ivory, lovely music is being played for your enjoyment. Kings' daughters are among your concubines.

*Standing beside you is the queen, wearing jewelry of finest
gold from Ophir. I advise you, O daughter, not to fret about
your parents in your homeland far away. Your royal husband
delights in your beauty. Reverence him, for he is your lord.
The people of Tyre, the richest people of our day, will shower
you with gifts and entreat your favors.*

*The bride, a princess, waits within her chamber, robed in
beautiful clothing woven with gold. Lovely she is, led beside
her maids of honor to the king! What a joyful, glad
procession as they enter in the palace gates! Your sons will
some day be kings like their father. They shall sit on thrones
around the world!*

*I will cause your name to be honored in all generations; the
nations of the earth will praise you forever.*

One could almost see Korah, representing the Jerusalem Press,
being invited to that future glorious event—the wedding of
the King! He describes vividly for us the glory of the Bridegroom (vs. 2–8), the expensive wedding gifts (v. 12), the love-
liness of the bride (vs. 13, 14), and the joyful rice-throwing
crowd (v. 15).

I. The certainty of the marriage.
Earthly marriages may be prevented because of various
unexpected problems.

    1. In an earthly wedding there can be a last-minute refusal
on the part of either the bride or groom. But not with
the heavenly marriage.

        a. The Bridegroom has already expressed his great love
for his bride (Eph. 5:25), and he never changes.
*This same Jesus, which is taken up from you into heaven,
shall so come in like manner as ye have seen him go into
heaven* (Acts 1:11).
*. . . Jesus Christ, the same yesterday, and today, and
forever* (Heb. 13:8).

        b. The bride has already been glorified and is sinless,
and therefore cannot be tempted into changing her
mind or losing her love for the Bridegroom.
*. . . a glorious church, not having spot, or wrinkle . . . but
. . . holy and without blemish* (Eph. 5:27).
For by one offering he hath perfected forever them that

48

are sanctified (Heb. 10:14).
2. In an earthly wedding a serious legal problem might arise, such as lack of age, or even that of a previous marriage— but not in the heavenly wedding (see Rom. 8:33–39).
3. In an earthly wedding the tragedy of death might intervene—but not in the heavenly wedding.
   a. The bride will never die.
   And whosoever liveth and believeth in me shall never die (Jn. 11:26).
   b. The Bridegroom will never die.
   I am he that liveth, and was dead; and, behold, I am alive for evermore; Amen (Rev. 1:18).

FOUR
THE STORY OF
TWO SONGS

The events described here in Revelation 4 and 5 are all too often overlooked in the study of prophecy. This is unfortunate, for the account records two songs which in themselves summarize God's two great works, that of creation and redemption.

A. Events leading up to the first song (Rev. 4).

John the apostle has been caught up into heaven (Rev. 4:1), where he writes about the marvelous things he sees and hears.

1. He sees the glory of the Father upon the throne (Rev. 4:2, 3). Will we actually see the Father in heaven? These verses almost seem to suggest that we will. The only other possible description of the Father is found in Daniel 7:8-14.

   John could distinguish no form or give no description of the awesome One upon this throne, save to say, "He that sat was to look upon like a jasper and a sardine stone" (4:3). Here the jasper, a white stone, and the sardine, a fiery red stone, may refer to God's two basic characteristics: his glory and his grace. These were also the first and last stones among the twelve that the Old Testament high priest bore upon his breastplate. These stones represented the twelve tribes of Israel, arranged according to the births of the twelve sons of Jacob (Ex. 28). Reuben was the first tribe, which name meant "behold a son," and Benjamin was the last, meaning, "son of my right hand." This then may be God's way of reminding all creatures throughout eternity of:

   a. The incarnation of Christ (his humanity) via the

50

jasper stone, Reuben—"behold a son."
   b. The exaltation of Christ (his deity) via the sardine
      stone, Benjamin—"son of my right hand."
2. He sees a beautiful green rainbow around this throne
   (Rev. 4:3).
3. He sees twenty-four elders with golden crowns (Rev.
   4:4). (These twenty-four may consist of a special
   representative body of both Old Testament and New
   Testament saints. The Greek text tells us they are all
   wearing *stephanos* crowns, or martyrs' crowns, rather
   than diadems, or monarchs' crowns. Thus they must be
   humans rather than angels.)
4. He sees and hears lightnings and thunderings, which
   means that the awful storm of the great tribulation is
   about to unleash its fury (Rev. 4:5).
5. He sees a crystal sea of glass (Rev. 4:6).
   Dr. Donald Barnhouse has written concerning this sea,

"Before the throne there was a glassy sea, like crystal.
The concordance immediately takes us to the temple built
by Solomon after the model of the tabernacle. 'And he
made a molten sea, ten cubits from the one brim to the
other; it was round all about, and its height was five
cubits' (1 Ki. 7:23). This great basin, fifteen feet in
diameter, was supported on the backs of twelve oxen of
brass, facing outward. Here the priests came for their
cleansing. Each time before they entered the holy place
they stopped for the cleansing ceremony. But thank God
the laver will be turned to crystal. The day will come
when none of the saints will ever need confession. One
of the greatest joys in the anticipation of Heaven is
that the laver is of crystal. I shall never have to go to the
Heavenly Father again to tell Him I have sinned. I shall
never have to meet that gaze of Christ that caused Peter
to go out and weep bitterly. The laver is of crystal only
because I and all the saints of all the ages will have been
made like unto the Lord Jesus Christ" (Donald G.
Barnhouse, *Revelation: An Expository Commentary*, Grand
Rapids: Zondervan, 1971, p. 94. Used by permission).

6. He sees and hears the testimony of four special angelic

creatures (Rev. 4:6–8). The first of these creatures had
the characteristics of a lion, the second of a calf, the
third of a man, and the fourth of an eagle. It is possible
that these beings are the same as described by Ezekiel the
Old Testament prophet (See Ezek. 1.) In chapter 10 he
identifies what he previously saw as the cherubims
(10:20–22). Some believe these four creatures may have
inherited Lucifer's responsibilities after his terrible
rebellion against God. (See Isa. 14:12–15; Ezek. 28:11–19.)
At any rate, there is a definite similarity between the
appearance of the four living creatures and the manner
by which the four Gospel writers present the earthly
ministry of Christ. For example:

Matthew presents Christ as the lion of the tribe of Judah.
Mark pictures him as the lowly ox.
Luke describes the Savior as the perfect man.
John paints him to be the lofty eagle.

Thus by their very features, these four heavenly beings
may serve to remind redeemed sinners throughout all
eternity of the Savior's blessed earthly ministry.

This then is the backdrop for the first song:

The Creation Hymn
Thou art worthy, O Lord, to receive glory and honour and power: for
thou hast created all things, and for thy pleasure they are and were
created (4:11).
Many of the Psalms were written to praise God for his great
work in creation. Note but a few:
When I consider thy heavens, the work of thy fingers, the moon and
the stars, which thou hast ordained (Ps. 8:3).
The heavens declare the glory of God; and the firmament sheweth
his handiwork. Day unto day uttereth speech, and night unto night
sheweth knowledge. There is no speech nor language, where their voice
is not heard. Their line is gone out through all the earth, and their
words to the end of the world. In them hath he set a tabernacle for the
sun (Ps. 19:1–4).
Know ye that the Lord he is God: it is he that hath made us, and
not we ourselves; we are his people, and the sheep of his pasture
(Ps. 100:3).

*Bless the Lord, O my soul. O Lord my God, thou art very great;
thou art clothed with honour and majesty. Who laid the foundations of
the earth, that it should not be removed for ever* (Ps. 104:1, 5).
B. Events leading up to the second song (Rev. 5).

THE PROCLAMATION
*And I saw in the right hand of him that sat on the throne a book
written within and on the backside, sealed with seven seals* (5:1).
John then hears an angel asking who was able to open this
book and loose its seals (5:2). What is this book (really a
rolled-up scroll), sealed so securely with seven seals? Whatever it contained, the scroll was extremely important, for
history informs us that under Roman law all legal documents
pertaining to life and death were to be sealed seven times. A
number of theologians believe that this is actually the legal
title deed to the earth. Thus the angels' proclamation was, in
effect, "Who is worthy to reclaim the earth's title deed? Who
is able to pour out the seven-sealed judgment, to purify this
planet, and to usher in the long-awaited golden-age millennium?" Who indeed was worthy?

THE INVESTIGATION
*And no man in heaven, nor in earth, neither under the earth, was
able to open the book, neither to look thereon* (Rev. 5:3).
Let us follow the angel as he begins his threefold search.
1. The search in heaven.
   Was there any among the redeemed worthy to claim the
   earth's title deed? There was not!
   a. Adam originally possessed this title deed (Gen. 1:28,
      29), but was cheated out of it by the devil (Gen 3:1–
      19).
   b. Noah, the hero of the flood, subsequently became the
      drunkard of the vineyard, thus disqualifying himself
      (Gen. 6–9).
   c. Abraham, the father of Israel, backslid and went to
      Egypt temporarily (Gen. 12).
   d. David, the man after God's own heart (1 Sam. 16:7),
      later broke God's heart through lust and murder
      (2 Sam. 11).
   e. John the Baptist, the forerunner of Christ, in a

moment of weakness doubted that same Messiah (Mt. 11:3).

 f. Peter, the "rock," denied his Lord in the hour of need (Mt. 26:70).

 g. Paul, perhaps the greatest Christian who ever lived, compromised his testimony (Acts 21).

2. The search on earth.

Who could accomplish in the sinful environment of earth what no man could achieve even in the sinless environment of heaven? Preachers and priests might minister to the earth, and kings rule over sections of it, but claim it they could not.

3. The search under the earth (in Hades).

If no saint or angel could purify this earth, then certainly no sinner or demon would, even if this were possible.

And I wept much, because no man was found worthy to open and to read the book, neither to look thereon (Rev. 5:4).

Why did John weep? Perhaps because (among other things) he realized that the ultimate resurrection and glorification of his own body was directly connected with the removal of the curse placed upon this earth. (See Rom. 8:17–23.)

THE MANIFESTATION

4. The search ended.

And one of the elders saith unto me, Weep not: behold, the Lion of the tribe of Juda, the Root of David, hath prevailed to open the book, and to loose the seven seals thereof. And I beheld, and, lo, in the midst of the throne and of the four beasts, and in the midst of the elders, stood a Lamb as it had been slain, having seven horns and seven eyes, which are the seven Spirits of God sent forth into all the earth. And he came and took the book out of the right hand of him that sat upon the throne (Rev. 5:5–7).

Who is this heavenly Hero who so boldly removes the scroll from the Father's right hand? We need not speculate for one second about his identity, for he is the Lord Jesus Christ himself. The proof is overwhelming.

a. He has the characteristics of a lamb.
Our Lord is referred to as a lamb twenty-nine times in the New Testament. In all but one instance (1 Pet. 1:19) it is the Apostle John who employs this title. Furthermore:

b. It is a pet lamb.
There are two words for "lamb" in the Greek New Testament. This one is *amnos* (a lamb in Christ himself, would come from his tribe, Gen. 49:8–10).

c. In 2 Samuel 7 God told David (who was of the tribe of Judah) that his kingdom would be eternal and that his household would rule forever (2 Sam. 7:8–17).

d. In Luke 1 the angel Gabriel explained to Mary (who was of the house of David) that her virgin-born son would inherit all the Old Testament promises as found in Genesis 49 and 2 Samuel 7 (Lk. 1:30–33).

Thus John sees Christ as a lamb, since he once came to redeem his people. This was his past work. John also sees him as a lion, for he shall come again to reign over his people. This will be his future work. The source of his claim to the earth's scepter is therefore related to his slain lamb characteristics, while the strength of his claim is due to his mighty lion characteristics. We are now given the words to the next song.

The Redemption Hymn

And they sung a new song, saying, Thou art worthy to take the book, and to open the seals thereof: for thou wast slain, and hast redeemed us to God by thy blood out of every kindred, and tongue, and people, and nation; and hast made us unto our God kings and priests: and we shall reign on the earth. And I beheld, and I heard the voice of many angels round about the throne, and the beasts and the elders: and the number of them was ten thousand times ten thousand, and thousands of thousands, saying with a loud voice, Worthy is the Lamb that was slain to receive power, and riches, and wisdom, and strength, and honour, and glory, and blessing. And every creature which is in heaven, and on the earth, and under the earth, and such as are in the sea, and all that are in them, heard I saying, Blessing, and honour, and glory, and power, be unto him that sitteth upon the throne, and unto the Lamb for ever and ever. And the four beasts said, Amen. And the four and twenty elders fell down and worshipped him that liveth for ever and ever (Rev. 5:9–14).

Worthy is the Lamb, is what they sing. The Bible is, in essence, a divine textbook on the subject of God's Lamb. In fact, the Scriptures can be aptly summarized by three statements about the Lamb: Isaac once asked, "Where is the Lamb?" (Gen. 22:7). John the Baptist would later answer, "Behold, the Lamb!" (Jn. 1:29). All creation will someday sing out, "Worthy is the Lamb!" (Rev. 5:12).

C. Two aspects of this choir.

1. Its diversity. Both angels and humans will participate. Inasmuch as angels had previously been allowed to be present at the creation of the world (Job 38:1, 4, 7) and its redemption (Lk. 2:8–14), it is only appropriate that they be permitted to join in this celebration.

2. Its universality. We note every creature, saved and unsaved alike, will give honor to the Lamb. This of course in no way suggests that all will be saved. A similar passage is found in Philippians 2:5–11:

   Let this mind be in you, which was also in Christ Jesus: Who, being in the form of God, thought it not robbery to be equal with God: But made himself of no reputation, and took upon him the form of a servant, and was made in the likeness of men: And being found in fashion as a man, he humbled himself, and became obedient unto death, even the death of the cross. Wherefore God also hath highly exalted him, and given him a name which is above every name: That at the name of Jesus every knee should bow, of things in heaven, and things in earth, and things under the earth; And that every tongue should confess that Jesus Christ is Lord, to the glory of God the Father.

   What these verses are saying is no creature has a choice concerning whether he or she will acknowledge the glory of Christ, but only how that acknowledgment will be made. He will either be recognized as one's Savior and Lord of all on earth, or as one's Judge and Lord of all throughout eternity.

FIVE
THE GREAT TRIBULATION

A discouraged and despondent Job once exclaimed in despair, "Man that is born of a woman is of few days, and full of trouble. He cometh forth like a flower, and is cut down; he fleeth also as a shadow, and continueth not" (Job 14:1, 2).

Job's pessimistic description is tragically true for the unsaved man, apart from the grace of God. Throughout his tortured and sinful history he has been subjected to calamities, disasters, and plagues which have tracked him as a wolf would a rabbit.

A. Some of the tragic disasters.

Epidemics
1. During 1340–1350 over 25,000,000 people in Asia and Europe died of the Black Death.
2. In 1545 typhus killed 250,000 in Cuba alone.
3. In 1560 over 3,000,000 died of smallpox in Brazil.
4. In 1680 diphtheria killed 8,000 in Naples, Italy.
5. In 1792 nearly 1,000,000 perished in Egypt of the Black Plague.
6. In 1802 yellow fever killed 30,000 of Napoleon's soldiers in Santo Domingo.
7. In 1827 Europe lost 900,000 due to cholera.
8. In 1851 tuberculosis killed 51,000 in England.
9. In 1863 30,000 died of scarlet fever in England.
10. In 1918 some 30,000,000 perished during the worldwide epidemic of influenza.

Volcanic action

In 1902 Mount Pelee erupted in the West Indies, killing over 30,000 people.

Earthquakes

On January 24, 1556, some 830,000 died in China after a massive earthquake.

Fires

On December 30, 1903, the most tragic fire in U.S. history killed 600 people who had packed the Iroquois Theater in Chicago, Illinois.

Tornadoes

On March 18, 1925, nearly 700 people living in Illinois, Indiana, and Missouri lost their lives in a tornado.

Famines

In 1877 nearly 1,000,000 people starved to death in Northern China alone.

Floods

In 1887 China lost 900,000 due to one mighty flood.

Landslides

On December 16, 1891, 200,000 died in China because of a landslide.

Cyclones

On November 12, 1970, over 500,000 fell victim to a killer waterstorm in East Pakistan.

The point of all the above gruesome statistics is this: Catastrophe has been man's constant companion throughout recorded history. But according to the Bible there is coming a calamity unlike any which this weary world has ever seen. Although this future period will be relatively short, it will nevertheless destroy more of this earth's population than all of the previously quoted figures combined. In fact, nearly one billion people will be struck down during the beginning of this terrible coming disaster.

B. The names for this period.

No less than twelve titles for this blood-chilling period can be found in the Bible.

1. The day of the Lord.

This title is used more frequently than any other. See, for example, Isaiah 2:12; 13:6, 9; Ezekiel 13:5; 30:3; Joel 1:15; 2:1, 11, 31; 3:14; Amos 5:18, 20; Obadiah 15; Zephaniah 1:7, 14; Zechariah 14:1; Malachi 4:5; Acts 2:20; 1 Thessalonians 5:2; 2 Thessalonians 2:2; 2 Peter 3:10. A distinction should be made between the day of the Lord and the day of Christ. The day of Christ is a reference to the millennium. See 1 Corinthians 1:8; 5:5; 2 Corinthians 1:14; Philippians 1:6, 10; 2:16.

2. The indignation (Isa. 26:20; 34:2).
3. The day of God's vengeance (Isa. 34:8; 63:1-6).
4. The time of Jacob's trouble (Jer. 30:7).
5. The overspreading of abominations (Dan. 9:27).
6. The time of trouble such as never was (Dan. 12:1).
7. The seventieth week (Dan. 9:24-27).
8. The time of the end (Dan. 12:9).
9. The great day of his wrath (Rev. 6:17).
10. The hour of his judgment (Rev. 14:7).
11. The end of this world (Mt. 13:40, 49).
12. The tribulation (Mt. 24:21, 29).

The word "tribulation" is derived from the Latin *tribulum*, which was an agricultural tool used for separating the husks from the corn. As found in the Bible, the theological implications would include such concepts as a pressing together, an affliction, a burdening with anguish and trouble, a binding with oppression. Keeping this in mind, it would seem that of all the twelve names for the coming calamity, the last one would most accurately describe this period. Therefore, from this point on, the term tribulation will be employed.

The following passages aptly describe this future and fearful time.

Howl ye, for the day of the Lord is at hand. . . . Therefore shall all hands be faint, and every man's heart shall melt. . . . For the stars of heaven and the constellations thereof shall not give their light; the sun shall be darkened in his going forth, and the moon shall not cause her light to shine. . . . And I will punish the world for their evil . . . (Isa. 13:6, 7, 10, 11).

And they shall go into the holes of the rocks and into the caves of the earth for fear of the Lord . . . when he ariseth to shake terribly the earth (Isa. 2:19).

Behold, the Lord maketh the earth empty . . . and turneth it upside down, and scattereth abroad the inhabitants thereof. . . . The earth is utterly broken down, the earth is clean dissolved, the earth is moved exceedingly. The earth shall reel to and fro like a drunkard . . . (Isa. 24:1, 19, 20).

For the indignation of the Lord is upon all nations, and his fury upon all their armies. . . . Their slain also shall be cast out, and their stink shall come up out of their carcasses, and the mountains shall be melted with their blood. And all the host of heaven shall be dissolved, and the heavens shall be rolled together as a scroll . . . (Isa. 34:2–4).

I have trodden the winepress alone . . . for I will tread them in mine anger, and trample them in my fury; and their blood shall be sprinkled upon my garments, and I will stain all my raiment. For the day of vengeance is in mine heart. . . . And I will tread down the people in mine anger, and make them drunk in my fury . . . (Isa. 63:3, 4, 6).

Thus saith the Lord of hosts, Behold, evil shall go forth from nation to nation, and a great whirlwind shall be raised up from the coasts of the earth. And the slain of the Lord shall be at that day from one end of the earth even unto the other end of the earth; they shall not be lamented, neither gathered, nor buried . . . (Jer. 25:32, 33).

Blow ye the trumpet in Zion, and sound an alarm in my holy mountain: let all the inhabitants of the land tremble, for the day of the Lord cometh . . . a day of darkness and of gloominess, a day of clouds . . . there hath not been ever the like, neither shall be any more after it . . . (Joel 2:1, 2).

The great day of the Lord is near . . . that day is a day of wrath, a day of trouble and distress . . . (Zeph. 1:14, 15).

For nation shall rise against nation, and kingdom against kingdom: and there shall be famines, and pestilences, and earthquakes, in divers places. . . . And many false prophets shall rise, and shall deceive many. And because iniquity shall abound, the love of many shall wax cold. . . . For then shall be great tribulation, such as was not since the beginning of the world to this time, no, nor ever shall be. And except those days should be shortened, there should no flesh be saved . . . (Mt. 24:7, 11, 12, 21, 22).

*And there shall be signs in the sun and in the moon and in the
stars, and upon the earth distress of nations, with perplexity, the
sea and the waves roaring, men's hearts failing them for fear . . .
for the powers of heaven shall be shaken* (Lk. 21:25, 26).

*. . . the day of the Lord so cometh as a thief in the night. For
when they shall say, Peace and safety, then sudden destruction
cometh upon them, as travail upon a woman with child; and they
shall not escape* (1 Thess. 5:2, 3).

*. . . and, lo, there was a great earthquake; and the sun became
black as sackcloth of hair, and the moon became as blood; and the
stars of heaven fell unto the earth, even as a fig tree casteth her
untimely figs, when she is shaken of a mighty wind. And the heaven
departed as a scroll when it is rolled together; and every mountain
and island were moved out of their places. And the kings of the
earth, and the great men, and the rich men, and the chief captains,
and the mighty men, and every bondman, and every free man, hid
themselves in the dens and in the rocks of the mountains, and said
to the mountains and rocks, Fall on us, and hide us from the face
of him that sitteth on the throne, and from the wrath of the Lamb:
for the great day of his wrath is come; and who shall be able to
stand?* (Rev. 6:12–17).

C. The length of the tribulation.

To establish this time-span we must now briefly consider the
most important, the most amazing, and the most profound
single prophecy in the entire Word of God! It is often referred
to as the prophecy of the seventy weeks, and was written by
Daniel, who was living in Babylon around 550 B.C. Daniel, a
former Jewish captive, had been reading Jeremiah's prophecy,
which predicted that after a seventy-year captivity period,
God would permit the Jews to return to Jerusalem
(Jer. 25:11; 29:10). As Daniel studied those words he began
to pray, confessing both his sins and the sins of Israel. During
this powerful and tearful prayer, the angel Gabriel appeared
to Daniel and related to him the prophecy of the seventy
weeks, which reads as follows:

*Seventy weeks are determined upon thy people and upon thy holy
city, to finish the transgression, and to make an end of sins, and to
make reconciliation for iniquity, and to bring in everlasting
righteousness, and to seal up the vision and prophecy, and to
anoint the most holy. Know therefore and understand, that from*

the going forth of the commandment to restore and to build Jerusalem
unto the Messiah the Prince shall be seven weeks, and threescore
and two weeks; the street shall be built again, and the wall, even
in troublous times. And after threescore and two weeks shall
Messiah be cut off, but not for himself: and the people of the
prince that shall come shall destroy the city and the sanctuary;
and the end thereof shall be with a flood, and unto the end of
the war desolations are determined. And he shall confirm the
covenant with many for one week: and in the midst of the week
he shall cause the sacrifice and the oblation to cease, and for the
overspreading of abominations he shall make it desolate, even
until the consummation, and that determined shall be poured
upon the desolate (Dan. 9:24–27).

1. To whom does this prophecy refer? It refers to Israel.
2. What is meant by the term "seventy weeks"?
   In his correspondence course on the book of Daniel, Dr.
   Alfred Martin of Moody Bible Institute writes the
   following helpful words:

   "The expression translated 'seventy weeks' is literally
   'seventy sevens.' Apart from the context one would not
   know what the 'sevens' were. One would have to
   inquire, 'seven of what?' This expression in Hebrew
   would be as ambiguous as if one were to say in English,
   'I went to the store and bought a dozen.' A dozen of
   what? One of the basic principles of interpretation is that
   one must always interpret in the light of the context, that
   is, in the light of the passage in which a given statement
   occurs. As one searches this context, remembering that
   the vision was given in answer to the prayer, one notes
   that Daniel had been reading in Jeremiah that God would
   'accomplish seventy years in the desolations of
   Jerusalem' (Dan. 9:2). This is the clue. Daniel is told in
   effect, 'Yes, God will accomplish seventy years in the
   captivity; but now he is showing you that the whole
   history of the people of Israel will be consummated in a
   period of seventy sevens of years'" (Alfred Martin,
   Daniel, the Framework of Prophecy, Chicago: Moody
   Correspondence School, 1963, pp. 85, 86).

To further clarify the meaning of the seventy weeks, it should be noted that Israel had in its calendar not only a week of seven days (as in Ex. 23:12), but also a "week" of seven years (Gen. 29:27, 28; Lev. 25:3, 4, 8–10).

In other words, God is here telling Daniel that he would continue to deal with Israel for another 490 years before bringing in everlasting righteousness. To summarize this particular point:

a. Israel was to allow its land to remain idle every seventh year (Lev. 25:1–4).

b. This command was disobeyed (Lev. 26:33–35; 2 Chron. 36:21; Jer. 34:12–22).

c. Finally, over a total of 490 years, the nation had built up a land rest debt of seventy years.

d. Daniel knew of all this and was praying about it. He recognized that the seventy years of captivity represented seventy sevens of years in which those violations had transpired.

e. Gabriel now tells him that another period, similar in length (490 years) to that which had made the exile necessary, was coming in the experience of the people.

3. When was the seventy-week period to begin? It was to begin with the command to rebuild Jerusalem's walls. The first two chapters of Nehemiah inform us that this command was issued during the twentieth year of Artaxerxes' accession. The *Encyclopedia Britannica* sets this date on March 14, 445 B.C.

4. What are the three distinct time periods mentioned within the seventy-week prophecy and what was to happen during each period?

a. First period
Seven weeks (forty-nine years), from 445 B.C. to 396 B.C. The key event during this time was the building of the streets and walls of Jerusalem "even in troublous times." This literally took place. See Nehemiah 2–6.

b. Second period
Sixty-two weeks (434 years), from 396 B.C. to A.D. 30. At the end of this second period the Messiah

was crucified. See Matthew 27, Mark 15, Luke 23,
and John 19.

The brilliant British scholar and Bible student, Sir Robert
Anderson, has reduced the first two periods into their
exact number of days. This he has done by multiplying
483 (the combined years of the first two periods) by 360
(the days in a biblical year, as pointed out in Gen. 7:11,
24; 8:3, 4).

The total number of days in the first sixty-nine weeks
(or 483 years) is 173,880. Anderson then points out
that if one begins counting on March 14, 445 B.C., and
goes forward in history, these days would run out on
April 6, A.D. 32.

It was on this very day that Jesus made his triumphal
entry into the city of Jerusalem. Surely our Lord must
have had Daniel's prophecy in mind when he said, "if
thou hadst known, even thou, at least in this thy day,
the things which belong to thy peace! But now they are
hid from thine eyes" (Lk. 19:42).

Of course, it was also on this same day that the
Pharisees plotted to murder Christ (Luke 19:47). Thus
Daniel, writing some five-and-one-half centuries earlier,
correctly predicted the very day of Christ's presentation
and rejection! (Note: Between the second and third
periods, there is a "time-out" period, unknown to
Daniel, called *The Church Age*.)

c. Third period

One-half week (three-and-a-half years), the first half
of the tribulation. At the beginning of this period the
antichrist will make a seven-year pact with Israel.

One-half week (three-and-a-half years), the last half
of the tribulation. At the beginning of this period the
antichrist will break his pact with Israel and will begin
his terrible bloodbath. At the end of the last week
(and of the entire seventy-week period), the true
Messiah will come and establish his perfect millennium.

5. Do the seventy weeks run continuously? That is to say, is
there a gap somewhere between these 490 years, or do
they run without pause until they are completed?

Dispensational theology teaches that these "weeks" do

not run continuously, but that there has been a gap or parenthesis of nearly 2,000 years between the sixty-ninth and seventieth week. The chronology may be likened to a seventy-minute basketball game. For sixty-nine minutes the game has been played at a furious and continuous pace. Then the referee for some reason calls time out with the clock in the red showing one final minute of play. No one knows for sure when the action will start again, but at some point the referee will step in and blow his whistle. At that time the teams will gather to play out the last minute of the game.

God has stepped in and stopped the clock of prophecy at Calvary. This divine "time out" has already lasted some twenty centuries, but soon now the Redeemer will blow his trumpet and the final "week" of action will be played upon this earth.

6. Does the Bible offer any other examples of time gaps in divine programs? It does indeed. At least three instances come to mind in which gaps of many centuries can be found in a single short paragraph.

a. Isaiah 9:6, 7:

For unto us a child is born, unto us a son is given: and the government shall be upon his shoulder: and his name shall be called Wonderful, Counsellor, The mighty God, The everlasting Father, The Prince of Peace. Of the increase of his government and peace there shall be no end, upon the throne of David, and upon his kingdom. . . .

In the first part of verse 6 a gap of at least twenty centuries is separated by a colon. The phrase "unto us a son is given" refers to Bethlehem, while the words "and the government shall be upon his shoulder" look forward to the millennium.

b. Zechariah 9:9, 10:

Rejoice greatly, O daughter of Zion; shout, O daughter of Jerusalem: behold, thy King cometh unto thee: he is just, and having salvation; lowly, and riding upon an ass, and upon a colt the foal of an ass. . . . And he shall speak peace unto the heathen: and his dominion shall be from sea even to sea, and from the river even to the ends of the earth.

Verse 9 is a clear reference to the triumphal entry of our Lord, but verse 10 looks ahead to the millennium.
c. Isaiah 61:1, 2:

The Spirit of the Lord God is upon me; because the Lord hath anointed me to preach good tidings unto the meek; he hath sent me to bind up the brokenhearted, to proclaim liberty to the captives, and the opening of the prison to them that are bound; to proclaim the acceptable year of the Lord, and the day of vengeance of our God. . . .

In verse 2 of this passage Christ's earthly ministry (to "proclaim the acceptable year of the Lord") and the tribulation (the "day of vengeance of our God") are separated by only a comma! It is extremely important to note that when Jesus read this passage during his sermon in Nazareth, he ended the reading at this comma, for "the day of vengeance" was not the purpose of his first coming. (See Lk. 4:18, 19.)

7. Review of the seventy weeks.
  a. The six main accomplishments of the seventy weeks.
    (1) To bring to an end all human transgressions and sins, especially those of the nation Israel (Ezek. 37:23; Acts 3:13–16; 28:25–31; Rom. 11:26, 27).
    (2) To make reconciliation for iniquity. This was done at Calvary when the Messiah was cut off (1 Cor. 5:18–20).
    (3) To vindicate by fulfillment all true prophets and their prophecies.
    (4) To prove the inability of the devil to rightfully rule this world.
    (5) To destroy him and his chief henchman, the antichrist (Rev. 19:20; 20:10).
    (6) To usher in the millennium (Ps. 45:3–7; Isa. 11:3–5; Jer. 23:3–8).
  b. The three main time-periods of the seventy weeks (490 years).
    (1) First period (forty-nine years, or seven weeks)— from 445 B.C. to 396 B.C.
    (2) Second period (434 years, or sixty-two weeks)— from 396 B.C. to A.D. 32.

(3) A time out period (which has already lasted almost twenty centuries). This time gap between the sixty-ninth and seventieth week was unrevealed and therefore unknown to the Old Testament prophets. (See Eph. 3:1-10; 1 Pet. 1:10-12.)

(4) Third period (seven years, or one week)—from the rapture until the millennium.

  c. The two main individuals of the seventy weeks.

    (1) Messiah—the Lord Jesus Christ.

    (2) The prince that shall come—the wicked antichrist.

D. The purpose of the tribulation.

Why this terrible period? At least seven scriptural reasons are:

  1. To harvest the crop that has been sown throughout the ages by God, Satan, and mankind.

This aspect is so important that our Lord took an entire sermon to discuss it. Portions of his message are as follows:

  a. The first part of the sermon proclaimed.

Behold, a sower went forth to sow. And when he sowed, some seeds fell by the way side, and the fowls came and devoured them up: Some fell upon stony places, where they had not much earth: and forthwith they sprung up, because they had no deepness of earth: And when the sun was up, they were scorched; and because they had no root, they withered away. And some fell among thorns; and the thorns sprung up, and choked them: But other fell into good ground, and brought forth fruit, some an hundredfold, some sixtyfold, some thirtyfold (Mt. 13:3-8).

  b. The first part of the sermon explained.

Hear ye therefore the parable of the sower. When any one heareth the word of the kingdom, and understandeth it not, then cometh the wicked one, and catcheth away that which was sown in his heart. This is he which received seed by the way side. But he that received the seed into stony places, the same is he that heareth the word, and at once with joy receiveth it; yet hath not root in himself, but dureth for a while: for when tribulation or persecution ariseth because of the word, by and by he is offended. He also that received seed among the thorns is he that heareth the word; and the care of this world, and the deceitfulness

*of riches, choke the word, and he becometh unfruitful. But
he that received seed into the good ground is he that
heareth the word, and understandeth it; which also beareth
fruit, and bringeth forth, some an hundredfold, some sixty,
some thirty* (Mt. 13:18–23).

c. The second part of the sermon proclaimed.
*The kingdom of heaven is likened unto a man which
sowed good seed in his field: but while men slept, his
enemy came and sowed tares among the wheat, and went
his way. But when the blade was sprung up, and brought
forth fruit, then appeared the tares also. So the servants of
the householder came and said unto him, Sir, didst not
thou sow good seed in the field? from whence then hath it
tares? He said unto them, An enemy hath done this. The
servants said unto him, Wilt thou then that we go and
gather them up? But he said, Nay, lest while ye gather up
the tares, ye root up also the wheat with them. Let both
grow together until the harvest: and in the time of harvest I
will say to the reapers, Gather ye together first the tares,
and bind them in bundles to burn them: but gather the
wheat into my barn* (Mt. 13:24–30).

d. The second part of the sermon explained.
*He that soweth the good seed is the Son of man; the field
is the world; the good seed are the children of the kingdom,
but the tares are the children of the wicked one; the enemy
that sowed them is the devil; the harvest is the end of the
world; and the reapers are the angels. As therefore the
tares are gathered and burned in the fire, so shall it be in
the end of this world. The Son of man shall send forth his
angels, and they shall gather out of his kingdom all things
that offend, and them which do iniquity; and shall cast
them into a furnace of fire: there shall be wailing and
gnashing of teeth. Then shall the righteous shine forth as
the sun in the kingdom of their Father* (Mt. 13:37–43).

2. To prove the falseness of the devil's claim.
Since his fall (Isa. 14:12–14), Satan has been attempting
to convince a skeptical universe that he rather than
Christ is the logical and rightful ruler of creation.
Therefore, during the tribulation the sovereign God will
give him a free and unhindered hand to make good his

boast. Needless to say, Satan will fail miserably.

3. To prepare a great martyred multitude for heaven.
   After this I beheld, and, lo, a great multitude, which no man could number, of all nations and kindreds and people and tongues, stood before the throne. . . . These are they which came out of great tribulation, and have washed their robes, and made them white in the blood of the lamb (Rev. 7:9, 14).

4. To prepare a great living multitude for the millennium.
   And before him shall be gathered all nations: and he shall separate them one from another, as a shepherd divideth his sheep from the goats: And he shall set the sheep on his right hand, but the goats on the left. Then shall the King say unto them on his right hand, Come, ye blessed of my Father, inherit the kingdom prepared for you from the foundation of the world (Mt. 25:32–34).

5. To punish the Gentiles.
   For the wrath of God is revealed from heaven against all ungodliness and unrighteousness of men . . . (Rom. 1:18).
   And for this cause God shall send them strong delusion, that they should believe a lie, that they all might be damned who believe not the truth, but had pleasure in unrighteousness (2 Thess. 2:11, 12).
   And out of his mouth goeth a sharp sword, that with it he should smite the nations (Rev. 19:15).

6. To purge Israel.
   And I will cause you to pass under the rod . . . and I will purge out from among you the rebels . . . (Ezek. 20:37, 38).
   And it shall come to pass, that in all the land, saith the Lord, two parts therein shall be cut off and die; but the third shall be left therein. And I will bring the third part through the fire, and will refine them as silver is refined, and will try them as gold is tried; they shall call on my name, and I will hear them: I will say, it is my people: and they shall say, The Lord is my God (Zech. 13:8, 9).
   And he shall sit as a refiner and purifier of silver; and he shall purify the sons of Levi, and purge them as gold and silver, that they may offer unto the Lord an offering in righteousness (Mal. 3:3).

7. To prepare the earth itself for the millennium.

The Bible indicates that prior to the great flood, our earth was surrounded by a watery canopy (Gen. 1:6, 7; 7:11) resulting in a universal semitropical paradise of a climate. The discovery of vast oil and coal deposits in the area of both North and South poles bears strong witness to this. In addition there were probably no deserts, ice caps, rugged mountains, or deep canyons, all of which so radically affect our weather today. But then came the flood, changing all this. (The psalmist may have written about this in Psalm 104:5–9.) However, during the millennium, pre-flood conditions will once again prevail. (See Isa. 4:5; 30:26; 40:3–5; 60:19, 20.) Mankind will once again experience longevity. (Compare Gen. 5 with Isa. 65:20.)

But by what process will all these tremendous changes come about? It is interesting that the King James Bible translators used the word "regeneration" on but two occasions. One is in reference to the conversion of repenting sinners (Titus 3:5), and the other describes the salvation of nature itself. Note:

And Jesus said unto them, Verily I say unto you, that ye which have followed me, in the regeneration when the Son of man shall sit in the throne of his glory, ye also shall sit upon twelve thrones, judging the twelve tribes of Israel (Mt. 19:28).

In other words, mother nature herself will be gloriously regenerated and give up her evil habits (droughts, tornadoes, floods, cyclones, earthquakes, volcanic action, etc.) at the beginning of the millennium. Here are the conditions which will lead up to her marvelous conversion:

a. Between the sixth and seventh judgment seals the winds of heaven are held back.
   And after these things I saw four angels standing on the four corners of the earth, holding the four winds of the earth, that the wind should not blow on the earth, nor on the sea, nor on any tree (Rev. 7:1).

b. During the fourth vial judgment, great solar heat proceeds from the sun.
   And the fourth angel poured out his vial upon the sun;

70

and power was given unto him to scorch men with fire. And men were scorched with great heat, and blasphemed the name of God, which hath power over these plagues: and they repented not to give him glory (Rev. 16:8, 9).

c. As a result of the seventh vial judgment, the mightiest earthquake of all times takes place.
There was a great earthquake, such as was not since men were upon the earth. . . . And every island fled away, and the mountains were not found (Rev. 16:18, 20).

d. During the tribulation the sun will boil away great quantities of water into the upper atmosphere.

e. However, the absence of wind will prohibit the formation of clouds, thus making it impossible for rain to fall. As a result, the original pre-flood canopy will be reestablished.

f. The world's greatest earthquake will level the mountains and fill up the deep canyons, thus creating the gentle geographical terrain existing before the flood.

What a wonderful and gracious God we have, who will use the very wrath of the tribulation as an instrument to prepare for the glories of the millennium. In performing this, God will answer a prayer once uttered by the prophet Habakkuk some six centuries B.C.
O Lord . . . revive thy work in the midst of the years . . . in wrath remember mercy (Hab. 3:2).

71

SIX
THE
PERSONALITIES IN
THE TRIBULATION

As in a play, a number of actors will render their parts and say their lines during the earth's most sobering drama, the tribulation.

A. The Holy Spirit.

Contrary to some, the Holy Spirit will not be removed when the church is raptured. He will instead (it would seem) perform a ministry similar to his work in the Old Testament. It is concluded that he will remain on earth due to the fact that many will be saved during the tribulation (Rev. 7:9-17). The Word of God makes it crystal clear that no mortal can ever be saved apart from the convicting ministry of the Holy Spirit. (See Jn. 3:5-8; 16:8-11; 1 Cor. 2:1-13.) At any rate, his presence will be felt in the tribulation, as indicated by the prophet Joel.

And it shall come to pass afterward, that I will pour out my spirit upon all flesh. . . . And I will shew wonders in the heavens and in the earth, blood, and fire, and pillars of smoke. The sun shall be turned into darkness, and the moon into blood, before the great and the terrible day of the Lord come. And it shall come to pass, that whosoever shall call on the name of the Lord shall be delivered (Joel 2:28, 30-32).

(See also Rev. 11:11; 17:3.)

B. The devil.

Woe to the inhabiters of the earth and of the sea! For the devil is come down unto you, having great wrath, because he knoweth that he hath but a short time (Rev. 12:12).

72

C. Two special Old Testament (?) witnesses.
And I will give power unto my two witnesses, and they shall prophesy a thousand two hundred and threescore days, clothed in sackcloth (Rev. 11:3).

D. The antichrist.
. . . that man of sin . . . the son of perdition, who opposeth and exalteth himself above all that is called God, or that is worshipped, so that he as God sitteth in the temple of God, shewing himself that he is God. . . . Even him, whose coming is after the working of Satan with all power and signs and lying wonders (2 Thess. 2:3, 4, 9).

E. The false prophet.
And I beheld another beast coming up out of the earth; and he had two horns like a lamb, and he spake as a dragon (Rev. 13:11).

F. A multitude of specialized angels.
Angels have been employed throughout the Bible to perform God's work, but at no other time will they be as busy as during the tribulation. The book of Revelation describes the following for us:
1. An angel with the seal of the living God (Rev. 7:2).
2. Seven angels with seven trumpets (Rev. 8, 9, 11).
3. An angel with a golden censer (Rev. 8:3).
4. An angel with a little book and a measuring reed (Rev. 10:1, 2; 11:1).
5. An angel with the everlasting gospel (Rev. 14:6).
6. An angel with a harvest sickle (Rev. 14:19).
7. Seven angels with seven vials of wrath (Rev. 16).
8. An angel with a message of doom (Rev. 18:1, 21).
9. An angel with a strange invitation (Rev. 19:17).
10. An angel with a key and a great chain (Rev. 20:1).
In the Old Testament, the prophet Daniel (Dan. 12:1) informs us that one of these angels will be Michael the Archangel himself.

G. One-hundred-forty-four-thousand Israelite preachers.
And I heard the number of them which were sealed: and there were sealed an hundred and forty and four thousand of all tribes of the children of Israel (Rev. 7:4).

H. An army of locust-like demons from the bottomless pit.
And he opened the bottomless pit; and there arose a smoke out of the pit, as the smoke of a great furnace; and the sun and the air

73

*were darkened by reason of the smoke of the pit. And there came
out of the smoke locusts upon the earth: and unto them was given
power, as the scorpions of the earth have power* (Rev. 9:2, 3).

I. An army of horse and rider demons from the Euphrates River.

*And the number of the army of the horsemen were two hundred
thousand thousand: and I heard the number of them* (Rev. 9:16).

J. Three evil spirits.

*And I saw three evil spirits disguised as frogs leap from the mouth
of the Dragon, the Creature, and his False Prophet. These miracle-
working demons conferred with all the rulers of the world to gather
them for battle against the Lord on that great coming Judgment Day
of God Almighty* (Rev. 16:13, 14, TLB).

K. A cruel, power-mad ruler from the north.

*And the word of the Lord came unto me, saying, Son of man, set
thy face against Gog, the land of Magog, the chief prince of
Meshech and Tubal, and prophesy against him, and say, Thus
saith the Lord God; Behold, I am against thee, O Gog, the chief
prince of Meshech and Tubal* (Ezek. 38:1-3).

L. Four symbolic women.

1. A persecuted woman (Israel).

   *And there appeared a great wonder in heaven; a woman
   clothed with the sun, and the moon under her feet, and upon
   her head a crown of twelve stars* (Rev. 12:1).

2. A vile and bloody harlot (the false church).

   *So he carried me away in the spirit into the wilderness: and I
   saw a woman sit upon a scarlet coloured beast, full of names
   of blasphemy, having seven heads and ten horns. And the
   woman was arrayed in purple and scarlet colour, and decked
   with gold and precious stones and pearls, having a golden cup
   in her hand full of abominations and filthiness of her
   fornication: And upon her forehead was a name written,
   MYSTERY, BABYLON THE GREAT, THE MOTHER
   OF HARLOTS AND ABOMINATIONS OF THE
   EARTH* (Rev. 17:3-5).

3. An arrogant queen (the world's political and economic systems).

   *And he cried mightily with a strong voice, saying, Babylon the
   great is fallen, is fallen, and is become the habitation of devils,
   and the hold of every foul spirit, and a cage of every unclean*

and hateful bird. How much she hath glorified herself, and lived deliciously, so much torment and sorrow give her: for she saith in her heart, I sit a queen, and am no widow, and shall see no sorrow (Rev. 18:2, 7).

4. A pure, chaste bride (the true church).
   Let us be glad and rejoice, and give honour to him: for the marriage of the Lamb is come, and his wife hath made herself ready. And to her was granted that she should be arrayed in fine linen, clean and white: for the fine linen is the righteousness of saints (Rev. 19:7, 8).

M. A mighty warrior from heaven.
   And I saw heaven opened, and behold a white horse; and he that sat upon him was called Faithful and True, and in righteousness he doth judge and make war. And he hath on his vesture and on his thigh a name written, KING OF KINGS, AND LORD OF LORDS" (Rev. 19:11, 16).

SEVEN
THE FIRST PART OF
THE TRIBULATION
(3½ YEARS)

THE ACTION OF THIS SEVEN-YEAR PERIOD.
1. The formal organization of the super harlot church. John the
   apostle writes about a bloodshedding, God-hating, gold-
   loving prostitute, calling her "mystery Babylon" (Rev. 17:5).
   This brutal, bloody, and blasphemous harlot is none other
   than the universal false church, the wicked wife of Satan.
   God had no sooner begun his blessed work in preparing for
   himself a people than the devil did likewise. In fact, the first
   baby to be born on this earth later became Satan's original
   convert. (See Gen. 4:8; 1 Jn. 3:12.) We shall now consider
   the historical, current, and future activities of this perverted
   prostitute.
   a. The harlot viewed historically.
      (1) Satan's church began officially at the tower of Babel
          in Genesis 11:1–9, nearly twenty-four centuries B.C.
          Here, in the fertile plain of Shinar, probably very
          close to the original Garden of Eden, the first spade
          of dirt was turned for the purpose of devil-worship.
      (2) The first full-time minister of Satan was Nimrod,
          Noah's wicked and apostate grandson (Gen.
          10:8–10).
          Secular history and tradition tell us that Nimrod
          married a woman who was as evil and demonic as
          himself. Her name was Semerimus. Knowing God's
          promise of a future Savior (Gen. 3:15), Semerimus

brazenly claimed that Tammuz, her first son, fulfilled this prophecy.

Semerimus thereupon instituted a religious system which made both her and her son the objects of divine worship. She herself became the first high priestess. Thus began the mother-child cult which later spread all over the world.

From Babylon it spread to Phoenicia under the name of Ashteroth and Tammuz.

From Phoenicia it traveled to Pergamos in Asia Minor. This is the reason for John's admonition to the church at Pergamos in the book of Revelation: "I know thy works, and where thou dwellest, even where Satan's seat is . . ." (Rev. 2:13).

In Egypt the mother-child cult was known as Isis and Horus.

In Greece it became Aphrodite and Eros.

In Rome this pair was worshiped as Venus and Cupid. Dr. J. Dwight Pentecost writes:

"Several years ago I visited an archeological museum in Mexico City. A recent find had just been put on display which Mexican archeologists had authenticated as belonging to the period about 200 years before Christ. The object was the center of religious worship among some of the early Indians in Mexico. To my amazement, it was an image of a mother with a child in her arms. This Babylonian religion spread abroad to become the religion of the world . . ." (*Prophecy for Today*, Moody Press, p. 133).

What was the teaching of Semerimus' satanic church? That Semerimus herself was the way to God. She actually adopted the title "Queen of Heaven." Adherents believed that she alone could administer salvation to the sinner through various sacraments, such as the sprinkling of holy water. They believed that her son Tammuz was tragically slain by a wild bear during a hunting trip, but was, however, resurrected from the dead forty days later. Thus, each year afterward the temple virgins of this cult would enter a forty-day fast as a memorial to Tammuz' death and resurrection.

After the forty-day fast, a joyful feast called Ishtar took place. At this feast colored eggs were exchanged and eaten as a symbol of the resurrection. An evergreen tree was displayed and a yule log was burned. Finally hot cakes marked with the letter T (to remind everybody of Tammuz) were baked and eaten.

About 2000 B.C. God called Abraham away from all this (see Josh. 24:2, 3) and led him into the Promised Land. But by the ninth century B.C., Israel had returned to this devil worship under the influence of wicked Jezebel (see 1 Ki. 16:30–33). At this time the cult was worshiped under the name of Baal.

Both Jeremiah and Ezekiel warned against this hellish thing.

The children gather wood, and the fathers kindle the fire, and the women knead their dough, to make cakes to the queen of heaven . . . to burn incense to the queen of heaven, and to pour out drink offerings unto her . . . (Jer. 7:18; 44:25).

Then he brought me to the door of the gate of the Lord's house which was toward the north; and behold, there sat women weeping for Tammuz (Ezek. 8:14).

By the time of Christ this cult had so influenced Roman life that the Caesars were not only crowned as Emperors of Rome but also bore the title Pontifex Maximus, meaning, "high priest." They were high priests of the Babylonian satanic church.

During A.D. 306 a Roman Emperor named Constantine was threatened by a very powerful enemy army. Realizing that his uneasy troops needed confidence, Constantine claimed to have seen a vision on the eve of the battle. He saw a large blue flag with a red cross on it and heard a mighty voice which said *In hoc signo vinces*—"in this sign conquer." He thereupon marched his troops into a shallow river, claimed them to be officially baptized, and ordered the sign of the cross painted on all his weapons. Thus inspired, he led his troops to victory and subsequently made Christianity the state religion of Rome.

The Roman priests of Tammuz soon discovered that they could easily make the transition into Christianity (with certain changes) and thereupon carried their traditions forward without interruption by promoting the madonna-child worship concept, the holy water sacrament, etc.

Thus for nearly 300 years the devil had desperately attempted to destroy the church from outside by his terrible persecutions. But with the advent of Constantine he changed his tactics, walking the aisle, applying for membership, and joining the church. To this very day he holds his church letter. The corrupted church was already flourishing in Christ's day, and the Savior delivered a scathing attack against some of its very deacons and elders. (See Mt. 23.)

b. The harlot viewed currently.

Is mystery Babylon at work today? She is indeed, stronger and more sinful than ever. At least three New Testament writers describe her latter-day activities and characteristics.

(1) Paul.

This know also, that in the last days perilous times shall come. For men shall be lovers of their own selves, covetous, boasters, proud, blasphemers, disobedient to parents, unthankful, unholy, without natural affection, trucebreakers, false accusers, incontinent, fierce, despisers of those that are good, traitors, heady, highminded, lovers of pleasures more than lovers of God; having a form of godliness, but denying the power thereof . . . (2 Tim. 3:1–5).

For the time will come when they will not endure sound doctrine; but after their own lusts shall they heap

to themselves teachers, having itching ears; and they
shall turn away their ears from the truth, and shall be
turned unto fables (2 Tim. 4:3, 4).

(2) Peter.

But there were false prophets also among the people,
even as there shall be false teachers among you, who
privily shall bring in damnable heresies, even denying the
Lord that bought them . . . (2 Pet. 2:1).

(3) John.

I know thy works, that thou art neither cold nor hot; I
would thou wert cold or hot. So then because thou art
lukewarm, and neither cold or hot, I will spue thee out
of my mouth. Because thou sayest, I am rich and
increased with goods, and have need of nothing, and
knowest not that thou art wretched, and miserable, and
poor, and blind, and naked (Rev. 3:15–17).

c. The harlot viewed prophetically.

Mystery Babylon is composed of apostate masses from
Protestantism, Catholicism, Judaism, and every other
major world religion. It is entirely possible that the
World Council of Churches will spearhead this latter-day
ungodly union. A recent event would strongly suggest
this. In 1955, as a celebration of the tenth anniversary of
the United Nations, a special "Festival of Faith" was held
in the San Francisco Cow Palace. This was reported in the
September issue of *The National Council Outlook*, the
official organ of the National Council of Churches. Here
are their own words:

"Today in the United Nations mankind finds new hope
for the achievement of peace. This hope was given
dramatic expression last June 19 when some 16,000 persons of every race, creed, and color assembled in San
Francisco's Cow Palace to pray for peace and pledge their
support to the United Nations. . . . There were Christians
and Jews, Buddhists and Confucianists, Hindus and
Moslems—men whose names are household words
around the world, and workaday folk.

They called God by different names—speaking to Him

in different tongues, but the dream for peace in their hearts was the same—and the prayers on their lips echoed the prayers of people around the world. Initiated by the San Francisco Council of Churches, the Festival of Faith was a symbol for all men of the oneness of their aspirations. . . . High point of the prayer meeting was the recitation together of the Responsive Reading, composed of sentences from the sacred books of the six faiths represented—Christian, Jewish, Moslem, Buddhist, Hindu, and Confucian."

2. The appearance of the antichrist and his false prophet. Since the days of Adam, it has been estimated that approximately 40 billion human beings have been born upon our earth. Four and one-half billion of this number are alive today.

However, by any standard of measurement one might employ, the greatest human (apart from the Son of God himself) in matters of ability and achievement is yet to make his appearance upon our planet.

The Scriptures give him various names and titles:

The little horn (Dan. 7:8).
The willful king (Dan. 11:36).
The man of sin (2 Thess. 2:3).
The son of perdition (2 Thess. 2:3).
The wicked one (2 Thess. 2:8).
The beast (Rev. 11:7—this title is found thirty-six times in the book of Revelation).

However, his most descriptive title is the antichrist. (1 Jn. 2:18, 22; 4:3). Note but a few scriptural references describing this satanic superman:
And he shall speak great words against the most High, and shall wear out the saints of the most High . . . (Dan. 7:25).
And the king shall do according to his will; and he shall exalt himself, and magnify himself above every god, and shall speak marvellous things against the God of gods . . . (Dan. 11:36).
. . . that man of sin . . . the son of perdition; who opposeth and exalteth himself above all that is called God, or that is worshipped; so that he as God sitteth in the temple of God,

shewing himself that he is God. . . . Even him whose coming is
after the working of Satan with all power and signs and lying
wonders (2 Thess. 2:3, 4, 9).

Who is a liar but he that denieth that Jesus is the Christ? He is
antichrist, that denieth the Father and the Son (1 Jn. 2:22).

And I saw, and behold a white horse: and he that sat on him
had a bow; and a crown was given unto him: and he went forth
conquering, and to conquer" (Rev. 6:2).

And I stood upon the sand of the sea, and saw a beast rise up
out of the sea. . . . And the beast which I saw was like unto a
leopard, and his feet were as the feet of a bear, and his mouth as
the mouth of a lion: and the dragon gave him his power . . . and
great authority. . . . And he opened his mouth in blasphemy
against God . . . (Rev. 13:1, 2, 6).

a. Historical and modern attempts to identify the antichrist.
The ink of the holy writ which spoke of the antichrist
had scarcely dried before speculation arose concerning his
identity.

(1) Some believe he will be a Gentile.
Tim LaHaye writes:

"One of the most frequently asked questions about
the Antichrist concerns his nationality. Revelation
13:1 indicates that he 'rises up out of the sea,'
meaning the sea of peoples around the
Mediterranean. From this we gather that he will be
a Gentile. Daniel 8:8, 9 suggests that he is the 'little
horn' that came out of the four Grecian horns,
signaling that he will be part Greek. Daniel 9:26
refers to him as the prince of the people that shall
come, meaning that he will be of the royal lineage of
the race that destroyed Jerusalem. Historically this
was the Roman Empire; therefore he will be
predominantly Roman" (Tim LaHaye, *Revelation*,
Zondervan, 1975, p. 172).

(2) Others affirm he will be a Jew, based on two Old
Testament passages and one New Testament
passage.

82

Ezekiel 21:25: "And thou, profane wicked prince of Israel, whose day is come when iniquity shall have an end."

Daniel 11:37: "Neither shall he regard the God of his fathers. . . ."

John 5:43: "I am come in my Father's name, and ye receive me not: if another shall come in his own name, him ye will receive."

(3) There are also those who feel he will come from the tribe of Dan, basing this upon the following:

(a) Jacob's prophecy upon his son Dan:
Dan shall be a serpent by the way, an adder in the path, that biteth the horse heels, so that his rider shall fall backward (Gen. 49:17).

(b) Dan was the first tribe to be guilty of idolatry. See Judges 18:30, 31; 1 Kings 12:29.

(c) Jeremiah's prophecy concerning the tribulation:
The snorting of his horses was heard from Dan: the whole land trembled at the sound . . . for they are come, and have devoured the land, and all that is in it; the city, and those that dwell therein. For, behold, I will send serpents, cockatrices, among you, which will not be charmed, and they shall bite you, saith the Lord (Jer. 8:16, 17).

(d) The tribe of Dan is omitted from the list in Revelation 7. This chapter records the tribal identity of the 144,000 Hebrew evangelists who will be saved and called to special service during the tribulation.

But the antichrist guessing game has gone much further than mere attempts to identify his racial or tribal origins.

(4) A number of overzealous Bible students have claimed he could be personally identified.

(a) The antichrist is Judas Iscariot
Some believe he will be Judas Iscariot, on the basis of the following verses:

Luke 22:3; John 13:27—here Satan actually enters Judas. This is never said of any other individual in the Bible.

John 6:70, 71—here Jesus refers to Judas as the devil.

John 17:12; 2 Thessalonians 2:3—the title "son of perdition" is found only twice in the New Testament. In the first instance Jesus used it to refer to Judas. In the second instance Paul used it to refer to the antichrist.

Acts 1:25—here Peter says that Judas after his death went "to his own place." Some have seen in this a reference to the bottomless pit, and, and believe that Satan has retained Judas there for the past 2,000 years in preparation for his future role as the antichrist!

(b) The antichrist is Nero

Nero committed suicide under somewhat mysterious circumstances in A.D. 68. Rumors then began to circulate that he would rise from the dead and lead a fierce army against God's people.

(c) The antichrist is Titus

Titus was the Roman general who destroyed the city of Jerusalem in A.D. 70.

(d) The antichrist is Domitian

Domitian was the Roman Emperor on the throne when John wrote the book of Revelation.

(e) The antichrist is Constantine the Great

He was the Roman ruler who declared Christianity to be the state religion in A.D. 325, and thereby corrupting it with gross worldiness and paganism.

(f) The antichrist is Mohammed

Mohammed was born in Mecca in A.D. 570 and later became the founder of the Islamic religion.

(g) The antichrist is various Roman Catholic Popes

St. Bernard in the twelfth century called Pope Leo the beast of Revelation. In the thirteenth century Frederick II, ruler of Germany, accused Pope Gregory IX of being the antichrist. Both Wycliffe and John Huss were convinced that the Pope during their day was the antichrist. John Whitgift, Professor of Divinity in Cambridge University, presented his doctoral thesis to the faculty of the university, in which he "proved" that the Pope was the antichrist. He was awarded a Doctor of Divinity Degree on the basis of this work. The Westminster Confession of Faith in 1646 stated this:

"There is no other head of the church but the Lord Jesus Christ: nor can the Pope of Rome in any sense be the head thereof; but is that antichrist, that man of sin and son of perdition, that exalteth himself in the church against Christ."

This was also the view of King James of England, who authorized the King James Bible. Walter Price writes:

"While only twenty years of age he wrote a paraphrase upon the Revelation of the Apostle John, in which he set forth the view that the locusts mentioned in the book of Revelation were different orders of monks, and their king was the pope" (*The Coming Antichrist*, Moody Press, 1974, p. 35).

(h) The antichrist is Napoleon
On the opening page of Tolstoy's famous novel *War and Peace*, there is an interesting reference to this belief that Napoleon is the antichrist.
(i) The antichrist is Benito Mussolini

In 1926 the famed missionary statesman, Oswald J. Smith, wrote a tract entitled, "Is the Antichrist at Hand?" In it he strongly hinted that the Italian dictator might well be the antichrist. Smith wrote:

"If our chronology is correct it means that all these things, including the great tribulation, the revival of the Roman Empire, the reign of the Antichrist, and the battle of Armageddon must take place before the year 1933."

Dr. Harry Ironside, former pastor of the famed Moody Memorial Church in Chicago, also felt Mussolini to be the antichrist. On January 8, 1930, he delivered a message to the students of the Bible Institute of Los Angeles. Walter Price records for us some of his quotes on that occasion concerning the rise of Mussolini:

"His bombastic utterances backed up by tremendous ability to perform have astonished the world. He declares himself the Man of Destiny, chosen to revive the Roman Empire and restore it to its pristine glory. The Mediterranean, he declares, shall yet become a Roman lake surrounded by nations in alliance with Italy. His grandiose plans move on to fulfillment in spite of all opposition" (*The Coming Antichrist*, Moody Press, 1974, p. 40).

(j) The antichrist is Adolph Hitler
During the late 1930s and early 1940s, many pamphlets appeared identifying Adolph Hitler as the antichrist. The most sensational attempt involved equating the 666 antichrist number of Revelation 13:18 with the name Hitler. To accomplish this, a unique numerical system was devised whereby the English letter A

equaled 100, B equaled 101, C, 102, D, 103,
etc. Thus:

H - 107
I - 108
T - 119
L - 111
E - 104
R - <u>117</u>
    666

(k) The antichrist is Henry Kissinger
This is one of the latest and perhaps most
foolish, futile attempts to identify the
antichrist. It also involves the use of a
makeshift numbering system. In this case A
equals 6, B, 12, C, 18, D, 24, etc. As a result:

K - 66
I - 54
S - 114
S - 114
I - 54
N - 84
G - 42
E - 30
R - <u>108</u>
    666

(l) The antichrist is whoever you don't especially
like!
It seems the foolish and futile antichrist
speculation syndrome has all but reached this
sorry stage.

b. Worldly preparations for the antichrist.
In the 60s and 70s a rash of movies from Hollywood
were released dealing with a subject previously untouched
by the film industry, the birth of the antichrist. The three
most famous were (1) "Rosemary's Baby," (2) "The
Omen," and (3) "Damien Omen II." The first to hit the
box office was "Rosemary's Baby." This amazing film has
for its plot the rape of a drugged girl by Satan himself,
arranged by her materialistic husband and a small band of
devil worshipers. After the birth, the once horrified

mother stoically accepts her chosen role and, as the movie ends, joins with the rest of the faithful in worshiping this child of perdition. The second film, "The Omen," begins with the birth of antichrist. The scene is a dimly lit hospital in Rome where a distraught American diplomat makes a decision that will involve him in a bizarre life of unrelenting terror. The doctor has just told him that his wife has delivered a child who lived but a moment. A priest appears from the shadows to arrange for him to "adopt" a mysterious baby to take the place of the one lost by his wife. Because she has wanted a child for so long, the husband agrees, hoping she will never discover the real truth. The name of this child, he is told, is Damien. Probably very few of the millions who saw this movie were aware of the fact that Damien is the English translation of the Greek word for *demon*. As the film unfolds, the husband discovers the horrible truth about his adopted son, but not before Damien kills both his nursemaid and mother. Finally, in desperation, the father attempts to knife the boy to death, but is himself slain.

The third movie, "Damien Omen II," was advertised as follows:

"Only thirteen-year-old Damien seems immune from the bizarre accidents claiming the lives of those around him. Damien, whose own father tried to kill him seven years ago . . . Damien, whose loving foster family is learning the meaning of hellish fear . . . Damien, who is discovering that it is not, after all, the meek, but the master of ultimate evil who shall inherit the earth!"

The theme of these three films is perhaps best summarized through a poem which is often quoted in "The Omen":

"When the Jews return to Zion,
And a Comet rips the sky,
And the Holy Roman Empire rises,
Then you and I must die.
From the eternal sea he rises,

Creating armies on either shore,
Turning man against his brother,
'til man exists no more."

Perhaps the most well known antichrist prophecy of
modern day, however, is found not in a film, but in a
book, written by the popular clairvoyant and newspaper
astrologer, Jeane Dixon. In her book, My Life and
Prophecies, Mrs. Dixon not only declares the existence of
antichrist on earth today, but actually identifies his
birthday as February 5, 1962. She writes concerning this
amazing revelation which came to her:

"I gazed out my window and, although the sun was still in
hiding, what I saw was almost beyond description.
   The bare-limbed trees of the city had given way to an
endless desert scene, broiled by a relentless sun. Glowing
like an enormous ball of fire, the sun had cracked the
horizon, emitting brilliant rays of scintillating light which
seemed to attract the earth like a magic wand.
   The sun's rays parted, facilitating the appearance of an
Egyptian Pharaoh and his queen. I immediately recognized
her as Queen Nefertiti; the man with her I took to be her
husband, reported by history to be Ikhnaton, the so-
called 'heretic' Pharaoh. Holding hands as lovers do, they
emerged from the brilliant rays, majestic in their bearing;
Ikhnaton's royal headdress was a sign of his power under
the sun . . . not of power under the Son.
   But my eyes were drawn to Nefertiti and the child she
tenderly cradled in her other arm. It was a newborn babe,
wrapped in soiled, ragged swaddling clothes. He was in
stark contrast to the magnificently arrayed royal couple.
   Not a sound broke the unearthly silence as they issued
forth with the child. I then became aware of a multitude
of people that appeared between the child and me. It
seemed as though the entire world was watching the royal
couple present the baby. Watching the baby over their
heads, I witnessed Nefertiti hand the child to the people.
Instantly rays of sunlight burst forth from the little boy,

carefully blending themselves with the brilliance of the sun, blotting out everything but him.

Ikhnaton disappeared from the scene. Nefertiti remained. I observed her walking away from the child and the people, into the past, into the secret past of the ancients. Thirsty and tired, she rested beside a water jug, and just as she cupped her hands to drink, a sudden thrust of a dagger in her back ended her life. Her death scream, piercing and mournful, faded out with her.

My eyes once again focused on the baby. By now he had grown to manhood, and a small cross which had formed above his head enlarged and expanded until it covered the earth in all directions. Simultaneously, suffering people, of all races, knelt in worshipful adoration, lifting their arms and offering their hearts to the man. For a fleeting moment I felt as though I were one of them, but the channel that emanated from him was not that of the Holy Trinity. I knew within my heart that this revelation was to signify the beginning of wisdom, but whose wisdom and for whom? An overpowering feeling of love surrounded me, but the look I had seen in the man when he was still a babe—a look of serene wisdom and knowledge—made me sense that here was something God allowed me to see without my becoming a part of it.

I also sensed that I was once again safe within the protective arms of my Creator.

I glanced at my bedside clock. It was still early—7:17 a.m.

What does this revelation signify? I am convinced that this revelation indicates a child, born somewhere in the Middle East shortly after 7:00 a.m. on February 5, 1962—possibly a direct descendant of the royal line of Pharaoh Ikhnaton and Queen Nefertiti—will revolutionize the world. There is no doubt that he will fuse multitudes into one all-embracing doctrine. He will form a new 'Christianity,' based on his 'almighty power,' but leading man in a direction far removed from the teachings and life of Christ, the Son" (Jeane Dixon, *My Life and Prophecies*, William Morrow & Co., pp. 178–180).

Dixon concludes by predicting mankind will begin feeling the great force of this man in the early eighties, and his power will grow mightily until 1999, at which time he will form his new religion.

What are we to conclude concerning these films and books? Certainly not that they are inspired prophecies in any sense of the word. But they do clearly reflect a growing unholy desire for the occult and a recognition by the world that a satanic superman is now on his way.

c. The Old Testament forerunners of the antichrist.

Just as there are many Old Testament characters which depict the person and work of the Lord Jesus (such as Melchizedek in Gen. 14 and Isaac in Gen. 22), there are a number of Old Testament men who describe for us the coming ministry of the antichrist:

Cain—by his murder of the chosen seed (Gen. 4:5-14; Jude 11; 1 Jn. 3:12).

Nimrod—by his creation of Babylon and the tower of Babel (Gen. 10, 11).

Pharaoh—by his oppression of God's people (Ex. 1:8-22).

Korah—by his rebellion (Num. 16:1-3; Jude 11).

Balaam—by his attempt to curse Israel (Num. 23, 24; 2 Pet. 2:15; Jude 11; Rev. 2:14).

Saul—by his intrusion into the office of the priesthood (1 Sam. 13:9-13).

Goliath—by his proud boasting (1 Sam. 17).

Absalom—by his attempt to steal the throne of David (2 Sam. 15:1-6).

Jeroboam—by his substitute religion (1 Ki. 12:25-31).

Sennacherib—by his efforts to destroy Jerusalem (2 Ki. 18:17).

Nebuchadnezzar—by his golden statue (Dan. 3:1-7).

Haman—by his plot to exterminate the Jews (Est. 3).

Antiochus Epiphanes—by his defilement of the Temple (Dan. 11:21-35).

Of all the Old Testament foreshadows of the antichrist, by far the most pronounced type is Antiochus Epiphanes. He was a Syrian. He came to the throne in 175 B.C. and ruled until 164 B.C. He was anti-Semitic to the core. He assaulted Jerusalem, murdering over 40,000 in three days, and selling an equal number into cruel slavery. He was the youngest son of Antiochus the Great and is immediately classified as a vile (or contemptible) person by the Word of God (Dan. 11:21). He was nicknamed "Epimanes" by those who knew him best, meaning "madman." He practiced deceit and pretended to be a second-century Robin Hood (1 Macc. 3:29-31).

Antiochus had hoped to capture Egypt, but was stopped coldly by the mighty Romans (Dan. 11:30). He took out his insane rage on the city of Jerusalem (11:28-35). He forbade the practice of Judaism. Anyone caught observing the Sabbath or circumcising a child would be killed. The Hebrew Scriptures were ordered destroyed. Josephus tells us that during this time a great group of faithful Jews were caught in a cave observing the Sabbath. The entrance was sealed and fires set to suffocate them. Two mothers had circumcised their infants. They were paraded about the city with the infants tied to their breasts and finally thrown over the wall.

On September 6, 171 B.C., he began his evil actions toward the Temple.

On December 15, 168, his Temple desecration reached its ultimate low, for on that day this Nero of the Old Testament sacrificed a giant sow on an idol altar he had made in the Jewish Temple. He forced the priests to swallow its flesh, also made a broth of it, and sprinkled all the Temple. He finally carried off the golden candlesticks, table of shewbread, altar of incense, various other vessels, and destroyed the sacred books of the law. A large image of Jupiter was placed in the Holy of Holies. All this was termed by the horrified Jews as "The abomination of desolation," and is referred to by Jesus in Matthew 24:15 as a springboard to describe the activities of the future antichrist.

All through Palestine, altars to Jupiter were set up and the Jews were forced to sacrifice at them. But at a little Jewish town called Modin (seventeen miles northwest of Jerusalem) there lived a Jewish priest named Mattathias, of the House of Hasmon. He had five sons and this brave old man not only refused to worship Antiochus' idols, but boldly slew the king's religious ambassador. The Jewish revolt was on. One of his sons was named Judas and he was called Maccabee (meaning, the hammer). For the next few years Judas successfully led an army of Jews against the Syrians. Their brave exploits are described in two Apocryphal books, First and Second Maccabees. On December 25, 165 B.C., the Jewish patriots cleansed and rededicated the Temple Antiochus had defiled. This day later became a Jewish holiday known as the feast of dedication. (See Jn. 10:22.)

Note: In 8:14 a time period of 2300 days is mentioned. This apparently began on September 6, 171 B.C. and ended on December 25, 165 B.C. It was, however, on the basis of this period that William Miller, founder of the modern Seventh Day Adventist movement, went astray. He made the days stand for years and arrived at the date of October 22, A.D. 1844 for the return of Christ.

Antiochus died in Babylon in 164 B.C. after being soundly defeated in battle.

As one studies the life of this vicious Syrian, a number of similarities soon surface between Antiochus and the coming antichrist.

(1) Each has a religious leader who helps him. Antiochus had an apostate Benjamite named Menelaus who murdered the legitimate high priest and assumed his office. He then enforced the worship of Antiochus. The antichrist will of course be aided by the false prophet. (See Rev. 13:11–18.)

(2) Both would be withstood by a godly Jewish remnant. Antiochus was opposed by the Maccabees while the antichrist will be withstood by the 144,000. (See Rev. 7.)

(3) Both are reported dead but appear alive again. (Compare 2 Macc. 5:5 with Rev. 13:3, 13, 14.)

(4) The Jews are to be saved from both these men by a great Jewish deliverer. Judas Maccabees performed this during Antiochus' day, while Christ himself will

deliver his people and personally end the ruthless reign of antichrist. (See Rom. 11:26; Rev. 19:11-21.)

(5) Both would conquer much (Dan. 8:9; Rev. 13:4).

(6) Both would magnify themselves (Dan. 8:11; Rev. 13:15).

(7) Both would be masters of deceit (Dan. 7:25; 2 Thess. 2:10).

(8) Both would offer a false "peace program" (Dan. (Dan 8:25; 1 Thess. 5:2, 3).

(9) Both would hate and persecute Israel (Dan. 8:25; Rev. 12:13).

(10) Both would profane the Temple (Dan. 8:11; Mt. 24:15).

(11) Both would be energized by Satan (Dan. 8:24; Rev. 13:2).

(12) Both would be active in the Middle East for about seven years (Dan. 8:14; 9:27).

(13) Both would speak against the Lord God (Dan. 8:25).

(14) Both would be utterly destroyed by God (Dan. 8:25; Rev. 19:19, 20).

d. The personal characteristics of the antichrist.

He will be an intellectual genius (Dan. 8:23).

He will be an oratorical genius (Dan. 11:36).

He will be a political genius (Rev. 17:11, 12).

He will be a commercial genius (Dan. 11:43; Rev. 13:16, 17).

He will be a military genius (Rev. 6:2; 13:2).

He will be a religious genius (2 Thess. 2:4; Rev. 13:8).

J. Vernon McGee writes:

"He will achieve the goal of present-day religionists: one religion for the whole world. Have you noticed today the tremendous move to bring together the religions of the world? A startling comment comes from a Jewish rabbi: 'Whether Messiah is a person or an assembly is of minor importance,' said Chief Rabbi Marcus Melchoir of Denmark. 'I believe Messianic times would come if the United Nations were made Messiah.'

If this rabbi would be willing to accept the UN as Messiah, do you think he would not recognize as Messiah a man who is able to do what the UN apparently cannot do—put Europe back together and bring about world peace?" (*Reveling Through Revelation*, p. 19).

Thus, to use various American presidents as an analogy, here is a world leader possessing:

The leadership of a Washington and Lincoln.
The eloquence of a Franklin Roosevelt.
The charm of a Teddy Roosevelt.
The charisma of a Kennedy.
The popularity of an Ike.
The political savvy of a Johnson.
The intellect of a Jefferson.

He shall do everything according to his own selfish will (Dan. 11:36). (See also Rev. 13:7; 17:13.) He shall magnify himself and malign God (11:36). (See also 2 Thess. 2:4; Rev. 13:6.) The word for "marvelous things" in this verse is literally "astonishing, unbelievable." The antichrist will scream out unbelievable blasphemies against God, insults no one else could ever think of, or would dare say if he could. He will be allowed by God to prosper (be given full rope) during the tribulation (the indignation) (see 11:36). (See also Rev. 11:7; 13:4, 7, 10.) The phrase "that which is determined shall be done," however, reminds us that God is still in absolute control, even during the terrible reign of this monster.

He will not regard "the gods of his fathers" (11:37). The word for God is plural. The antichrist will carry out a vendetta against all organized religion. In fact, it is he who will destroy that great harlot, bloody Babylon, which is the super world church. (See Rev. 17:5, 16.) He will not have the desire for (or of) women (11:37). Here three theories are offered to explain this phrase.

(1) The normal desire for love, marriage, and sex. (See 1 Tim. 4:3.)

(2) Those things characteristic of women, such as mercy, gentleness, and kindness.

(3) That desire of Hebrew women to be the mother of
the Messiah (1 Tim. 2:15).

His god will be the god of fortresses (11:38). The
antichrist will spend all his resources on military
programs.

e. His rise to power.
  (1) Through the power of Satan (2 Thess. 2:3, 9–12;
    Rev. 13:2).
  (2) Through the permission of the Holy Spirit. His
    present-day manifestation is being hindered by the
    Holy Spirit until the rapture of the church. God is
    in control of all situations down here and will
    continue to be. (See Job 1–2, 2 Thess. 2:6, 7.)
  (3) Through the formation of a ten-nation organizat'on.
    He will proceed from a ten-dictatorship
    confederation which will come into existence
    during the tribulation. These dictators are referred
    to as "ten horns" in Daniel 7:7; Revelation 12:3;
    13:1; 17:7, 12. In his rise to power he will defeat
    three of these dictators (Dan. 7:8, 24). This ten-
    horned confederation is the revived Roman
    Empire. This is derived from the fact that the most
    important prophetic details concerning the old
    Roman Empire in Daniel 2:40–44 are still
    unfulfilled.

    The revived Roman Empire is the last of seven
    Gentile world powers to plague the nation Israel.
    These powers are referred to as seven heads in
    Revelation 12:3; 13:1; 17:7. They are:

Egypt, which enslaved Israel for 400 years (Ex.
  1–12).
Assyria, which captured the northern kingdom of
  Israel (2 Ki. 17).
Babylon, which captured the southern kingdom of
  Israel (2 Ki. 24).
Persia, which produced wicked Haman (Est. 3).
Greece, which produced, indirectly, Antiochus
  Epiphanes (Dan. 11).
Rome, which destroyed Jerusalem in A.D. 70 (see
  Lk. 21) and which will hound Israel in the

revived Empire as never before in all history
(Rev. 12).

(4) Through the cooperation of the false religious
system (Rev. 17).

(5) Through his personal charisma and ability.

(6) Through a false (or real?) resurrection (Rev. 13:3).

(7) Through a false peace program, probably in the
Middle East (Dan. 8:25).

(8) Through a master plan of deception and trickery
(Mt. 24:24; 2 Thess. 2:9; Rev. 13:14). Out of the
ninety-one occurrences in the New Testament of
the words meaning "to deceive," or "to go astray,"
twenty-two of them belong definitely to passages
dealing with the antichrist and the tribulation. (See
Mt. 24:4, 5, 11, 24; 2 Thess. 2:3, 9–11; 2 Tim.
3:13; Rev. 12:9; 18:23; 19:20; 20:3, 8, 10.) Three
reasons explain this fearful deception.

Universal ignorance of God's Word (see Mt. 22:29).
Fierce demonic activity (see 1 Tim. 4:1).
The empty soul (see Lk. 11:24–26).

f. His activities.

(1) He begins by controlling the western power block
(Rev. 17:12). The antichrist will defeat three of
these ten kingdoms (horn) in his rise to power
(Dan. 7:8).

(2) He makes a seven-year covenant with Israel but
breaks it after three and a half years (Dan. 9:27).

(3) He gains absolute control over the Middle East
after the Russian invasion (Ezek. 38, 39).

(4) He attempts to destroy all of Israel (Rev. 12).

(5) He destroys the false religious system, so that he
may rule unhindered (Rev. 17:16, 17).

(6) He thereupon sets himself up as God (Dan. 11:36,
37; 2 Thess. 2:4, 11; Rev. 13:5).

(7) He briefly rules over all nations (Ps. 2; Dan. 11:36;
Rev. 13:16). He will have a universal rule during
the final three and a half years of the tribulation
(Dan. 7:25). (See also Rev. 13:5; Mt. 24:21.)
He will shed blood upon this earth in an

unprecedented manner (Dan. 7:7, 19). He will wear out the saints of God (Israel) (7:25). (See also Rev. 12:13.) He will attempt to change seasons and laws (7:25). He will blaspheme God (7:25). (See also Rev. 13:5, 6.)

In the latter days of the tribulation, he will be attacked by the king of the south (Egypt) and the king of the north (Russia), (Dan. 11:40). According to Ezekiel (38–39) these two nations, especially Russia, are destroyed upon the mountains of Israel by God himself. After the defeat of Russia, the antichrist will occupy Palestine (Dan. 11:41). Edom and Moab will not be occupied by him. Some believe God will not allow him dominion over these areas, because Petra is located there, the mountainous city where the Jewish remnant will take shelter from the antichrist during the last part of the tribulation. (See Rev. 12:14.)

Upon establishing control in Palestine, the antichrist marches into Egypt and controls that land (Dan. 11:42, 43). While he is in Egypt he hears alarming rumors from the east and the north (11:44). The exact nature of these rumors is uncertain. Several suggestions have been offered: This concerns a report about a Jewish uprising. Dr. Leon Wood advocates this position in his book, *A Commentary on Daniel* (see p. 313). It concerns an invasion of a vast horde of some 200,000,000 warriors from the far east (Rev. 9:16) under the leadership of "kings of the east" (Rev. 16:12) who now challenge him for world leadership. These nations would include China, India, and others. Dr. J. Dwight Pentecost suggests this possibility (*Things to Come*, p. 356). It concerns a report that thousands of Jews are escaping Jerusalem and fleeing into Petra. This theory is offered as a possibility by the author.

He quickly returns and in great fury destroys many (Dan. 11:44). Here again the identity of those who are destroyed cannot be dogmatically stated. He apparently successfully deals with the threat and establishes his worldwide headquarters on Mt. Zion. Here he remains until his total destruction by the King of kings at the end of the tribulation (11:45). (See also Rev. 19:11–21.)

(8) He is utterly crushed by the Lord Jesus Christ at the battle of Armageddon (Rev. 19).

(9) He is the first creature to be thrown into the lake of fire (Rev. 19:20).

g. His ability to imitate.

The antichrist would surely have been a tremendously successful mimic on any late-night TV talk show! Note the following areas in which he will attempt to imitate the person and work of Christ.

(1) The antichrist comes in the very image of Satan, as Christ came in the image of God (2 Thess. 2:9; Rev. 13:4; cf. Col. 1:15 and Heb. 1:3).

(2) The antichrist is the second person in the hellish trinity, as Christ is in the heavenly Trinity (Rev. 16:13; cf. Mt. 28:19).

(3) The antichrist comes up from the abyss, while Christ comes down from heaven (Rev. 11:7; 17:8; cf. Jn. 6:38).

(4) The antichrist is a savage beast, while Christ is a sacrificial lamb (Rev. 13:2; cf. 5:6–9).

(5) The antichrist receives his power from Satan, as Christ received his power from his Father (Rev. 13:2; cf. Mt. 28:18).

(6) The antichrist will experience a resurrection (perhaps a fake one), just as Christ experienced a true one (Rev. 13:3, 12; cf. Rom. 1:4).

(7) The antichrist will receive the worship of all unbelievers, as Christ did of all believers (Jn. 5:43; Rev. 13:3, 4, 8; cf. Mt. 2:11; Lk. 24:52; Jn. 20:28; Phil. 2:10, 11).

(8) The antichrist will deliver mighty speeches, as did Christ (Dan. 7:8; Rev. 13:5; cf. Jn. 7:46). Satan will doubtless give to the antichrist his vast knowledge of philosophy, science, and human wisdom

accumulated through the centuries (Ezek. 28:12).

(9) The greater part of the antichrist's ministry will last some three and a half years about the time span of Christ's ministry (Rev. 13:5; 12:6, 14; cf. Jn. 2:13; 6:4; 11:55).

(10) The antichrist will attempt (unsuccessfully) to combine the three Old Testament offices of prophet, priest, and king, as someday Christ will successfully do.

(11) The antichrist's symbolic number is six, while the symbolic number of Christ is seven (Rev. 13:18; cf. 5:6, 12).

(12) The antichrist will someday kill his harlot wife, while Christ will someday glorify his holy bride (Rev. 17:16, 17; cf. 21:1, 2).

In past years a number of novels have been written concerning the story of the tribulation. The oldest and perhaps most famous was written by Sidney Watson, entitled, *In the Twinkling of an Eye.* However, from both a biblical and literary standpoint, one of the best is by William Hull, entitled, *Israel, Key to Prophecy.* Mr. Hull presents a vivid picture of the person and ministry of the antichrist in this book. As a summary of our study on the antichrist, an extended section of Hull's presentation is now given:

"The United Nations Organization had ceased to exist as such. There was now one world leader and a super world cabinet. This council had been formed to take over all activities of the former U.N.O. with this difference: it had force to back up its decisions. All authority was now in the hands of the President and he delegated this as he wished to his council. The council consisted of seven ecclesiastical leaders and ten secular leaders. The seven were former cardinals of Rome. The office of Pope no longer existed, all the former power and authority of this position now rested in the President. He was infallible both in religious and secular affairs. The seven cardinals had complete control over all religious matters in every country and all religions had been unified. The only exceptions to this were the Jewish and Moslem religions. Members of these two religions were permitted to observe their form of worship, with certain reservations, but could not receive converts.

The ten secular leaders were individually dictators in their respective countries, subject always to instructions from the President. They had control over all affairs of state in all countries. The combined council, with the President at its head, ruled the world. The President had for many years been a popular TV figure. His appearances had been watched with interest and admiration, not only by Roman Catholics but also by Protestants. His smooth, glib speech, his bright piercing eyes, had all combined to win him a great following of admirers.

Religious worship was on an entirely new basis. Except for Jews and Moslems there was only the one religion in the world. Everyone was compelled to attend at least one service each week. The Bible was not used, nor were people permitted to have copies of this book in their homes. In place of it a new 'Bible,' based on philosophy, and setting forth the perfect way of life for each day, had been published. It contained in addition a catechism to be used for moral and religious instruction, a statement of doctrine and faith, information on a practical application of the suggested principles for everyday living and a long dissertation by the President setting forth the superiority and advantages of the new religion, as contrasted with the former religions of superstition and tradition.

Many were surprised when it was announced that Judaism would be permitted to continue and that Jews could worship their God in their own way. The reason for this favor was not evident. The ruling had come directly from the President himself, overriding the advice of his religious council. For some reason the world ruler seemed to desire to cultivate Jewish goodwill and friendship.

Shortly after assuming office the President called the leaders of Israel—the Chief Rabbis of Jerusalem, the Prime Minister, the Minister of Foreign Affairs and the Minister of Finance—to a conference in Washington. The

matters discussed were not made public but it was learned
that a secret agreement had been entered into between the
World Authority and the Government and Rabbinate of
Israel. Rumor was that Israel had signed a seven year
contract. This was to guarantee Israel sufficient funds to
restore her land to its original condition of productivity,
both agriculturally and commercially. Much more than
this, however, was the rumor (as yet only spoken in a
whisper among the Jews), that the Temple Area was to be
given to Israel and funds furnished to build a magnificent
temple outshining any previous temple or any building in
the world. What Israel was to give in return for all this
was not yet clear. What had Israel to offer for such
munificence?

As the months went by Jerusalem became aware of
activity on the former Temple Area. Solomon's Temple
had stood there thousands of years ago, but since the
destruction of Herod's Temple in 70 A.D. by the Romans
under Titus, no Jewish building had occupied this site.
Since the occupation of Jerusalem by the Moslems in 637
A.D. the former Temple Area had been considered a
"Holy Place." Next to Mecca and Medina, Jerusalem was
the third most holy site in the world to Mohammedans.
However, the activity observed was not that of Moslems.
Only Jews were seen now on this site, where formerly
they had been forbidden and where it had meant instant
death for any Jews to enter.

Then the story broke. It was a seven-day wonder and
papers all over the world revealed details of the secret
agreement made between the President and the Jews. The
Temple Area was to be made available to the Jews on
which to build once again a temple for the worship of
Jehovah. Moslem leaders had been secretly informed by
personal representatives of the World Ruler. There had
been no public outcry, for the Moslems had been told
that for them it was a case of give up the Haram
Esh-Sherif or Islam would cease as a permitted religion.
There was no doubt that the Leader was able to enforce
such an ultimatum and to eliminate this religion from the
face of the earth. It was clear that the President was

favoring the Jews and seemingly could not do enough for them. Yet why this should be was still a mystery to the world, and to the Jews. What had the Jews to offer to pay for all these favors and help?

Some years were to pass before the Temple would be completely finished and shine in all its glory. This, however, would not hinder the restoration of worship at an early date. Work was ordered so that the central part of the Temple would be rushed to a degree of completion which would enable services to be held and the priests to officiate. The great altar and the laver also were to be erected at once. The choosing of the High Priest was to be made an event of outstanding importance in the history of Israel.

With the appointment of the High Priest the whole set-up of government was changed and put on a theocratic basis. The High Priest was supreme and in a short time had organized both the secular ruling authority and the priesthood.

The last Jewish sacrifice had been made three weeks before the Temple had been destroyed in 70 A.D. Jerusalem had been besieged at the time by the Romans and finally all the sacrificial animals had been slain and no further living animals were available. The priests had carried on the Temple worship without sacrifices for another three weeks. Then, on the ninth of Av, the inner walls of the city fell; the Temple was desecrated and destroyed and there had been neither temple nor sacrifice since that day nearly two thousand years ago.

It was decided that the daily sacrifices must be renewed at the earliest possible moment.

As the day for the renewal of Temple service and sacrifices drew near, people poured into Jerusalem from all parts of the world. The President was unable to attend but a vast television screen had been prepared on the front of the Temple building, and with the development of world television relay in recent years, his image, as he spoke in Washington, would appear on the screen. This new development was called Rayscreen. The relay was produced by reflecting rays back and forth from earth stations to satellites suspended five hundred miles above the earth. In this way the above could be encircled in any direction. Hundreds of thousands of people would face the screen in Jerusalem and see the World Leader and hear him speak.

The day dawned bright and clear. Hours before, people had begun to assemble in the Temple courtyard. At dawn the first sacrificial lamb was led out to the altar. The knife of the priest flashed, smoke began to rise from under the altar and the sacrifice was consumed in the flames. Suddenly the sky darkened, a most unusual phenomenon at that time of year. Lightning flashed from one end of the heavens to the other, accompanied by peal after peal of deafening thunder. Then came a downpour of rain which threatened to wash away sacrifice, altar, priests and the great concourse of people. The storm was over in ten minutes but the sky remained dark and the sun did not appear again that day. People asked one another, 'What did this portend? Was God displeased?'

At seven in the morning (midnight in Washington) the face of the President appeared on the great screen. A smile lighted up his face, but his words were like steel bullets pouring forth from the many loud-speakers.

'High Priest, leaders and citizens of Israel, visitors in Jerusalem,' he orated. 'On this day which is outstanding in the history of Israel I offer my congratulations to a nation revived, restored and rebuilt in its land after an absence of nineteen hundred years. It has been my pleasure to help restore both your land and your Temple.

'On this occasion of the restoration of your Temple worship it is well to remember that this site was chosen by your God as His dwelling place on earth. Here you worshiped and sacrificed to your God. Here your God put His name and accepted your worship. Here I have permitted and enabled you to rebuild your Temple and to worship. I have kept my word. I have fulfilled my covenant. I will continue to be your protector and herewith command you to worship in this Temple. I have spoken.'

The cheers which followed the brief and abrupt speech

of the President were given dutifully, in view of the presence of many high representatives of the President and hundreds of secret police ever ready to report any lack of enthusiasm for the World Leader. However, most of those present sincerely rejoiced, believing that the God of Israel would be pleased with the renewal of Israel's sacrifices on the Temple altar, and would henceforth smile on their nation.

In spite of the beauty and richness of the great buildings there was one thing lacking. Israel sensed this lack and wondered—there was no glory cloud, no feeling of God in their midst. Where was God? Was their return to Temple worship and sacrifices not pleasing to Him? 'Oh God of Abraham, Isaac and Jacob, bless Your people and Your Temple. We have wandered nineteen hundred years. We are weary and tired of our wandering and would solace our souls once more in Your presence. Return, Oh God, and bless Your people Israel! Speak again, and Your servants will hear and answer.'

Three and one half years had passed since the renewal of Temple worship. Israel, by now, was accustomed to the form of worship. The smoke and fire of the altar, the bleating and bellowing of the sacrifice animals and the daily ministration of the priests had become almost commonplace to the Jews. For the last few months, however, there had been some strange foreign activity in the Temple courtyard which no one seemed to be able to explain.

It had started shortly after the receipt of a note which came from the President. The note had informed the High Priest that certain construction work would be undertaken in a small area of the Temple courtyard. The work was to be done by workmen sent from America, who would require no assistance from the Jews but must be permitted to work unhindered. Work would be suspended on Saturdays and Sundays.

The workmen arrived and began to construct a tall wooden structure, one hundred feet square and a hundred fifty feet high. All material had been brought on their ship and moved to the site in closed trucks of great size.

All the workers were close-mouthed and kept entirely to themselves. They never entered into conversation with any of the Jews, and from the beginning the construction work had been guarded night and day by a large force of World Police, changed and replaced every three days. None were permitted to approach near the hastily built building. Some, however, had said that they had heard the sound of hammers on stone coming from within the building.

Eventually it became evident that a new stage had been reached in the work. The rough covering forming the building was now being dismantled board by board. Within could be seen a small building or covered object. When all the wooden framework was removed there remained what appeared as a steel frame of four uprights encircled by iron loops. The actual frame could only be conjectured at, for it was covered and almost concealed by a rich tapestry covering. Not the slightest hint was offered as to what was inside this queer tent-like structure.

Jerusalem, Tel Aviv and other cities and villages were enjoying the end of their Sabbath. As usual the main streets of the cities were thronged with strolling couples and groups of Jews dressed in their Sabbath clothes and filling both sidewalks and roadways and making it almost impossible for cars to push their way through. They were gay happy throngs, all well-clothed and prosperous looking.

Not only prosperity but peace had finally come and it seemed as though the 'controversy of Zion' was ended. Sabbath was surely a time when all Israel could show its enjoyment of its new freedom and liberty. The future outlook was bright, even beyond the dreams of the early Zionist 'dreamers.' This night was much as other end-of-Sabbath nights, until a trumpet suddenly sounded through the streets. The blast had come from the loudspeakers put up at the strategic points in all cities, villages and kibbutzim throughout the country. It indicated a special message to be issued from World Headquarters in Washington. First the message would be given in English, immediately followed by a Hebrew translation.

The laughing, moving throngs became tense, rigid, as words began to pour forth. All gathered as close as possible to the many speakers and hung on every word.

The message stated that next Sabbath, at twelve noon, an event of outstanding importance would take place in the Temple Area in Jerusalem. The President himself was flying to Israel to take part and to make a personal announcement at that time. All Jews that could be accommodated in Jerusalem were to proceed there immediately for this event. The message was repeated every hour through the night and next day, so that none could be ignorant of its content. It brought amazement and wonderment in Israel and was a headline story in the world press. What could it be? What could be so important to bring the great World Leader to Jerusalem? Not only Jerusalem, but throughout the world people discussed the announcement and what it presaged.

Exactly on the dot of twelve a tremendous blast from one hundred trumpets heralded the arrival of the President. As he slowly proceeded along the carpeted way every eye was upon him. At least two million people watched him reach the steps and ascend to the platform. On the platform a large golden throne had been placed and the President, the ruler of the world, seated himself.

Following the President, at a distance of fifty paces, the seven cardinals had come in, two by two, with the seventh bringing up the rear. They too presented a dazzling sight, with pure white robes almost hidden under crimson dyed capes of beautiful marten fur. On their heads were golden framed headpieces covered with Russian sable dyed crimson to match their capes. They too ascended the platform and took their seats in a semicircle facing, and at the foot of, the throne.

Then came a brilliant array of ecclesiastics and representatives of all nations. The head of this column stopped at the foot of the steps to the platform and remained standing facing the President, while the long column of dignitaries closed ranks until they too presented a great mass of faces as they stood on the carpeted pathway between the two ranks of Bodyguard troops.

Thus was arrayed the greatest pageant the world had ever witnessed. There was an element of mystery to it all, for only a few knew what was to follow. The plans and preparations had been executed with such secrecy that not a whisper had reached the ears of any except those involved in the work. Now the stage was prepared. The setting was magnificent, with the great Temple building, its golden roof shining in the bright sun, as a background, and the vast concourse of people crowding almost every inch of space in the courtyard, on the walls and buildings and on the Mount of Olives. The bright colored robes of the chief participants and leaders were as brilliant jewels in a massive setting. Dominating all was the beautifully tapestried tower, before which the President sat on this throne. The covering of the tower was woven in brilliant colors forming most extraordinary patterns. Four scenes were depicted on this tapestry. One was of fiery red serpents crawling out of a pit. The second was a beast of most unusual ferociousness, its right paw lying heavily on a prostrate human form. The third depicted a huge golden image of a man, the face vaguely familiar to those able to see it from their positions, and the fourth showed the figure six, appearing three times, each figure entwined with the other, giving the appearance of a chain hanging down the tapestry. The figures were in gold on purple.

Rising slowly, as every eye watched and every tongue was stilled, the President stood to his feet. His raised hand may have been a gesture of salutation or a demand for silence. If the latter, it was unnecessary, for the air seemed hushed and still awaiting the revelation to come.

'My people,' the leader began, 'this day is unique in the history of man. You are gathered before me in this city of Jerusalem or you view me on your Rayscreens. You are gathered at my command. I speak to all people but my remarks apply specifically to those of the Jewish religion.

'It was on this site, at the command of your God, that your father King David prepared for the erection of your first Temple. This Temple was erected by King Solomon and in it you worshiped your God, Jehovah. You believed that your God dwelt in this Temple and your Bible claims that He supernaturally revealed His presence at the time of its dedication.

'And now, after nineteen hundred years, I have graciously permitted you to once more worship your God in this newly erected Temple which I enabled you to build. I have restrained all opposition, and have restored to you opportunity for worship as it existed when your fathers dwelt in this land and possessed all authority.

'For three and a half years you have worshiped your God according to your ancient rites and laws. Now the time has come for you to be enlightened and you will know why I have sponsored the reorganization of your Temple worship and sacrifices. Give honor to whom honor is due. In years gone by your God was not able to maintain His residence in the Temple nor to protect it from destruction by His enemies. Your God could not protect you as you were forced to flee from your land and to serve nineteen hundred years in bondage. Your God could not enable you to build your Temple again, BUT I DID!

'Let all the world behold!'

At this cry the great tapestries covering the high tower slowly parted at the front and gathered together at the back of the metal frame. Then was disclosed to all eyes a huge stone image one hundred feet high. It was an image of the President, a perfect likeness, standing with arms folded and a sardonic smile on the face. Suddenly, while the people gazed with mingled feelings of awe, fear and admiration, the image began to speak.

'Men and women of the earth: For millenniums of time, since you first lived on this earth, you have worshiped gods. In your ignorance you have worshiped gods many, or god singular, yet you have not known me.

'Today, I have chosen to reveal myself. This day is the most important in all the history of man. This day I am opening your eyes and permitting you to see and to acclaim the true God. I AM GOD! WORSHIP ME! I AM THE CREATOR! I MADE HEAVEN, I MADE

THE KING IS COMING

EARTH. THERE IS NO GOD BESIDE ME. SEE MY POWER!'

Suddenly the sky was rent, a great pillar of fire flashed down and rested upon the dome of the Temple. The earth trembled and rocked.

Then the image continued to speak:

'Henceforth you will worship me as God. You will bow down to me. You will be marked with my mark and everyone who fails to bow to me and to receive my mark will be ostracized from society. You will not be able to purchase the necessities of life, you will not be able to sell your time or produce. You will die the death which I have ordained.

'Israel—I am your true God. You have ignorantly worshiped your false god—Jehovah—but now I have opened your eyes. For this purpose I enabled you to erect your Temple and to restore worship as in the days of your fathers. NOW I COMMAND YOU TO WORSHIP ME—I AM GOD, WORSHIP ME!'

His closing words ended on such a high pitch as to be almost a screech" (W. Hull, *Israel, Key to Prophecy*, Zondervan, 1964, pp. 51–63, 67–71).

Having examined in some detail the activities of antichrist, let us now turn to his evil cohort, the false prophet.

And I beheld another beast coming up out of the earth (Rev. 13:11).

h. His identity.

Who is this second beast of Revelation 13 who is also called on three later occasions "the false prophet"? (See Rev. 16:13; 19:20; 20:10.) Some believe he will be a Jew (while the antichrist will be a Gentile), and that he will head up the apostate church.

It is entirely possible that the antichrist will come from the United Nations, while the false prophet may well proceed from the World Council of Churches. It is also entirely feasible that both personages are alive and active in this world right now, and are waiting for the rapture to remove the final barrier, thus allowing them to begin their deadly and damnable work!

There are a number of examples in church history of the unholy union between a political and a religious leader. The Emperor Charlemagne and Pope Leo III had this in the ninth century. Centuries later Henry VIII and Cardinal Wolsey would also create such a union.

i. His activities.

It has already been pointed out that the antichrist will attempt to mimic Christ; it would appear that the false prophet will try to copy the work of the Holy Spirit. Thus the following analogy has been suggested between the Spirit of God and the second beast.

(1) The Holy Spirit is the third person of the heavenly Trinity (Mt. 28:19), while the false prophet is the third person of the hellish trinity (Rev. 16:13).

(2) The Holy Spirit leads men into all truth (Jn. 16:13), while the false prophet seduces men into all error (Rev. 13:11, 14).

(3) The Holy Spirit glorifies Christ (Jn. 16:13, 14), while the false prophet glorifies the antichrist (Rev. 13:12).

(4) The Holy Spirit made fire to come down from heaven at Pentecost (Acts 2:3), while the false prophet will do likewise on earth in view of men (Rev. 13:13).

(5) The Holy Spirit gives life (Rom. 8:2), while the false prophet kills (Rev. 13:15).

(6) The Holy Spirit marks with a seal all those who belong to God (Eph. 1:13), while the false prophet marks those who worship Satan (Rev. 13:16, 17).

j. His mark.

And he causeth all, both small and great, rich and poor, free and bond, to receive a mark in their right hand, or in their foreheads: and that no man might buy or sell, save he that had the mark, or the name of the beast, or the number of his name. Here is wisdom. Let him that hath understanding count the number of the beast: for it is the number of a man; and his number is six hundred threescore and six (Rev. 13:16–18).

THE KING IS COMING

Perhaps no other single passage in the Word of God has been the object of more silly and serious speculation. We shall quote from two well-known authors:

"In Greek (as in Hebrew and in Latin) the letters of the alphabet serve likewise as signs for the figures. Alpha signifies one; beta, two, etc. For any name it is, therefore, possible to add together the numerical value of each letter and to arrive at a total which forms 'the number of a man.' The name of the antichrist will give the total of 666. Men have sought to apply this method with reference to all the persons in history who have seemed to be the antichrist. By more or less arranging the letters of the titles of these persons they have arrived at the number 666 for the names of Nero, Mohammed, the Pope, Napoleon, and even Hitler, not to speak of many others. In our opinion the proof that these interpretations are still premature is that they are all contradictory. We are convinced that when the last and great antichrist appears, the true believers of the entire world will recognize him. The Holy Spirit will give to him enough light to calculate unanimously the number of his name" (Rene Pache, *The Return of Jesus Christ*, p. 183).

"Probably the simplest explanation here is the best, that the triple six is the number of a man, each digit falling short of the perfect number seven. Six in the Scripture is man's number. He was to work six days and rest the seventh. The image of Nebuchadnezzar was sixty cubits high and six cubits broad. Whatever may be the deeper meaning of the number, it implies that this title, referring to the first beast, Satan's masterpiece, limits him to man's level, which is far short of the deity of Jesus Christ" (Dr. John Walvoord, *The Revelation of Jesus Christ*, p. 210).

Whatever is involved in this hellish mark, it is apparently very important, for it is referred to again no less than six times. (See Rev. 14:9, 11; 15:2; 16:2; 19:20; 20:4.)

3. The revival of the Roman Empire (Dan. 2:41; 7:7, 8; Rev. 13:1; 17:12).

During his Olivet Discourse our Lord uttered the following sober sentence concerning Jerusalem. It was both historical and prophetical in its scope. He proclaimed:

. . . *and Jerusalem shall be trodden down of the Gentiles, until the times of the Gentiles be fulfilled* (Lk. 21:24).

Concerning this, Scofield observes:

"The 'times of the Gentiles' began with the captivity of Judah under Nebuchadnezzar (2 Chron. 36:1-21), since which time Jerusalem has been under Gentile overlordship" (*Scofield Bible*, p. 1106).

Both the history and prophecy of Christ's statement are explained by a dream and a vision in the book of Daniel. A Babylonian king had the dream, while Daniel saw the vision. One occurred in chapter 2, the other in chapter 7. Both referred to the same events.

The dream of King Nebuchadnezzar (Dan. 2:31-35). He saw a huge and powerful statue of a man. It was made up of various materials. Its head was gold. Its breast and arms were silver. Its belly and thighs were brass. Its legs were iron and its feet part iron and clay. This statue was then utterly pulverized into small powder by a special rock, supernaturally cut from a mountain-side, which fell upon it. The rock then grew until it filled the entire earth.

The vision experienced by Daniel (Dan. 7). He saw vicious animals fighting with each other. One was like a lion, the second like a bear, the third as a leopard, while the fourth (the most horrible of all) was somewhat of a composite of the first three. At the end of this vision Daniel saw a mighty figure from heaven who destroyed these beasts and set up an everlasting kingdom upon earth.

Just what did Nebuchadnezzar's dream and Daniel's vision mean? From these two extended passages and from secular history we learn that:

a. Four major powers (or kingdoms) will rule over Palestine.

b. These powers are viewed by mankind as gold, silver, brass, iron, and clay.

c. These powers are viewed by God as four wild animals: a winged lion, a bear, a winged leopard, and an

113

indescribably brutal and vicious animal.

d. These four powers stand for: Babylon—from 625 B.C. to 539 B.C.; Medo-Persia—from 539 B.C. to 331 B.C.; Greece—from 331 B.C. to 323 B.C.; and Rome. For Rome three periods are to be noted here:

The first period—the original Empire—from 300 B.C. to A.D. 476.

The second period—the intervening influence—from A.D. 476 to the present.

We are amazed at Rome's continuing world influence, centuries after the official collapse of its empire. As Erich Sauer observes:

"The Roman *administration* lives on in the Church of Rome. The ecclesiastical provinces coincided with the State provinces; and Rome, the chief city of the world empire, became the chief city of the world church, the seat of the Papacy.

The Roman *tongue* lives on in the Latin of the Church, and is still in use in the international technical language of law, medicine, and natural science.

Roman *law* lives on in legislation. The Corpus Juris Romanum (body of Roman law) of the Eastern Roman Emperor Justinian (A.D. 527-565) became the foundation of jurisprudence among the Latin and Germanic peoples throughout the Middle Ages and far into modern times.

The Roman *army* lives on in military systems. It became the model for armaments and western defense. We still use Latin words such as captain, major, general, battalion, regiment, army, infantry, artillery, and cavalry" (Erich Sauer, *The Triumph of the Crucified*, Grand Rapids: Eerdmans Publ. Co., 1951, p. 132).

The third period—the revived Empire—from the rapture to Armageddon. This is definitely implied, for the prophecies concerning the fourth power were not fulfilled in the history of ancient Rome. The smiting rock (Christ himself) did not shatter those earthly kingdoms. On the contrary, he was put to death by the sentence of an official representing the fourth power. Thus it is concluded this last empire—the Roman Empire—will be revived at the end of the age, and during its revival will be utterly crushed by Christ himself.

e. This revived Roman Empire will consist of ten nations.

f. The antichrist will personally unite these Western nations. One has only to consult his newspaper in order to follow the rapid present-day fulfillment of this revived Roman Empire prophecy. Students of history will readily agree that the unity of any empire of nations depends upon three factors. These are the military, the economic, and the political. With this in mind, consider the following recent developments in Western Europe:

    (1) The military aspect.
         On April 4, 1949, the North Atlantic Treaty Organization (NATO) was formally brought into being.

    (2) The economic and political aspects.
         Dr. Donald Barnhouse has written:

"Many men have been haunted with the idea of a revival of this empire, but it has never yet been revived. Charlemagne attempted it, and the pope who crowned him Emperor on Christmas Day of the year 800 no doubt saw a revival of Caesar's power. But at Charlemagne's death the dream vanished, and the division of his kingdom at the treaty of Verdun in 843 laid the foundation for all the wars of Western Europe since that time. The Holy Roman Empire was then established, and it moved in spectral fashion across the history of the centuries that followed—never achieved, yet never forgotten. Napoleon found himself on an island in the South Atlantic after he had consolidated European power for a few brief moments and named his own little boy 'the king of Rome.' Mussolini added a worthless African plateau to the territory of Rome and immediately proclaimed a 'Roman Empire,' a haunting name, evoking thoughts of grandeur and glory that have never been forgotten since the Roman legions wrote their laws

115

in letters of blood across the Mediterranean lands.
But the death stroke of the Roman Empire most
certainly will be healed. God's word will never pass
away. Every jot and tittle must be fulfilled" (Dr.
Donald Barnhouse, *Revelation*, Grand Rapids:
Zondervan, 1971, p. 237, 238).

And so it shall! In fact, since 1948, zealous
European statesmen have worked day and night to
resurrect this ancient corpse. Consider:

June 8, 1948. Three European nations, Belgium,
the Netherlands, and Luxembourg signed the
Benelux Agreement which coordinated their
domestic, economic, and financial policies.

March 25, 1957. The Treaty of Rome was signed
in Rome, paving the way for the present-day
European Common Market. Jean Monnet, a French
economist and often described as the Father of the
Common Market, said on that occasion: "Once a
common market interest has been created, then
political union will come naturally."

December 28, 1958. The Treaty of Rome is
formally ratified. Two national magazines described
this meeting as follows:

"On Capitoline Hill in Rome, nearly 2,000 years
ago, Caesar's legions went forth to bring the first
unified rule to Europe's warring tribes. Since the
Roman Empire's fall the unification of Europe has
been a dream which neither the sword of Napoleon
nor Hitler could realize. But on Rome's Capitoline
Hill last week six statesmen, with the peaceful
stroke of a pen, took the biggest step yet made
toward this dream of centuries" (*Life* magazine, 9
January 1959).

"When the history of the 20th century is written,
last week is likely to prove one of its water-sheds.
For in the seven days which spanned 1958 and
1959, Western Europe began to flex its economic
muscles for the first time in a decade, and took its

biggest step toward unity since the death of Charlemagne 1,145 years ago" (*Time* magazine, 12 January 1959, p. 23).

December 5, 1978. The European monetary system (EMS) was agreed upon in Brussels, Belgium.

January 1, 1979. A fund of 32.5 billion dollars was set aside for EMS countries to borrow from.

May 28, 1979. Greece voted in as the tenth member nation with membership to be in full force beginning January 1, 1981. These ten nations (as of January 1, 1981) are as follows:

Belgium	Italy
Denmark	Luxembourg
France	Netherlands
West Germany	United Kingdom
Ireland	Greece

June, 1979. The first direct election was held to elect members to the European Parliament.

July 17, 1979. The first session of the newly elected 410-member legislative body. Simone Weil, a Jewish Frenchwoman who had survived Auschwitz death camp, served as the Common Market's first president.

So here we see, step by step, the tremendous progress already achieved leading to the revived Roman Empire! In 1978 its 260 million people turned out 1.94 trillion dollars in goods and services, as compared to the United States' 2.1 trillion. Its exports outstrip America by more than 50 percent. It accounts for 21 percent of the world's production and 35 percent of the trade.

One final thing: As we have already mentioned in passing, the antichrist himself will eventually head up and rule over this federation of Western nations. With this in mind, consider this shocking statement made by Paul Henry Spaak, first President of the Council of Europe, former president of the U.N. General Assembly, and one of the chief architects of the European Common Market:

"Send us a man who can hold the allegiance of all the people, and whether he be God or the devil, we will receive him!" (*Moody Monthly Magazine*, March, 1974).

4. The antichrist's seven-year covenant with Israel.

And your covenant with death shall be disannulled, and your agreement with hell shall not stand (Isa. 28:18).

And he shall confirm the covenant with many for one week (Dan. 9:27).

a. The background of this covenant.

From June 4 through June 8, 1967, the world-famous six-day war between Israel and Egypt took place. When the smoke had cleared, Israel had won a stunning and fantastic victory. Her land area had increased from 7,992 square miles to over 26,000 square miles. With less than 50,000 troops she had all but annihilated Nasser's 90,000 soldiers. During that fateful week, Egypt suffered 30,000 casualties, 197 planes, and 700 tanks, and had watched two billion dollars go up in smoke. Israel, on the other hand, lost sixty-one tanks, and suffered 275 dead and 800 wounded. But in spite of all this, Israel's position in Palestine today is anything but secure. She continues to find herself surrounded by powerful enemies who have sworn by their gods to drive her into the sea. In addition to this, her northern neighbor, Soviet Russia, views her land with growing interest. Consider for example, just a few "bad days" for this little nation in the past few years.

October 14, 1974. The United Nations by an overwhelming vote (105 yes, four no, twenty abstentions) recognized Israel's mortal enemy, the Palestinian Liberation Organization (P.L.O.).

November 13, 1974. Yasir Arafat, Israel's enemy and leader of the P.L.O., by special invitation addressed the U.N.

November 11, 1975. A U.N. General Assembly resolution equated Zionism with racism. This Arab-sponsored resolution was approved by a vote of seventy-two to thirty-five, with thirty-two abstentions.

July 4, 1975. A bomb concealed in an old refrigerator exploded in Jerusalem's Zion Square, killing fourteen and wounding eighty. This was the bloodiest terrorist incident since the founding of Israel in 1948.

July 2, 1976. Arab terrorists held 100 Israeli hostages in Uganda. This episode, of course, would end in a thrilling victory, for on July 4, Israeli storm troopers rescued their countrymen in an amazing midnight raid.

November 20, 1978. Two of Israel's enemies, Ethiopia and the U.S.S.R., signed a twenty-year treaty of peace and friendship in Moscow.

October 25, 1979. Another Israeli enemy, South Yemen, joined with Russia to sign a peace and friendship pact.

The Word of God indicates that this already intolerable situation will worsen. Then (shortly after the rapture), to Israel's astonishment and relief, a powerful Western leader (the antichrist) will pretend to befriend Israel. In fact, he will propose a special seven-year security treaty, guaranteeing to maintain the status quo in the Middle East. Israel will swallow this poisoned bait, hook, line, and sinker.

b. The betrayal of the covenant.

This king will make a seven-year treaty with the people, but after half that time, he will break his pledge and stop the Jews from all their sacrifice and their offerings; then, as a climax to all his terrible deeds, the Enemy shall utterly defile the sanctuary of God . . . (Dan. 9:27, TLB).

5. The pouring out of the first six seal judgments (Mt. 24:4–8; Rev. 6:1–17).

a. The first seal (Rev. 6:2).

And I saw, and behold, a white horse; and he that sat on him had a bow; and a crown was given unto him; and he went forth conquering and to conquer.

This is doubtless a symbolic picture of the antichrist as he subdues to himself the ten nations of the revived Roman Empire. This may be thought of as the "Cold War" period. We note he carries no arrow, which may indicate conquest by diplomacy rather than shooting war.

b. The second seal (Rev. 6:3, 4).

And when he had opened the second seal, I heard the second beast say, Come and see. And there went out another horse that was red; and power was given to him that sat thereon to

take peace from the earth, and that they should kill one
another; and there was given unto him a great sword.
The uneasy peace which the rider on the white horse
brings to earth is temporary and counterfeit. The
antichrist promises peace, but only God can actually
produce it!

As Isaiah would write, "But the wicked are like the
troubled sea, when it cannot rest, whose waters cast up
mire and dirt. There is no peace, saith my God, to the
wicked! (Isa. 57:20, 21). Now open and bloody hostility
breaks out among some of the nations.

  c. The third seal (Rev. 6:5, 6).

And when he had opened the third seal, I heard the third beast
say, Come and see. And I beheld, and lo a black horse; and
he that sat on him had a pair of balances in his hand. And I
heard a voice in the midst of the four beasts say, A measure of
wheat for a penny, and three measures of barley for a penny;
and see thou hurt not the oil and the wine.

Dr. Charles Ryrie writes the following concerning this
seal:

"The third judgment brings famine to the world. The
black horse forebodes death, and the pair of balances
bespeaks a careful rationing of food. Normally, a 'penny'
(a Roman denarius, a day's wages in Palestine in Jesus'
day, Mt. 20:2) would buy eight measures of wheat or
twenty-four of barley. Under these famine conditions the
same wage will buy only one measure of wheat or three
of barley. In other words, there will be one-eighth of the
normal supply of food. The phrase 'see thou hurt not the
oil and the wine' is an ironic twist in this terrible
situation. Apparently luxury food items will not be in
short supply, but of course most people will not be able
to afford them. This situation will only serve to taunt the
populace in their impoverished state" (*Revelation*, Moody
Press, 1968, pp. 45, 46).

Will the food problem really be as bad as all this
during the tribulation? One of the best-selling books of

the late sixties was titled *The Population Bomb*, and was written by Stanford University biology professor Dr. Paul R. Ehrlich. The following are but a few of the frightening quotes from his pen:

"While you are reading these words four people will have died from starvation, most of them children [from the cover].
The battle to feed all of humanity is over. In the 1970's the world will undergo famines—hundreds of millions of people are going to starve to death in spite of any crash programs embarked upon now [from the Prologue].
The rich are going to get richer, but the more numerous poor are going to get poorer. Of these poor, a minimum of three and one half million will starve to death this year, mostly children. But this is a mere handful compared to the numbers that will be starving in a decade or so" (p. 17).

d. The fourth seal (Rev. 6:7, 8).
And when he had opened the fourth seal, I heard the voice of the fourth beast say, Come and see. And I looked, and behold a pale horse: and his name that sat on him was Death, and Hell followed with him. And Power was given unto them over the fourth part of the earth, to kill with sword, and with hunger, and with death, and with the beasts of the earth.
  (1) The identity of these riders. John calls them "death" and "hell," apparently referring to physical and spiritual death. Thus the evil will destroy the bodies and damn the souls of multitudes of unbelievers during this third-seal plague.
  (2) The damage done by these riders. One fourth of all humanity perishes during this plague. It is estimated that during the Second World War one out of forty persons lost their lives, but this seal judgment alone will claim one out of four persons—nearly one billion human beings! We note the phrase, "with the beasts of the earth." Here John Phillips has written:

"The beasts are closely linked with the pestilence, and this might be a clue. The most destructive creature on earth as far as mankind is concerned, is not the lion or the bear, but the rat. The rat is clever, adaptable, and destructive. If ninety-five percent of the rat population is exterminated in a given area, the rat population will replace itself within a year. It has killed more people than all the wars in history, and makes its home wherever man is found. Rats carry as many as thirty-five diseases. Their fleas carry bubonic plague, which killed a third of the population of Europe in the fourteenth century. Their fleas also carry typhus, which in four centuries has killed an estimated two hundred million people. Beasts, in this passage, are linked not only with pestilence, but with famine. Rats menace human food supplies, which they both devour and contaminate, especially in the more under-developed countries which can least afford to suffer loss" (*Exploring Revelation*, Moody Press, 1974, p. 116).

Also to be noted are the words of Dr. Frank Holtman, head of the University of Tennessee bacteriological department.

"While the greater part of a city's population could be destroyed by an atomic bomb, the bacteria method might easily wipe out the entire population within a week. The virus causing parrot fever, one of the most deadly of human diseases, is appraised by scientists as being the most preferable for this purpose. While the cost of producing psittacosis bombs is comparatively cheap, its lethal potency is extremely high. According to Thomas R. Henry, science editor, less than one cubic centimeter of this virus is required to infect 20 million human beings when released in the air as an infinitesimal spray" (quoted by J. Vernon McGee, *Reveling Through Revelation*, Thru the Bible Books, 1971, p. 56).

e. The fifth seal (Rev. 6:9-11).

And when he had opened the fifth seal, I saw under the altar the souls of them that were slain for the word of God, and for the testimony which they held: and they cried with a loud voice, saying, How long, O Lord, holy and true, dost thou not judge and avenge our blood on them that dwell on the earth? And white robes were given unto every one of them; and it was said unto them, that they should rest yet for a little season, until their fellowservants also and their brethren, that should be killed as they were, should be fulfilled.

Here is religious persecution as never before. These three verses are loaded with theological implications.

(1) They refute the false doctrine of soul-sleep.
(2) They correct the error of one general resurrection. It is evident that these martyred souls did not receive their glorified bodies at the rapture, as did the church-age saints. Therefore it can be concluded that these are Old Testament saints who will experience the glorious bodily resurrection after the tribulation. (See Rev. 20:4-6.)
(3) They suggest the possibilities of an intermediate body. (See also 2 Cor. 5:1-3.) Dr. John Walvoord writes:

"These martyred dead here pictured have not been raised from the dead and have not received their resurrection bodies. Yet it is declared that they are given robes. The fact that they are given robes would almost demand that they have a body of some sort. A robe could not hang upon an immaterial soul or spirit. It is not the kind of body that Christians now have, that is, the body of earth; nor is it the resurrection body of flesh and bones of which Christ spoke after His own resurrection. It is a temporary body suited for their presence in heaven but replaced in turn by their everlasting resurrection body given at the time of Christ's return" (*The Revelation of Jesus Christ*, Moody Press, 1966, p. 134).

f. The sixth seal (Rev. 6:12–17).

And I beheld when he had opened the sixth seal, and lo, there was a great earthquake; and the sun became black as sackcloth of hair, and the moon became as blood; and the stars of heaven fell unto the earth, even as a fig tree casteth her untimely figs, when she is shaken of a mighty wind. And the heaven departed as a scroll when it is rolled together; and every mountain and island were moved out of their places. And the kings of the earth, and the great men, and the rich men, and the chief captains, and the mighty men, and every bondman, and every free man, hid themselves in the dens and in the rocks of the mountains; and said to the mountains and rocks, Fall on us, and hide us from the face of him that sitteth on the throne, and from the wrath of the Lamb: For the great day of his wrath is come; and who shall be able to stand?

As it can be seen, this fearful judgment ushers in:

(1) The greatest earthquake in history. There have, of course, been hundreds of severe earthquakes in man's history. The earliest recorded was in July, A.D. 365, in the Middle East. The most destructive was in January, 1556, in China, in which nearly one million lost their lives.

The worst earthquakes in the United States:

The San Francisco earthquake, April 18, 1906. Killed 700 people. Cost $500 million.

The Anchorage, Alaska, earthquake, March 27, 1964. Killed 114. Cost $750 million. But at the end of the tribulation there will be one even worse than the one occurring in the sixth seal. (See Rev. 16:18.)

(2) The greatest cosmic disturbances in history. This may be a result of nuclear war. Hal Lindsey writes:

"Do you know what happens in a nuclear explosion? The atmosphere rolls back on itself! It's this tremendous rush of air back into the vacuum that causes much of the destruction of a nuclear explosion. John's words in this verse are a perfect picture of an all-out nuclear exchange. When this happens, John continues, every mountain and island will be jarred from its present position. The whole world will be literally shaken apart!" (*There's a New World Coming,* p. 110).

(3) The greatest prayer meeting in history.
But they prayed for the wrong thing. The only object to protect the sinner from the wrath of the Lamb is the righteousness of the Lamb.

g. Interlude (7:1–17).
Between the sixth and seventh seal judgments, God calls a divine time-out. During this pause two significant events take place.

(1) The conversion and call of the 144,000 (Rev. 7:1–8).
And after these things I saw four angels standing on the four corners of the earth, holding the four winds of the earth, that the wind should not blow on the earth, nor on the sea, nor on any tree. And I saw another angel ascending from the east, having the seal of the living God: and he cried with a loud voice to the four angels, to whom it was given to hurt the earth and the sea, saying, Hurt not the earth, neither the sea, nor the trees, till we have sealed the servants of our God in their foreheads. And I heard the number of them which were sealed: and there were sealed an hundred and forty and four thousand of all the tribes of the children of Israel.
No ink will be wasted here refuting the unscriptural claim of that sect known as the Jehovah's Witnesses, who brazenly claim that their group today comprises this 144,000. The Bible clearly teaches that the 144,000 will consist of 12,000 saved and commissioned preachers from each of the twelve tribes of Israel (Rev. 7).
This passage does not mean that God will save only Jews during the tribulation, for in Revelation 7:9–17, the Bible declares that a great multitude

125

from every nation will be saved. What this chapter
does teach, however, is that God will send out
144,000 "Hebrew Billy Sundays" to evangelize the
world. This will be a massive number indeed,
especially when we consider that there are less than
35,000 missionaries of all persuasions in the world
today! Our Lord doubtless had the ministry of the
144,000 in mind when he said, "And this gospel of
the kingdom shall be preached in all the world for
witness unto all nations; and then shall the end
come" (Mt. 24:14).

Judah heads up this list, and not Reuben, the first
born. Both Dan and Ephraim are missing. Both
tribes were guilty of going into idolatry (Jdg. 18;
1 Ki. 11:26; Hosea 4). The tribes of Levi and
Manasseh here take their place. However, both are
listed in Ezekiel's millennial temple (Ezek. 48), so
they simply forfeit their chance to preach during the
tribulation. Some have concluded on the basis of
Genesis 49:17 and Jeremiah 8:16 that the antichrist
will come from the tribe of Dan.

Dr. J. Dwight Pentecost offers the following
interesting words concerning the conversion of the
144,000:

"In 1 Corinthians 15:8 is a clue concerning the way
God will work after the church's rapture. After the
apostle had listed those to whom the resurrected
Christ appeared, so as to authenticate His
resurrection, he says, 'And last of all he was seen of
me also, as of one born out of due time.' This
phrase, 'born out of due time,' means a premature
birth. That is exactly what the apostle Paul is
saying—'I was one that was born prematurely.'
What did he mean? Comparing Revelation 7 with
Paul's statement in 1 Corinthians 15, we conclude
that after the rapture of the church, God will
perform the same miracle He performed in Saul of
Tarsus on the Damascus Road 144,000 times over"
(*Will Man Survive?*, p. 148).

126

(2) The conversion of "a great multitude" (Rev. 7:9–17).
  (a) Their number: Countless! (7:9).
  (b) Their praise: "Salvation to our God which sitteth upon the throne, and unto the Lamb!" (7:10).
  (c) Their background: "These are they which came out of great tribulation, and have washed their robes, and made them white in the blood of the Lamb" (7:14).
  (d) Their service: serving God continuously (7:15).
  (e) Their reward: to be both fed and led by the Lamb (7:17).

6. The mass return of the Jews to Palestine.
   One of the most remarkable chapters in all the Bible concerns itself with the latter-day return of the Jews to Palestine.

The power of the Lord was upon me and I was carried away by the Spirit of the Lord to a valley full of old, dry bones that were scattered everywhere across the ground. He led me around among them, and then he said to me: "Son of dust, can these bones become people again?" I replied, "Lord, you alone know the answer to that." Then he told me to speak to the bones and say: "O dry bones, listen to the words of God, for the Lord God says, See! I am going to make you live and breathe again! I will replace the flesh and muscles on you and cover you with skin. I will put breath into you, and you shall live and know I am the Lord."

So I spoke these words from God, just as he told me to; and suddenly there was a rattling noise from all across the valley, and the bones of each body came together and attached to each other as they used to be. Then, as I watched, the muscles and flesh formed over the bones, and skin covered them, but the bodies had no breath. Then he told me to call to the wind and say: "The Lord God says: Come from the four winds, O Spirit, and breathe upon these slain bodies, that they may live again." So I spoke to the winds as he commanded me and the bodies began breathing; they lived, and stood up—a very great army. Then he told me what the vision meant: "These bones," he said, "represent all the people of Israel. They say: 'We have become a heap of dried-out bones—all hope is gone.' But tell them, the Lord God says: My

127

*people, I will open your graves of exile and cause you to rise
again and return to the land of Israel. And, then at last, O my
people, you will know I am the Lord. I will put my Spirit into
you, and you shall live and return home again to your own land.
Then you will know that I, the Lord, have done just what I
promised you"* (Ezek. 37:1-14, TLB).

Even today we see the beginning of this future Israelite
ingathering. Note the following figures:

In 1882 there were approximately 25,000 Jews in
Palestine.

In 1900 there were 50,000.

In 1922 there were 84,000.

In 1931 there were 175,000.

In 1948 there were 650,000.

In 1952 there were 1,421,000.

Today there are approximately 3,500,000 Jews in
Palestine.

Thus the number of Jews has increased over 120 times in
less than 100 years! They have been gathered from over one
hundred countries. Three additional passages bear out his
latter-day Jewish return:

*For thus saith the Lord God, Behold, I, even I, will both search
my sheep, and seek them out. As a shepherd seeketh out his flock
in the day that he is among his sheep that are scattered; so will I
seek out my sheep, and will deliver them out of all places where
they have been scattered in the cloudy and dark day. And I will
bring them out from the people, and gather them from the
countries, and will bring them to their own land . . .* (Ezek.
34:11-13).

*For I will take you from among the heathen, and gather you
out of all countries, and will bring you into your own land* (Ezek.
36:24).

*Fear not: for I am with thee: I will bring thy seed from the east,
and gather thee from the west; I will say to the north, Give up;
and to the south, Keep not back: bring my sons from far, and my
daughters from the ends of the earth* (Isa. 43:5, 6).

7. The rebuilding of the Jewish Temple.

There is ample scriptural evidence to show that the antichrist
will allow (and perhaps even encourage) the building of the

128

Temple and the rendering of its sacrifices during the tribulation. See Daniel 9:27; 12:11; Matthew 24:15; 2 Thessalonians 2:4; Revelation 11:2; 13:14, 15.

In his book *Will Man Survive?* Dr. J. D. Pentecost quotes from a Jewish ad that appeared in the *Washington Post* during May 1967.

"A project to rebuild the temple of God in Israel is now being started. With divine help and guidance the temple will be completed. It will signal a new era in Judaism. Jews will be inspired to conduct themselves in such a moral way that our maker will see fit to pay us a visit here on the earth. Imagine the warm feelings that will be ours when this happy event takes place."

The history of Israel can be aptly summarized by simply studying their three holy buildings. These include a tabernacle and two Temples.

a. The Tabernacle of Moses.
  (1) The instructions were given to Moses by God on Mt. Sinai (Ex. 25:9).
  (2) Was to be patterned after the heavenly tabernacle (Ex. 25:9, 20; Isa. 6:1-8; Heb. 8:2, 5; 9:24; Rev. 11:9; 14:15, 17; 16:1, 7).
  (3) Time of construction—six months.
  (4) Date of completion—April, 1444 B.C. (Ex. 40).
  (5) Description and size.
      (a) Consisted of three sections: Outer court, Inner court, and Holy of Holies.
      (b) Outer court: Similar to a picket fence, 150 feet long, seventy-five feet wide, seven and a half feet high.
      (c) Inner court: The eastern enclosed section of a two-room tent.
      (d) Holy of Holies: The western enclosed section of this tent. The entire length of the tent was forty-five feet; it was fifteen feet high, and fifteen feet wide.
  (6) Furniture.

    (a) In the Outer Court: A bronze altar and laver.

    (b) In the Inner Court: Shewbread table, lamp-stand, and incense altar.

    (c) In Holy of Holies: The Ark of the Covenant.

(7) The tabernacle lasted for approximately 400 years.

(8) It was set up at Shiloh (Josh. 18:1; 19:51; Jdg. 18:31; 1 Sam. 1:9; 3:3).

(9) It was eventually destroyed by the Philistines (1 Sam. 4; Ps. 78:60; Jer. 7:12-14; 26:6).

b. The first Temple.

  (1) Construction began under Solomon in April, 966 B.C., and was completed seven and a half years later in October, 959 B.C. (2 Chron. 2-7; 1 Ki. 5-8).

  (2) God had given the blueprints to David, who passed them on to his son (1 Chron. 28:11, 12, 19).

  (3) Construction crew:

    (a) Hiram of Tyre was the main contractor (1 Ki. 7:13).

    (b) Under him 30,000 Israelites served to cut and carry the Lebanese cedars (1 Ki. 5:13, 14).

    (c) Also 153,000 non-Israelites were employed (2 Chron. 2:17).

    (d) These were superintended over by 3600 foremen (2 Chron. 2:18).

  (4) David began gathering vast materials for the Temple while Solomon was still a boy (1 Chron. 22:5). They consisted of 100,000 talents of gold (120 million ounces) and one million talents of silver (1.2 billion ounces), plus untold quantities of bronze and wood. At today's prices, the gold and silver alone would surpass 75 billion dollars. The total cost for the Temple probably approached one tenth of a trillion dollars.

  (5) David himself personally gave 3,000 talents of gold (3.6 million ounces), $1,800,000,000; and 7,000 talents of silver (8.4 million ounces), or $84,000,000 (1 Chron. 29:4, 5).

  (6) At the dedication, 22,000 oxen and 120,000 sheep

and goats were sacrificed. The celebration lasted fourteen days (1 Ki 8: 62–66).

(7) The Temple proper was ninety feet long, twenty feet wide, and forty-five feet high (1 Ki. 6:2). The total size of the courtyard was 600 feet long by 300 feet wide.

(8) It was built of blocks of stone quarried in the nearby hills. The inside was paneled with finely carved cedar wood overlaid with gold. The floors were made of cypress boards (1 Ki. 6:16, 21, 22). All this was done without sound of hammer, axe, or any other tool (1 Ki. 6:7).

(9) It had ten lampstands and ten tables of shewbread (2 Chron. 4:7, 8).

(10) The altar of bronze was thirty feet long by fifteen feet high, with a circumference of thirty feet (2 Chron. 4:1).

(11) The laver measured fifteen feet across, seven and a half feet deep, with a circumference of forty-five feet. It rested on the back of twelve oxen in four groups of three, facing the cardinal points of the compass (2 Chron. 4:2–5). This bowl weighed over thirty tons and could hold some 16,000 gallons of water.

(12) Two huge pillars stood at the entrance of the Temple. These were named "Jachin" (sustainer) and "Boaz" (smitten).

(13) History of the first Temple:
  (a) It was sacked by Egypt during Rehoboam's time (2 Chron. 12).
  (b) Joash was hidden there during the bloody reign of Athaliah (2 Chron. 22–23).
  (c) The High Priest Zechariah stoned there (2 Chron. 24).
  (d) Uzziah became a leper there (2 Chron. 26).
  (e) Manasseh set up idols to devil gods there (2 Chron. 33).
  (f) Josiah found a copy of God's Word there (2 Chron. 34).

(14) Both Isaiah (64:10, 11) and Jeremiah (7:11–15; 26:6–9) predicted the destruction of the Temple because of Judah's sin.

(15) Nebuchadnezzar destroyed the Temple on the ninth of Av, 586 B.C. (2 Chron. 36:16–19; 2 Ki. 24:13, 14). It had lasted 373 years.

c. The second Temple.

(1) Construction was begun by Zerubbabel in June, 535 B.C. (See Ezra 3 for the dedication service.)

(2) It was completed in February, 516 B.C. The prophet Haggai was the prompter God used to get the Temple built. (See his book.)

(3) Its dimensions were ninety feet long by ninety feet high (Ezra 6:3).

(4) Herod the Great began rebuilding and adding to the Temple in 20 B.C.

(5) Construction continued after his death. In Jesus' day work was still going on. (See Jn. 2:20.)

(6) It was finally completed in A.D. 64.

(7) On the ninth of Av, A.D. 70, Titus totally destroyed it.

(8) The glory cloud of God did *not* fill this Temple as it had the tabernacle and Solomonic Temple (Ex. 40:34–38; 1 Ki. 8:10, 11; 2 Chron. 5:13, 14).

(9) The dimensions of Herod's Temple proper was 150 feet by 150 feet. The total Temple, including courts, etc., was 750 feet long by 600 feet wide. The bronze altar inside was forty-eight feet square and twenty-four feet high.

(10) The Temple history between Zerubbabel and Christ.

(a) Josephus says Alexander the Great visited the Temple in 332 B.C.

(b) On December 15, 168 B.C., Antiochus Epiphanes defiled the Temple by slaughtering a sow on the altar. He then looted the Temple and burned the copies of the Law of Moses.

(c) This led to a Jewish revolt, instigated by Mattathias and his five sons, John, Simon, Judas, Eleazer, and Jonathan. Judas became nicknamed "the hammer" (Maccabee).

(d) On December 25, 165 B.C., the Maccabees captured and cleansed the Temple. This originated the feast of dedication (also called Lights and Hanukkah). (See Jn. 10:22.)

(e) In 63 B.C. Pompey took the Temple after a three-month siege on the day of atonement.

(11) The Temple in the time of Jesus.

(a) It was the most beautiful building in the world. Herod had trained 1000 priests in building arts, and had employed 10,000 skilled masons. He then secured 1,000 wagons to have stones from the quarries. The Temple was made of beautiful marble and gold—so gleaming that it appeared from afar as a mountain of snow glittering in the sun. It could easily hold 120,000 worshipers.

(12) The Temple personnel:

(a) The high priest.

(b) The chief priests (200 highborn Jews who could trace their descent back to Zadok). They had charge of the weekly Temple services, Temple treasury, and maintenance of the sacred vessels.

(c) The regular priests—7,200 in number. They were divided into twenty-four priestly clans, each serving a week at a time. Their job was lighting the altar fires, burning incense, baking the unleavened bread, and sacrificing the animals.

(d) The Levites—9,600 in number. They also served one week at a time, as guards, policemen, doorkeepers, singers, musicians, and servants.

(e) The daily Temple ritual required the services of 1,000 chief priests and Levites. During the three great feast days (Passover, Weeks, Booths) all twenty-four clans were required to attend—thus there were some 18,000 priests on hand.

(13) Christ and the Temple.

(a) He was dedicated in the Temple (Lk. 2:27).

      (b) He asked questions in the Temple (Lk. 2:46) at the age of twelve.

      (c) He was taken to the pinnacle of the Temple by the devil (Lk. 4:9).

      (d) He taught there (Mt. 21:23; 26:55; Jn. 7:14).

      (e) He healed there (Mt. 21:14).

      (f) He cleansed the Temple, at the beginning and conclusion of his ministry (Jn. 2:14, 15; Mt. 21:12).

      (g) He predicted its destruction (Mt. 23:37—24:2).

      (h) Its veil was torn at his death (Mt. 27:51).

  (14) The apostles and the Temple.

      (a) The twelve met, taught, and worked miracles in the Temple (Acts 2:46; 3:1; 5:42).

These then are the tabernacle and two historical temples. The Jews, of course, have enjoyed no temple since September of A.D. 70 when Titus burned Jerusalem. But there are a number of biblical passages which clearly predict the future construction of yet another holy place.

d. The third temple.

And he [antichrist] shall confirm the covenant [his false treaty] with many [Israel] for one week [seven years]; and in the midst of the week he shall cause the sacrifice and the oblation to cease, and for [because of] the overspreading of abominations he shall make it [the temple] desolate . . . (Dan. 9:27).

When ye therefore shall see the abomination of desolation, spoken of by Daniel the prophet, stand in the holy place . . . (Mt. 24:15).

. . . that man of sin . . . the son of perdition, who opposeth and exalteth himself above all that is called God, or that is worshipped; so that he as God sitteth in the temple of God, showing himself that he is God (2 Thess. 2:3, 4).

And there was given me a reed like unto a rod: and the angel stood, saying, Rise, and measure the temple of God, and the altar, and them that worship therein (Rev. 11:1). (See also Rev. 13.)

Several questions may be raised at this point. Where

will the third temple be built? There seems little doubt it
will be constructed on the same spot where the first and
second temples once stood—Mount Moriah. Note its
eventful history:

(1) The place where Abraham offered up Isaac (Gen.
22:2).

(2) The place where the hand of the death angel was
stayed in David's time (1 Chron. 21:15-29). David
then bought this area from a Jebusite named Ornan.

(3) The place where Solomon built the first Temple
(2 Chron. 3:1).

(4) The place where the second Temple was constructed.
(a) Begun by Zerubbabel (Ezra 3).
(b) Greatly enlarged by King Herod (Jn. 2:20).

(5) In A.D. 135 Roman Emperor Hadrian built a statue
of Jupiter on this spot.

(6) The earliest Christians looked upon Moriah as a
place cursed by God.

(7) In A.D. 534 Emperor Justinian built a church
dedicated to St. Mary.

(8) In A.D. 639 Jerusalem fell to Islam and Moriah
became a Moslem shrine.

(9) In A.D. 691 the famous Dome of the Rock was
completed. This shrine, the third holiest in the
Moslem world, is an octagonal building, each side
measuring sixty-six feet, for a total of 528 feet in
circumference. The diameter is 176 feet, and the
height 108 feet. The walls are thirty-six feet high.
It remains standing today.

(10) In the tenth century the crusaders captured
Jerusalem and worshiped God in this building on
Mt. Moriah, believing it was actually the second
Temple. They called it the Lord's Temple.

(11) A century later the Arabs took it again, this time
for keeps.

In ancient times Moriah covered twenty-five acres.
Today it occupies thirty-five acres. It is 2,425 feet above
sea level.

Jewish legend has it that in the beginning Moriah was

suspended in midair and the rest of the world created around it. Moslem legend teaches that the rock inside their dome on Moriah is the gate to paradise. They say believers can hear the roar of the five rivers of the Garden of Eden beneath Moriah. Here they believe is the rock Adam was created upon and the spot where Noah's ark rested. Here final judgment will take place. True believers will then be ushered by the angel Gabriel into paradise. Moslems believe Mohammed, riding on Burak (a winged horse with a woman's face and peacock's tail), accompanied by Gabriel, came from Mecca to this rock, before his ascent into the seventh heaven. Moslems also believe the souls of the dead pray there twice each week.

What will happen to the Dome of the Rock, which must be removed to allow the construction of the third temple? Of course, no one knows. Perhaps an earthquake will destroy it, or it may be bombed or burned. It could be the antichrist himself will relocate it on another nearby site.

What will cause the Jews to rebuild the third temple? First of all, it can be stated that there is a growing desire in the heart of some Jews to rebuild the third temple. This ancient yearning was fanned to white heat during the days following the six-day war in June of 1973, at which time the Jews recaptured the old walled city of Jerusalem, including their beloved western (or wailing) wall!

The western wall is sixty feet high and 200 feet long. It extends below the ground for seventy feet. It is the holiest spot in Israel to the Jew. The western wall was a part of the old retaining Temple wall during the time of Jesus. It may rest on the ancient Solomonic wall. It was left by Titus to show the power of Rome in defeating a city surrounded by such a wall.

The Jews began coming here during the third century to lament the destruction of both Temples on the ninth of Av. It thus became known as the wailing wall. Pieces of paper containing prayers can be seen stuffed in cracks of the wall.

The divine Presence is believed to rest eternally upon

the wall. On the eve of Av, legend holds that in the dead of the night a white dove—the divine Presence—appears and coos sadly with the mourners. At night the stones are covered with drops of dew, declared to be the tears of the wall, shed over Israel.

From 1948 to 1967 no Jew was allowed to come near the wall. On June 6, 1967, Israeli paratroopers took the wall from the Arab legionnaires.

The actual capture of the wall was in itself a thrilling story. It began on Monday, June 5, 1967. On that day, Uzi Narkiss, Major General and Central Commander of the Israeli forces, felt great disappointment in not being able to see any action in Sinai or the Golan Heights. He was ordered simply to maintain a defensive posture on Mt. Scopus. At that time Israel did not expect Jordan would enter the war against them, as Egypt and Syria had done. But King Hussein did attack. Thus, on Wednesday, June 7, 1967, at 6:00 a.m., the order was given Narkiss to take the Old City. His soldiers entered the city via the Lion's Gate (St. Stephen's Gate) and at 9:50 a.m. they reached the Temple mount. En route, Narkiss met Brigadier General Rabbi Goren and offered him a ride. He refused, saying: "No, for 2,000 years we have waited for this moment. Now I am not going to the Wall in a jeep. I'll walk!"

Narkiss later wrote of his feelings as he stood by the wall.

"It was as though I was in another world. . . . I felt a part of the whole Jewish people, who for 2,000 years had longed for this moment. It was an emotion far bigger than myself, bigger than the whole generation. I stood there before the Wall and I didn't know what to do. When the Rabbi arrived, he knew what to do. He prayed and blew the shofar (ram's horn). I then seized myself and led in the singing of the National Anthem. . . ."

The next week (June 14), on the feast of weeks, 200,000 Jews gathered to pay homage at the wall. Two arches sweep out from the wall: Robinson's and Wilson's arches. Warren's shaft is under Wilson's arch. Excavations have found a drinking vessel used in the Temple rituals, and a jar fragment inscribed "Korban" (Hebrew word for sacrifice). Below Robinson's arch, a large stone engraved with a Hebrew inscription has been brought to light. It carries the words of Isaiah's prophecy: "And when ye see this, your heart shall rejoice, And your bones shall flourish like young grass" (Isa. 66:14).

Zola Levitt observes:

"One is reminded of the succinct prophecy of our Lord in Luke 21:24 which reviews this situation: 'And they shall fall by the edge of the sword, and shall be led away captive into all nations: and Jerusalem shall be trodden down of the Gentiles, until the times of the Gentiles be fulfilled.'
The scope of our Lord's foreknowledge is breathtaking. The prophecy has clearly been justified. The Jews hold the Temple site, and in the words of their brilliant military commander Moshe Dayan, 'No power on earth will remove us from this spot again.' And rebuilding the Temple at this time has not escaped the Jews as a real possibility. Rabbi Sinai Halberstam, writing in *The Jewish Press*, August 2, 1968, noted, 'When Jerusalem was in foreign hands the question always arose, "When can we rebuild our beloved Temple?" Even more so does this question arise today when, with the blessing of the Almighty, Jerusalem has been returned to the caretaking of Jewish hands. The Temple grounds are again under the control of the descendants of those who stood upon Mount Sinai. When will the Temple be rebuilt?'
Time magazine, ordinarily no valuable source of biblical commentary, speculated on the possibilities only one month after the Six-Day War, and published an article entitled 'Should the Temple Be Rebuilt?' On June 30, 1967, that potent secular periodical asked, 'Assuming that Israel keeps the Western Wall, which is one of the few

remaining ruins of Judaism's Second Temple, has the time now come for the erection of the Third Temple?'

An Israeli guide reports that he attended the recent rededication of the restored main Jewish Synagogue in the Jewish quarter in Old Jerusalem, with hundreds of Israelis present. The officiating rabbi stirred the crowd by predicting, 'As the city has been reunited in our lifetime, so will the rebuilding of the Temple be accomplished in our lifetime.'

The *Time* article goes on to review the nineteen centuries of hope that have passed among the scattered Jews, and says, 'Although Zionism was largely a secular movement, one of its sources was the prayers of Jews for a return to Palestine so that they could rebuild a new Temple.'

Looking at the 1967 situation, *Time* went on to say, 'Such is Israel's euphoria today that some Jews see plausible theological grounds for discussing reconstruction. They base their argument on the contention that Israel has already entered its "Messianic Era" (the time of the coming of the Jewish Messiah, as expected in Jewish theology). In 1948, they note, Israel's chief rabbis ruled that with the establishment of the Jewish state and the ingathering of the exiles, the age of redemption had begun.

'Today many of Israel's religious leaders are convinced that the Jews' victory over the Arabs has taken Judaism well beyond that point. Says historian Israel Eldad: "We are at the stage where David was when he liberated Jerusalem. From that time until the construction of the Temple by Solomon, only one generation passes. So will it be with us." And what about that Moslem shrine (standing directly on the Temple site)? Answers Eldad: "It is of course an open question. Who knows? Perhaps there will be an earthquake." '

Fascinating. Our time is compared to that of David and Solomon, when all Israel focused on the construction of the splendid first Temple. And perhaps God will act to clear the site. This has been the generation of liberation comparable to the coming of David's armies. The next generation, as the Jewish scholar sees it, will be like that of Solomon—the actual building" (Zola Levitt, *Israel and Tomorrow's Temple*, Chicago: Moody Press, 1977, pp. 24, 25).

In the May 14, 1974, issue of *The Jerusalem Post* a group of Jews ran a half-page ad with the following headline:

"May it be Thy will, O Lord our God that our holy temple be rebuilt in Jerusalem in our days."

Those who responded to this amazing plea were told:

"Why We Need the Third Temple"

We look in our houses of worship and find our youth noticeably absent. They do not attend because they feel the services do not relate to their day to day problems.

The real problem we feel is that a state of mourning still exists for the destruction of the first and second Temples (Ps. 137). We find today instrumental music and dance on a very limited basis as a means of worship. The restriction of prayers primarily to reading and singing prayers is frustrating the personality of our people. It would appear that to reach fulfillment in prayer, we must find various ways to cater to the diverse talents and personalities amongst us. Those whose personality will not allow them to learn how to pray in the accepted form must find outlets for prayer. The third Temple would close this gap of emptiness that prevents millions of us from participating in prayer.

Most assuredly through the talents of each of us, additional methods of praising the Lord will be found, and the subject of prayer will take on new dimensions.

With the third Temple, we end our period of mourning, and a new world should begin for us. Our personality as a people will find new directions toward a brotherhood of man.

Finally, consider this article appearing in a New York paper:

"Second Coming Linked to New Jewish Temple"

New York—An aura of mystery surrounds the idea of restoring the Jewish Temple in Jerusalem. Both for many Christians and Jews, it's a longed-for dream, a Messianic sign. It is not yet. But something like it is happening.

Construction is due to begin on the first large, central Jewish house of worship in the Holy City since the destruction of the Temple 1,904 years ago.

"No one is suggesting that this means the restoration of the Temple," says Rabbi Dr. Maurice A. Jaffee, president of the Union of Israel Synagogues which is sponsoring the project. "But there are parallels."

For one thing, the prospective new "Jerusalem Great Synagogue" is planned as a central, representative sanctuary to which Jewish pilgrims from all over the world may come to pray—just as they did in the Temple of old.

In another respect, every Jew everywhere is being encouraged to contribute something to the building of the new edifice, even if it amounts to no more than a half shekel—the basic tribute of each practicing Jew to the ancient Temple.

Furthermore, the new house of worship is being built of a special radiant stone like that of the Temple of Bible times, and is to be situated next to the headquarters of Israel's rabbinic authority, as was the historic Temple.

"There are many analogies, but we're wary of drawing comparisons," Dr. Jaffee said in an interview. "One gets in hot water even to hint at such a thing. Conditions are out of the question for re-establishing the Temple."

Doing so, to many Christians who interpret the Bible literally, would be a prophetic indication of the imminent return of Christ. Many Jews also link restoration of the Temple to a coming Messiah (George W. Cornell, July 1974).

Frank Allnutt writes:

"Evidently the Orthodox Jews are serious about rebuilding the Temple, because college studies in the ritual of the temple sacrifices and offerings have recently been introduced into the curriculum for rabbinical students at Israel University. The newly-ordained rabbis are prepared to make sacrifices and offerings in a new temple which they expect to see built during their lifetime!

The priesthood that is being trained is called 'Kohane.' According to Israel's former military chaplain, Ashkenazic Chief Rabbi Shlomo Goren: 'The priesthood does exist. It is a concept handed down to us by Moses and it goes back to the first "Kohane," Aaron. Its significance apart from its present partly-ceremonial meaning is now based entirely on our future as a people. I believe we will have to establish a third Temple in modern Israel, and without a Kohanim that would be impossible. The third Temple will come in our time. It is part and parcel of our Messianic tradition' (cited in the *Times of Israel*, March 1974)" (Frank Allnutt, *After the Omen*, Van Nuys, Calif.: Bible Voice Publishers, 1976, p. 74).

So then, it is obvious that the desire in the hearts of many Jews is burning brightly concerning the rebuilding of the third temple. But what will trigger the actual project itself? Of course, no one knows, but it may well be connected with that mysterious and missing box known as the Ark of the Covenant. Here a little background will prove helpful.

Description: A five-feet long, three-feet high, three-feet wide box made of acacia wood, overlaid by gold. It contained a pot of manna, Aaron's rod that budded, and the two tablets of the Law of Moses. The lid was called the Mercy Seat. Two golden angels overlooked the Mercy Seat.

History:
God ordered Moses to build it while he was on Mt. Sinai (Ex. 25:10–22).
To be placed in the Holy of Holies (Ex. 26:33, 34).
Was anointed (Ex. 30:26).

142

Overshadowed by the glory cloud (Ex. 40:34-38; Lev. 16:2).

Covered by blue cloth when transported and carried by priests, on staves placed through four golden rings on the corners of the ark (Num. 4:5).

God spoke to Moses from the Mercy Seat (Num. 7:89).

The ark led Israel across the desert.

And the cloud of the Lord was upon them by day, when they went out of the camp. And it came to pass, when the ark set forward, that Moses said, Rise up, Lord, and let thine enemies be scattered; and let them that hate thee flee before thee. And when it rested, he said, Return, O Lord, unto the many thousands of Israel (Num. 10:34-36).

The ark led Israel and Joshua across the Jordan (Josh. 3-4).

The ark was carried around the city of Jericho (Josh. 6:1-17).

God spoke to Joshua from the ark after Israel's tragic defeat at Ai (Josh. 7:6).

The ark was in view as blessings and curses of the law were read from Mt. Ebal and Mt. Gerizim (Josh. 8:30-35).

High priest Phinehas received counsel from God concerning the civil war with Benjamin (Jdg. 20:27).

The ark resided in Shiloh during Samuel's and Eli's day (1 Sam. 3:3).

It was captured by the Philistines (1 Sam. 4).

The ark among the Philistines (1 Sam. 5-6).

The ark returned to Israel, resting at Kirjath-jearim (1 Sam. 6-7).

Saul brought the ark into battle against the Philistines (1 Sam. 14:18).

David brought the ark into Jerusalem (2 Sam. 6). It was ignored by Saul during his reign (1 Chron. 13:3); contrast with Psalm 132.

David planned to build the Temple to house the ark (2 Sam. 7:2).

It remained, however, in a tent until the time of

Solomon (2 Sam. 11:11). However, David donated the gold for the cherubims (2 Chron. 28:18).

The ark was carried out of Jerusalem and back during Absalom's rebellion (2 Sam. 15:24, 25-29).

Solomon worshiped God before the ark after receiving his gift of wisdom (1 Ki. 3:15).

Solomon placed ark in the Temple (1 Ki. 8).

Solomon then moved his pagan wife (daughter of Pharaoh) away from the area of the ark (2 Chron. 8:11).

The ark was placed back in the Temple during King Josiah's reign. It had apparently been removed previously. This is the last reference to it in the Old Testament (2 Chron. 25:3).

The ark was not in the Temple of Herod. Edersheim says there was simply a stone called the stone of foundation, three fingers high.

Theories concerning its whereabouts:

That Jeremiah carried it with him to Egypt.

That Jeremiah hid it on Mt. Nebo (2 Macc. 2:1-7).

That it is hidden beneath the Dome of the Rock.

That it resides in a church at Aksum in Ethiopia. A tradition says Solomon fathered a son called Menelik through the Queen of Sheba. As a young man, Menelik visited Solomon, who presented the boy with an exact reproduction of the ark. However, during a farewell party, Menelik got the priests drunk and substituted the replica for the original. The late Haile Selassie claimed to come from the line of Menelik. He called himself the King of kings, the Lion of Judah, Defender of the Christian Faith, Emperor of the Ancient Kingdom of Ethiopia, the Chosen of God.

That it is buried in a secret place under Mount Moriah, where the two Temples once stood. This is by far the most commonly believed theory.

Here it may be asked just what all this has to do with the building of the third temple. Simply, it is this. When David became king over all Israel in 1004 B.C., he did two significant things. First, he captured Jerusalem from pagan Jebusites (1 Chron. 11:4-9). The second thing he did was to locate the Ark of the Covenant and bring it into Jerusalem (1 Chron. 13). We then read:

Now it came to pass, as David sat in his house, that David said to Nathan, the prophet, Lo, I dwell in an house of cedars, but the Ark of the Covenant of the Lord remaineth under curtains [in a tent] (1 Chron. 17:1).

David then decided to build a Temple to house the ark. Of course, as things turned out, God appointed Solomon (David's son) to erect the Temple rather than David. But the point to be made here is that the taking of Jerusalem and the location of the ark resulted in the building of the first Temple!

What is the situation today? The Jews now possess Jerusalem. Is the ark still intact somewhere? If so, God may allow its discovery once again to trigger the construction of a temple—the third temple.

An extremely interesting article appeared in the March 23, 1980, *Jerusalem Post* which serves as one more reminder of the intense interest in Israel concerning the site of the first two temples.

"Temple Site Riddle"

Remains of a wall said to contain Herodian-style stones were found on the Temple Mount 10 years ago—almost precisely where a controversial researcher places the eastern wall of Herod's Temple. Knowledge of this wall— the first possible remains of the Jerusalem Temple ever uncovered—has been suppressed for the past decade because of its possible political implications. Although some scholars were aware of it, at least one of Israel's senior archaeologists heard about it for the first time last week from a reporter. The Western Wall, the focus of Jewish prayer for centuries, is not a remnant of the Temple but of the massive wall supporting the Temple Mount. The wall was uncovered in 1970 when the Supreme Moslem Council excavated a pit for water storage just off the northeast edge of the platform supporting the Dome of the Rock. A government archaeologist, who asked last week to remain anonymous, visited the site after being informed that ancient remains had been uncovered. He told *The Jerusalem Post* that he saw several courses of a massive wall, some of whose stones had the smooth margins typical of the Herodian stones seen in the Western Wall. By the time he returned with other archaeologists, however, the remains—five metres long, two metres thick and several courses high—had been knocked down.

The archaeologist said he wrote a report on his find, including sketches of the stones, but did not publish it. "I just felt the matter was too sensitive," he said. The sensitivity lay in the proximity of the Jews' most holy site with the Islamic shrine.

The water reservoir was being dug as a precautionary move against fire dictated by the arson at Al Aksa Mosque the previous year. That fire had been set by a crazed Australian Christian who wanted to destroy the mosques so that the Temple could be rebuilt.

Two years ago, word of the report reached Dr. Asher Kaufman, a Hebrew University physicist of Scottish origin who for the past few years has been devoting most of his time to research into the exact site of the First and Second Temples. Basing himself mainly on written sources, particularly the Mishna, his own archaeological observations and complicated scientific calculations, the Orthodox scientist had already drawn up a detailed plan of the Second Temple. He contacted the archaeologist who let him read his report. They saw that the wall whose remains had been found was parallel to and 2.6 metres from where Kaufman had placed the eastern wall of the Temple complex. Kaufman deduced that the 2.6 metre difference was due to his having erred in the thickness of the wall between the Temple's two main courts. "This is the only wall to which there is no written reference and its thickness had to be guessed," he said last night. By readjusting its thickness to that of the outer walls of the Temple—five cubits, or 2.18 metres, according to his calculation of a cubit—he could place the eastern wall of his plan within a few centimetres of the wall uncovered.

Departing from the universally accepted notion that the Dome of the Rock was built on the ruins of the Temple,

Kaufman places the Temple about 50 metres north of the Islamic landmark. He described a roughly rectangular complex 149 meters long, 43.7 metres wide (100 cubits) and containing a sanctuary 43.7 metres high, equivalent of a 15-story building. Kaufman's temple is oriented east-west with the Holy of Holies—the room entered only by the high priest and then only on Yom Kippur—near the western edge. In First Temple days, the Holy of Holies contained the foundation stone and the two tablets of the law. In the Second Temple, only the foundation stone remained. There is no description of what this stone looked like or what purpose it served. Some have even assumed that it was a meteorite. A more general belief identifies the foundation stone as the bare rock around which the Dome of the Rock is built, as-Sakhra.

Kaufman, however, is convinced that the foundation stone is a virtually unnoticed bedrock floor beneath a cupola at the northwestern end of the Temple platform known as the Dome of the Spirits or the Dome of the Tablets. The Arabic names, he says, associate the site both with divine presence and tablets of the law. The stone fits precisely into the chamber designated on Kaufman's plan as the Holy of Holies.

Also, an event took place in Jerusalem on the eighth of Tammuz, 5729 (June 24, 1969), which may possibly play a role in the erection of the third temple. On that day the ceremony of the laying of the foundation stone of the Jerusalem synagogue occurred. Present at this function was the President of Israel, the chief rabbis, cabinet and diplomatic members, Jerusalem's mayor, and distinguished Jewish leaders from around the world. This synagogue, called the Jerusalem Great Synagogue, to be completed sometime in 1982, is to be the most beautiful, costly, and spacious in the world. In May of 1980 it was my privilege to visit this unfinished project. I now quote from the descriptive brochure given me at that time by a rabbi.

"The Jerusalem Great Synagogue will be built from that beautiful Jerusalem stone which is known to change its

147

color throughout the day, the sun giving it a golden tinge
toward evening—hence the expression, 'Jerusalem the
Golden.'

The exterior architecture of the building has . . . its
own individual style, the central feature being a high
tower depicting the two tablets of stone bearing the Ten
Commandments.

Special materials to insure the maximum acoustics have
been used so that the service can be heard in every part
of the synagogue without the need for a microphone.

There will be twelve stained glass windows and a
specially designed window which will divide the two
tablets forming the central tower. This window, facing the
ancient city and site of the Temple, will be twenty metres
in length."

This building, of course, cannot actually become the
third temple itself, for neither its location nor features
could fulfill prophetical requirements. But it may very
well serve as a halfway house of some kind to bridge the
long gap between the second Temple and the present, and
to pave the way for the third temple.

EIGHT
THE MIDDLE PART
OF THE
TRIBULATION

RECENT DEVELOPMENTS IN THE LAND OF RUSSIA
(Ezekiel 38–39)

Some years back, Dr. Joshua Kunitz, a professor at London University, wrote a book about Russia and titled it, *Russia, the Giant That Came Last*. No better words could have been chosen to describe the U.S.S.R. The rise of Russia has been nothing less than phenomenal. Even though her land began to be peopled by the Slavs as early as the fifth century, A.D., Russia remained a geographical void for the next thousand years. Then came Peter the Great and the world began to take notice. In 1712 he transferred the capital from Moscow to St. Petersburg. After this, Catherine the Great appeared upon the scene (1762–1796) with her attempts to westernize Russia. Russia's place in world history was now assured. But how clumsy she was in those days. She was soundly defeated by tiny Japan in 1905.

In 1914 she entered World War I only to suffer crushing defeat. In October of 1917 the Communist Lenin took over all of Russia with some 40,000 followers. The statistics of growth of Communism from this point on are beyond comparison: from 40,000 in 1917 to over one billion today. This amounts to an increase of more than two million percent. God-hating and Christ-rejecting Communism continues to control Russia today as it did on that black October.

Some 2600 years ago, the Hebrew prophet Ezekiel prophesied

that such a nation would rise to the north of Palestine just prior to the Second Coming of Christ. He writes of this in chapters 38 and 39, giving the following:

A. Ezekiel's prophecy concerning Russia.
  1. That the name of his land would be Rosh (see Ezek. 38:2 in the American Standard Version). He continues by mentioning two cities of Rosh. These he calls Meshech and Tubal (38:2). The names here are remarkably similar to Moscow and Tobolsk, the two ruling city capitals of Russia today.
  2. That this land would be anti-God, and therefore God would be against it (Ezek. 38:3).
  3. That Russia (Rosh) would invade Israel in the latter days (Ezek. 38:8).
  4. That this invasion would be aided by various allies of Rosh (Ezek. 38:5, 6), such as: Iran (Persia), South Africa (Ethiopia), North Africa (Libya), Eastern Europe (Gomer), and the Cossacks of Southern Russia (Togarmah). In 38:15 Ezekiel describes the major part that horses will play during this invasion. The Cossacks of course have always owned and bred the largest and finest herd of horses in history.
  5. That the purpose of this invasion was "to take a spoil" (Ezek. 38:12). If one but removes the first two letters from this word "spoil," he soon realizes what Russia will really be after.

B. Russia's involvement in the Middle East.
  In 1979, events transpiring in two Middle East countries made world headlines. Russia was totally involved in each case. These nations were Iran and Afghanistan.
  1. Events happening in Iran. Three important dates are to be noted here:

  January 16: The Shah of Iran went into exile.
  February 1: The Ayatollah Khomeini arrived in Teheran.
  November 4: Moslem militants seized the U.S. embassy in Teheran and took (originally) some ninety persons hostage.

  For thousands of years prior to 1935 Iran was known as Persia. In 1953 Mohammed Reza Pahlavi, commonly known

150

as the Shah of Iran, came into power. From that moment on the Shah became a staunch and steady friend of the Western world, especially the United States. At times during the troublesome post-war years his voice was the only friendly one coming from the Middle East. All this is well known.

But a problem was seen here in prophetical matters, for according to Ezekiel 35:5, in the last days, Persia (Iran) is to join Russia in an all-out attack upon Israel. In other words, the Scriptures predicted Iran would become decidedly anti-West and pro-communist during the tribulation.

With the tragic betrayal of the Shah by his Western friends (especially the U.S.) in 1979, this of course began its fulfillment. Numerous reports now confirm that the Ayatollah, far from being simply a religious fanatic, was in reality a dedicated communist. Furthermore, several known Russian agents have been identified (as seen on national TV) posing as students who guarded the fifty-two American hostages.

All this was dramatically illustrated during the Iraqi-Iranian war which began over water rights in September, 1980. Of all Arabic nations, Iraq has been especially favored by the Russians. Iraq was the first Middle East country to free itself from Western European domi-nation as far back as 1932. In 1958 the monarchy was overthrown in a bloody military coup. Since then Russia has been to Iraq what America was to Iran. But then came the September war. Russia suddenly turned from Iraq and began supplying Iran war materials through North Korea.

2. Events happening in Afghanistan. Here two dates should be noted:

February 16: The U.S. ambassador was assassinated in Afghanistan. This act was believed to have been arranged by Russia to help prepare for a plan already drawn up which would take place at the end of 1979.

December 27: Soviet Russia invaded Afghanistan. This was nothing less than a trial run for the real thing when

Russia will overrun the entire Middle East during the tribulation.

"More than any other recent event, last winter's Soviet invasion of Afghanistan should awaken Americans to the peril that confronts us. The invasion shows that an expansionist Soviet dictatorship is now prepared, given the right circumstances, to strike out toward the oil fields of the Middle East. If we fail to contain the Russians now, we may wake up some morning to find that the oil America depends on to maintain itself as a great power has come under Moscow's control.

Worse still, Moscow's thrust into Afghanistan has brought Soviet military power within 300 miles of the Strait of Hormuz, the strategic chokepoint, just 30 miles wide, that dominates the entrance to the Persian Gulf. Thirty percent of our imported oil—about 15 percent of our total requirement—must come through Hormuz.

We will confront the Russians in the Gulf for years to come. The Soviet Union is the world's largest producer of oil, surpassing even Saudi Arabia. But, according to most experts, by the mid-1980's its supply of cheaply available oil will become inadequate to meet its demands. Faced with a growing pinch, Moscow has warned its satellites in Eastern Europe that it will have to decrease oil deliveries to them. In the next few years, many experts believe, the Soviet Union will have to import substantial amounts of oil. The Middle East, as a result, has suddenly become much more important to Moscow.

Where will the Soviets strike next? Iran, which borders on the Soviet Union and Afghanistan, must be tempting. But the main prize is clearly Saudi Arabia, along with the small Arab oil emirates of the Persian Gulf" (*Reader's Digest*, June 1980, pp. 147, 150).

This then is Ezekiel's prophecy concerning Russia. Of course, there are many who would criticize all this, and accuse Bible believers of simply waiting to see what happens and then twisting current events into their own peculiar prophetical scheme. To answer this, the following quotes are given. It will be observed by the dates that both statements were written long before Russia became the power she is today.

"Russia is evidently destined to become the master of Asia. Her frontier line across Asia will be 5000 miles in length. We believe, from the place assigned to Russia in the Word of God, that her legions will sweep over the plains and mountains of Asia and will become the dominant power over all the East" (Walter Scott, *The Prophetical News and Israel's Watch*, June 1888).

"This king of the North I conceive to be. . .Russia. Russia occupies a momentous place in the prophetic word" (John Cumming, in 1864).

We have already suggested that the seven-year tribulation may be broken up into three sections. The first part is three and a half years, the middle perhaps just a few days, and the last again three and a half years. We shall now observe five important events which may, with some degree of certainty, be placed in this brief middle period.

C. The five events.

  1. The Gog and Magog invasion into Palestine (Ezek. 38–39).

Son of man, set thy face toward Gog, of the land of Magog, the prince of Rosh, Meshech, and Tubal, and prophesy against him, and say, thus saith the Lord Jehovah; Behold, I am against thee, O Gog, prince of Rosh, Meshech, and Tubal . . . (Ezek. 38:2, 3; American Standard Version, 1901). In these two remarkable chapters, Ezekiel describes for us an invasion into Palestine by a wicked nation north of Israel in the latter days.

  a. The identity of the invaders.

Where is the land of Magog? It seems almost certain that these verses in Ezekiel refer to none other than that red communist bear, the U.S.S.R. Note the following threefold proof of this.

    (1) Geographical proof.

Ezekiel tells us in three distinct passages (38:6,

15; 39:2) that this invading nation will come from the "uttermost part of the north" (as the original Hebrew renders it). A quick glance at any world map will show that only Russia can fulfill this description.

(2) Historical proof.

The ancient Jewish historian Josephus (first century A.D.) assures us that the descendants of Magog (who was Japheth's son and Noah's grandson) migrated to an area north of Palestine. But even prior to Josephus, the famous Greek historian Herodotus (fifth century B.C.) writes that Meshech's descendants settled north of Palestine.

(3) Linguistic proof.

Dr. John Walvoord writes concerning this:

"In Ezekiel 38, Gog is described as 'the prince of Rosh' (ASV). The Authorized Version expresses it as the 'chief prince.' The translation 'the prince of Rosh' is a more literal rendering of the Hebrew. 'Rosh' may be the root of the modern term 'Russia.' In the study of how ancient words come into modern language, it is quite common for the consonants to remain the same and the vowels to be changed. In the word 'Rosh,' if the vowel 'o' is changed to 'u' it becomes the root of the modern word 'Russia' with the suffix added. In other words, the word itself seems to be an early form of the word from which the modern word 'Russia' comes. Genesis, the famous lexicographer, gives the assurance that this is a proper identification, that is, that Rosh is an early form of the word from which we get Russia . The two terms 'Mesheck' and 'Tubal' also correspond to some prominent words in Russia. The term 'Mesheck' is similar to the modern name 'Moscow' and 'Tubal' is obviously similar to the name of one of the prominent Asiatic provinces of Russia, the province of Tobolsk. When this evidence is put together, it points to the conclusion that these terms are early references to portions of Russia; therefore the geographic argument is reinforced by the linguistic argument and supports the idea that this invading force comes from Russia" (*The Nations in Prophecy*, Zondervan, 1967, p. 107, 108).

b. The allies in the invasion.
Ezekiel lists five nations who will join Russia during her invasion. These are Persia, Ethiopia, Libya, Gomer, and Togarmah. These may (although there is some uncertainty) refer to the following present-day nations:
   (1) Persia—modern Iran
   (2) Ethiopia—Black African nations (South Africa)
   (3) Libya—Arabic African nations (North Africa)
   (4) Gomer—East Germany
   (5) Togarmah—Southern Russia and the Cossacks, or perhaps Turkey.

c. The reasons for the invasion.
   (1) To cash in on the riches òf Palestine (Ezek. 38:11, 12).
   (2) To control the Middle East.
      Ancient conquerors have always known that he who would control Europe, Asia, and Africa must first control the Middle East bridge which leads to these three continents.
   (3) To challenge the authority of the antichrist (Dan. 11:40–44).

d. The chronology of the invasion.
Here it is utterly impossible to be dogmatic. The following is therefore only a suggested possibility, based on Ezekiel 38 and Daniel 11:40–44.
   (1) Following a preconceived plan, Egypt attacks Palestine from the south (Dan. 11:40a).
   (2) Russia invades Israel from the north by both an

amphibious and a land attack (Dan. 11:40b).

(3) Russia continues southward and doublecrosses her ally by occupying Egypt also (Dan. 11:42, 43).

(4) While in Egypt, Russia hears some disturbing news coming from the East and North and hurriedly returns to Palestine. We are not told what the content of this news is. Several theories have been offered:

(a) That it contains the electrifying news that the antichrist has been assassinated, but has risen from the dead. (See Rev. 13:3.)

(b) That it concerns itself with the impending counterattack of the Western leader (the antichrist).

(c) That it warns of a confrontation with China and India ("Kings of the East"), who may be mobilizing their troops.

It should be noted at this point, however, that some Bible students identify the he of Daniel 11:42 as being the antichrist, and not the Russian ruler. If this is true, then the above chronology would have to be rearranged accordingly.

(5) Upon her return, Russia is soundly defeated upon the mountains of Israel. This smashing defeat is effected by the following events, caused by God himself:

(a) A mighty earthquake (Ezek. 38:19, 20).

(b) Mutiny among the Russian troops (Ezek. 38:21).

(c) A plague among the troops (Ezek. 38:22).

(d) Floods, great hailstones, fire and brimstone (Ezek. 38:22; 39:6).

e. The results of the invasion.

(1) Five sixths (83 percent) of the Russian soldiers are destroyed (Ezek. 39:2).

(2) The first grisly feast of God begins (Ezek. 39:4, 17, 18, 19, 20). A similar feast would seem to

take place later, after the battle of Armageddon (Rev. 19:17, 18; Mt. 24:28).

(3) The communist threat will cease forever.

(4) Seven months will be spent in burying the dead (Ezek. 39:11–15).

(5) Seven years will be spent in burning the weapons of war (Ezek. 39:9, 10). Dr. John Walvoord writes the following concerning this seven-year period:

"There are some . . . problems in the passage which merit study. A reference is made to bows and arrows, to shields and chariots, and to swords. These, of course, are antiquated weapons from the standpoint of modern warfare. The large use of horses is understandable, as Russia today uses horses a great deal in connection with their army. But why should they use armor, spears, bows and arrows? This certainly poses a problem. There have been two or more answers given. One of them is that Ezekiel is using language with which he was familiar—the weapons that were common in his day—to anticipate modern weapons. What he is saying is that when this army comes, it will be fully equipped with the weapons of war. Such an interpretation, too, has problems. We are told in the passage that they used the wooden shafts of the spears and the bows and arrows for kindling wood. If these are symbols, it would be difficult to burn symbols. However, even in modern warfare there is a good deal of wood used. . . . A second solution is that the battle is preceded by a disarmament agreement between nations. If this were the case, it would be necessary to resort to primitive weapons easily and secretly made if a surprise attack were to be achieved. This would allow a literal interpretation of the passage. A third solution has also been suggested based on the

157

premise that modern missile warfare will have developed in that day to a point where missiles will seek out any considerable amount of metal. Under these circumstances, it would be necessary to abandon the large use of metal weapons and substitute wood such as is indicated in the primitive weapons" (*The Nations in Prophecy*, Zondervan Press, 1967, pp. 115, 116).

2. The ministry and martyrdom of the two witnesses.
And I will give power unto my two witnesses, and they shall prophesy a thousand two hundred and threescore days, clothed in sackcloth (Rev. 11:3).
   a. Their identity.
   Some hold that they are Elijah and Enoch. Hebrews 9:27 states that all men are appointed to die, and since these two men did not experience physical death, they will be sent back to witness and to eventually die a martyr's death. Some hold that they are Elijah and Moses.
   (1) Elijah.
      (a) Because of Malachi 4:5, 6, which predicts that God will send Elijah during that great and dreadful day of the Lord.
      (b) Because Elijah appeared with Moses on the Mount of Transfiguration to talk with Jesus (Mt. 17:3).
      (c) Because Elijah's Old Testament ministry of preventing rain for some three years will be repeated by one of the witnesses during the tribulation. (Compare 1 Ki. 17:1 with Rev. 11:6.)

      The Jews definitely felt Elijah would come again. When the Sanhedrin sent out a delegation from Jerusalem to check out the preaching and baptizing ministry of John the Baptist, the second question they asked was: "Art thou Elijah?" (Jn. 1:21).

      The Jewish work, *The Twelve Prophets*, is a

commentary on the Hebrew text of the Old Testament. It also advocates Elijah's return:

"Elijah the prophet . . . the messenger who will prepare the way for the coming of the Lord . . . is to later generations the helper and healer, the reconciler and peace-bringer, the herald of the days of the Messiah . . ." (*Books of the Bible*, London: Soncino Press, 1948, p. 356).

Even today at every Passover meal in Jewish homes there is an empty chair set in place for the prophet Elijah.

    (2) Moses.

        (a) Because of Jude 9, where we are informed that after the death of Moses Satan attempted to acquire his dead body, so that God would not be able to use him against the antichrist during the tribulation.

        (b) Because Moses' Old Testament ministry of turning water into blood will be repeated by one of the witnesses during the tribulation. (Compare Ex. 7:19 with Rev. 11:6.)

        (c) Because Moses appeared with Elijah on the Mount of Transfiguration (Mt. 17:3).

b. Their ministry.

    (1) To prophesy in sackcloth before men as God's anointed lampstands.

    (2) To destroy their enemies in the same manner that their enemies would attempt to destroy them.

    (3) To prevent rain for three and a half years.

    (4) To turn waters into blood.

    (5) To smite the earth with every kind of plague.

c. Their death.

The antichrist is finally allowed to kill them. The word "beast" is first mentioned here in 11:7. There are thirty-five other references to him in Revelation. It

should also be noted that he could not kill the witnesses until "they shall have finished their testimonies." Satan cannot touch one hair on the head
of the most humble saint until God gives him specific
permission. (See Job 1:12; 2:6.)

These two, like Paul, finished their testimonies
(2 Tim. 4:7). Contrast this with Belshazzar's sad death
(Dan. 5:26). To show his contempt for them, he
refused to permit their dead bodies to be buried, but
leaves them to rot in the street of Jerusalem. All the
earth celebrates their deaths through a hellish Christmas; men actually send gifts to each other. This
is the only reference to the word "rejoice" in the
entire tribulation.

The dead bodies of these two prophets are viewed
in a three and a half day period. Their bodies will
be on display in Jerusalem (11:8). It is called
Sodom because of its immorality, and Egypt because
of its worldliness. It is interesting to note that this
prophecy (Rev. 11:9) could not have been fulfilled
until the middle sixties. The following article explains
why:

"The first link in a worldwide, live television system
was taken on May 2, 1965, when the Early Bird
Satellite, hovering 22,300 miles in space between
Brazil and Africa, united millions of American and
European viewers in an international television
exchange" (Reader's Digest Almanac, 1966 edition).

d. Their resurrection.
    (Here the word "great" appears three times.)
    (1) A great voice calls them up to heaven (Rev.
        11:12).
    (2) A great fear falls upon those who witness this
        (Rev. 11:11).
    (3) A great earthquake levels one tenth of Jerusalem
        and kills 7,000 prominent men (Rev. 11:13).
        John Phillips writes:

"Death cannot hold them, and they arise from the grave. John tells us that they have a triumphant resurrection. He says, 'And after three days and a half the Spirit of life from God entered into them and they stood upon their feet; and great fear fell upon them which saw them.' Picture the scene—the sun-drenched streets of Jerusalem, the holiday crowds flown in from the ends of the earth for a firsthand look at the corpses of these detested men, the troops in the beast's uniform, the temple police. There they are: devilish men from every kingdom under heaven, come to dance and feast at the triumph of the beast. And then it happens! As the crowds strain at the police cordon to peer curiously at the two dead bodies, there comes a sudden change.

Their color changes from a cadaverous hue to the blooming, rosy glow of youth. Those stiff, stark limbs—they bend, they move! Oh, what a sight! They rise! The crowds fall back, break, and form again.

They also have a triumphant rapture. John says, 'And they heard a great voice from heaven saying unto them, Come up hither. And they ascended up to heaven in a cloud; and their enemies beheld them.' But will these evil men repent when faced with this, the greatest of all miracles! Not a bit of it! 'Father Abraham!' cried the rich man from the flames of a lost eternity. 'Father Abraham . . . if one went unto them from the dead, they will repent.' Back came the solemn reply, 'If they hear not Moses and the prophets, neither will they be persuaded though one rose from the dead' (Lk. 16:30, 31). And here not just one, but two arise, and repentance is the farthest thing from the minds of men" (*Exploring Revelation*, Moody Press, 1974, p. 158).

3. The martyrdom of the 144,000 Hebrew evangelists
   Rev. 14:1–5).
   And I looked, and, lo, a Lamb stood on the Mount Sion, and
   with him an hundred forty and four thousand, having his
   Father's name written in their foreheads (Rev. 14:1).
   What a far-reaching and fruitful ministry these Hebrew
   evangelists will have performed. The amazing results of
   their labor are recorded in Revelation 7:9, 13, 14.
   After this I beheld, and, lo, a great multitude, which no man
   could number, of all nations, and kindreds, and people, and
   tongues, stood before the throne, and before the Lamb, clothed
   with white robes, and palms in their hands. And one of the
   elders answered, saying unto me, What are these which are
   arrayed in white robes? and whence came they? And I said
   unto him, Sir, thou knowest. And he said to me, These
   are they which came out of great tribulation, and have washed
   their robes, and made them white in the blood of the Lamb.

   Jesus himself during his Mt. Olivet sermon predicted
   the tremendous scope of their ministry: "And this gospel
   of the kingdom shall be preached in all the world for a
   witness unto all nations . . ." (Mt. 24:14). In other
   words these future evangelists will accomplish in a few
   short years that which the Christian church has not been
   able to do in the past twenty centuries, namely, fulfill
   the Great Commission.
   Go ye therefore, and teach all nations, baptizing them in the
   name of the Father, and of the Son, and of the Holy Ghost:
   Teaching them to observe all things whatsoever I have
   commanded you: and lo, I am with you alway, even unto the
   end of the world. Amen (Mt. 28:19, 20).
4. The casting out of heaven's monster (Rev. 12:3–15).
   a. The identity of this monster.
      There is no doubt whatever concerning the identity of
      this "creature from the clouds." He is pinned down
      by no less than five titles.
      (1) The great red dragon (12:3).
          (a) Great, because of his vast power (see Mt.
              4:8, 9).
          (b) Red, because he was the first murderer (see
              Jn. 8:44).

(c) Dragon, because of his viciousness (see 2 Cor. 6:15).
(2) The old serpent (12:9).
   (a) Old, which takes us back to the Garden of Eden (Gen. 3).
   (b) Serpent, which reminds us of the first body he used (Gen. 3).
(3) The devil (12:9), one who slanders (see 12:10; also Job 1, 2; Zech. 3:1-7; Lk. 22:31).
(4) Satan (12:9), the adversary (see 1 Pet. 5:8).
(5) The deceiver of the world (12:9).
   Note: He not only deceives men but angels as well! In 12:4 we are told that his tail "drew [literally, 'pulled down,' or 'to drag'; see Acts 14:19 where the same word is used] the third part of the stars of heaven. . . ." This is apparently a reference to the number of angels Satan persuaded to join him in his original revolt against God (Isa. 14:12-15; Ezek. 28:11-19).
   b. The location of this monster.
   Satan has been, is now, or shall be in one of the following locations:
   (1) In heaven, as God's anointed angel (past location—Ezek. 28:14).
   (2) In heaven, as God's chief enemy (present location—Job 1, 2).
   (3) On earth, as the antichrist's spiritual guide (future location, during the tribulation—Rev. 12:12).
   (4) In the bottomless pit (future, during the millennium—Rev. 20:1-3).
   (5) On earth again (future, after the millennium—Rev. 20:8, 9).
   (6) In the lake of fire (future and forever—Rev. 20:10).
   c. The activities of this monster.
   (1) He deceives all living unbelievers (Rev. 12:9).
   (2) He accuses all living believers (Rev. 12:10).
   (3) He persecutes the nation Israel (Rev. 12:13).
5. The destruction of the false church (Rev. 17:16).

And the ten horns which thou sawest upon the beast, these shall hate the whore, and shall make her desolate and naked, and shall eat her flesh and burn her with fire.

One of the most ironical turn of events in all history will be the destruction of the false church. For this evil organization will meet its doom not at the hands of Gabriel, or the Father, or the Son, or the Spirit, but the antichrist!

What will the future hold for this vile and vicious vixen? According to Revelation 17 the false church lends all her evil strength to elevate the antichrist during the first part of the tribulation. For awhile she flourishes, luxuriating in surpassing wealth and opulence. But suddenly things change drastically. John describes this for us:

The scarlet animal and his ten horns (which represent ten kings who will reign with him) all hate the woman, and will attack her and leave her naked and ravaged by fire (17:16).

The probable reason for all this is that after she has put the antichrist into power, the harlot then attempts to control him. History gives us many examples of the Roman Catholic Church (and indeed other religious systems) attempting to control kings and rulers. Note the edict of Pope Gregory VII in the eleventh century:

"It is laid down that the Roman Pontiff is universal bishop, that his name is the only one of its kind in the world. To him alone it belongs to dispose or reconcile bishops. . . . He alone may use the ensigns of empire; all princes are bound to kiss his feet; he has the right to depose emperors, and to absolve subjects from their allegiance. He holds in his hands the supreme mediation in questions of war and peace, and he alone may adjudge contested succession to kingdoms—all kingdoms are held in fiefs under Peter . . . the Roman church has never erred . . . the Pope is above all judgment" (*Short Paper on Church History*, p. 355).

But the antichrist won't bow! He will turn on her, destroy her buildings, burn her holy books, and murder her priests. It has been suggested that the antichrist will begin by detesting the harlot, then despoiling her, then disgracing her, then devouring her, and finally destroying her.

This hatred is based on both providential and practical reasons. To summarize the future activities of this horrible harlot, we note: Her influence will be worldwide (17:1). This influence will be used to corrupt the entire earth (17:2). She will possess vast and unlimited wealth (17:4). She is drunken with the blood of God's saints (17:6). Only eternity will reveal how many tens of millions of believers have been cruelly murdered in the name of religion.

She teams up (for awhile) with the beast (antichrist) (17:3, 7). She has her name written on her forehead (17:5). In the time of John it was common for prostitutes to wear their name in jewelry form upon their forehead, thus advertising their trade. She may have her headquarters in Rome (17:9)—Rome sits upon seven mountains.

NINE
THE LAST PART OF
THE TRIBULATION
(3½ YEARS)

A. The full manifestation of the antichrist.

After the judgment of Russia, the destruction of the false church, and the murder of most of God's preachers (the 144,000 and the two witnesses), an unbelievable vacuum will undoubtedly settle down upon the world. The antichrist will immediately exploit this. The following is but a suggestion of the chronology of events which may take place at this critical time.

1. The antichrist and his false prophet make their headquarters in Jerusalem after God destroys Russia.
2. Here in the holy city, perhaps during a television speech, the antichrist is suddenly assassinated, as millions of astonished viewers watch (Rev. 13:3, 14).
3. Before his burial—perhaps during the state funeral— he suddenly rises from the dead. The world is electrified.

A well-known reporter who had covered every important news story during his long professional life was once asked the question: "In your expert opinion, what would be the greatest news story of all time?"

He replied: "If a famous dead person could suddenly rise from his coffin and tell us what it's like on the other side of the grave—that, my friend, would be the greatest news story of all time!"

To illustrate this, let us imagine the following: The date is November 22, 1988. A group of mourners have gathered beside the eternal flame in Arlington Cemetery near Washington, D.C., to observe the twenty-fifth anniversary of President John F. Kennedy's tragic assassination. Suddenly, as the TV cameras record the action, an earthquake-like rumbling comes from the earth. Great chunks of dirt are thrown aside and a coffin slowly rises. The lids opens and before the horrified eyes of the millions viewing by television, John F. Kennedy stands to his feet! Obviously, Mr. Kennedy will not be the antichrist. But can you imagine the unbelievable world reaction if a similar situation happened to a famous personality?

4. The antichrist is immediately worshiped by the world as God.
5. The false prophet thereupon makes a statue of the antichrist, causes it to speak, and places it in the Holy of Holies (Mt. 24:15; Dan. 9:27; 12:11; 2 Thess. 2:4).
6. A law is passed which stipulates that no one can buy, sell, work, or obtain any necessity of life unless he carries a special mark on his right hand or his forehead to identify him as a worshiper of the beast (Rev. 13:16, 17).
7. The number of this mark is 666 (Rev. 13:18).

B. The worldwide persecution of Israel.
And there appeared a great wonder in heaven: a woman clothed with the sun, and the moon under her feet, and upon her head a crown of twelve stars (Rev. 12:1).

These words are unquestionably symbolic, but to whom do they refer?

1. Identification of this woman.
   a. She is not Mary. Mary never spent three and a half years in the wilderness, as does this woman (Rev. 12:6, 14). Neither was Mary personally hated, chased, and persecuted, as we see here (Rev. 12:13, 17). While Mary did give birth to that One who will someday "rule all nations with a rod of iron" (Rev. 12:5), the language in this chapter has a wider reference than to Mary.
   b. She is not the church. The church did not bring the manchild into existence, as does this woman (Rev.

167

12:5), but rather the opposite. See Matthew 16:18.
c. She is Israel. A Jewish Christian who reads Revelation 12:1 will undoubtedly think back to the Old Testament passage in which Joseph describes a strange dream to his father and eleven brothers:
Behold, I have dreamed a dream . . . the sun and the moon and eleven stars made obeisance to me (Gen. 37:9).
This was of course fulfilled when Joseph's eleven brothers bowed down to him in Egypt (Gen. 43:28).

2. Persecution of this woman.
   a. Persecution in the past.
   Throughout the long history, Satan has made every attempt to exterminate Israel. This he has done by resorting to:
   (1) Enslaving (Ex. 2).
   (2) Drowning (Ex. 14).
   (3) Starving (Ex. 16).
   (4) Tempting (Ex. 32; Num. 14).
   (5) Cursing (Num. 23).
   (6) Capturing (2 Ki. 17, 24).
   (7) Swallowing (Jonah 2).
   (8) Burning (Dan. 3).
   (9) Devouring (Dan. 6).
   (10) Hanging (Est. 3).
   (11) Gassing (the gas ovens of Adolph Hitler).
   b. Persecution in the future.
   But the most vicious attack is yet to come. John Phillips writes:

"What a time of terror lies ahead for Israel! The world has seen dress rehearsals for this coming onslaught already—the knock on the door at the dead of night; the dreaded secret police; the swift ride through the darkened streets to the sidings where the boxcars wait; the dreadful ordeal of days and nights without food, drink or sanitation, with men and women and children herded like cattle in the dark, and with little babies flung on top of the struggling heap of humanity like so many sacks of flour; the lonely sidings; the barbed wire; the concentration camps; the callous treatment and cruel tortures; and then the gas ovens and the firing squads. It has been rehearsed already in preparation for the full-stage production of terror" (*Exploring Revelation*, Moody Press, 1974, p. 174).

And at that time shall Michael stand up, the great prince which standeth for the children of thy people; and there shall be a time of trouble, such as never was since there was a nation even to that same time . . . (Dan. 12:1).

For, lo, I will raise up a shepherd in the land which shall not visit those that be cut off, neither shall seek the young one, nor heal that that is broken, nor feed that that standeth still; but he shall eat the flesh of the fat, and tear their claws in pieces (Zech. 11:16).

For then shall be great tribulation, such as was not since the beginning of the world to this time, no, nor ever shall be (Mt. 24:21).

And when the dragon saw that he was cast unto the earth, he persecuted the woman which brought forth the manchild (Rev. 12:13).

This marks the last and most severe anti-Semitic movement in history. It will apparently begin at the recognition by Israel that the Roman world dictator is in reality the antichrist, and their refusal to worship him as God or receive his mark (Mt. 24:15-24). A. W. Kac writes:

"Next to the survival of the Jews, the most baffling historical phenomenon is the hatred which he has repeatedly encountered among the nations of the earth. This hostility to the Jews, which goes under the name of antisemitism, is as old as Jewish existence. It is endemic; i.e., like many contagious diseases it is always with us to some degree. But under certain circumstances it assumes epidemic proportions and characteristics. It is prevalent wherever Jews reside in sufficiently large numbers to make their presence. 'The growth of antisemitism,' Chaim Weizman declares, 'is proportionate to the number of Jews per square kilometre. We carry the germs of antisemitism in our knapsack on our backs'" (*Rebirth of the State of Israel*, p. 306).

When the Israelites see the statue of the antichrist standing in their Holy of Holies, the words of Christ will come to their minds. He had warned them of this very thing many centuries earlier (Mt. 24:15-20). At this point the Jews of the world will travel down one of three roads:

(1) Many Israelites will be killed by the antichrist.
   And it shall come to pass that in all the land, saith the Lord, two parts therein shall be cut off and die; but the third shall be left therein (Zech. 13:8).

(2) Some Israelites will follow the antichrist.
   And then shall many be offended, and shall betray one another, and shall hate one another. And many false prophets shall rise, and shall deceive many. And because iniquity shall abound, the love of many shall wax cold (Mt. 24:10-12).
   . . . I know the blasphemy of them which say they are Jews, and are not, but are the synagogue of Satan (Rev. 2:9).
   Behold, I will make them of the synagogue of Satan which say they are Jews, and are not, but do lie; behold, I will make them to come and worship before thy feet, and to know that I have loved thee (Rev. 3:9).

(3) A remnant of Israel will be saved.
   And to the woman were given two wings of a great eagle, that she might fly into the wilderness, into her place, where she is nourished for a time, and times, and half a time, from the face of the serpent (Rev. 12:14).
   And I will bring the third part through the fire, and will refine them as silver is refined, and will try them as gold is tried; they shall call on my name, and I will hear them: I will say, It is my people: and they shall say, The Lord is my God (Zech. 13:9).

Thus, it would seem that at least one third of Israel will remain true to God and be allowed by him to escape into a special hiding place for the duration of the tribulation. We shall now consider the location of this hiding place. While it is not actually specified in Scripture, many Bible students believe that this place will be Petra. This is based on the following three passages:

And ye shall flee to the valley of the mountains; for the valley of the mountains shall reach unto Azal: yea, ye shall flee . . . and the Lord my God shall come, and all the saints with thee (Zech. 14:5).

(The "Azal" mentioned here is thought to be connected with Petra.)

Who is this that cometh from Edom, with dyed garments from Bozrah? (Isa. 63:1).

The first few verses of Isaiah 63 deal with the Second Coming of Christ. He comes to Edom (of which Petra is capital) and Bozrah (a city in Edom) for some reason, and many believe that reason is to receive his Hebrew remnant who are hiding there.

He shall enter also into the glorious land, and many countries shall be overthrown: but these shall escape out of his hand, even Edom (Dan. 11:41).

Thus, for some reason the land of Edom will not be allowed to fall into the hands of the antichrist. It is assumed by some that the reason is to protect the remnant.

Many years ago the noted Bible scholar W. E. Blackstone, on the basis of these verses, hid thousands of copies of the New Testament in and around the caves and rocks of Petra. He felt that someday the terrified survivors of the antichrist's bloodbath will welcome the opportunity to read God's Word, preferring it even over the Dow-Jones stock average and the Wall Street Journal. On October 14, 1974, I had the opportunity to visit Petra. Before

171

leaving America my students were asked to sign their names, along with their favorite Scripture verse, in the front pages of a large Bible. I then included the following letter:

"Attention to all of Hebrew background: This Bible has been placed here on October 14, 1974, by the students and Dean of the Thomas Road Bible Institute in Lynchburg, Va., U.S.A. We respectfully urge its finder to prayerfully and publicly read the following Bible chapters. They are Daniel 7 and 11; Matthew 24; 2 Thessalonians 2; Revelation 12 and 13.

We then wrapped the Bible in heavy plastic and placed it in one of the remote caves among the thousands in Petra.

Petra has been called "the rainbow city," and once had 267,000 inhabitants. It was a large market center at the junction of a great caravan route. The city is inaccessible except through the gorge or canyon in the mountains, which is wide enough for only two horses abreast. The perpendicular walls of the gorge are from 400 to 700 feet high and are brilliant in splendor, displaying every color of the rainbow. The old buildings, cut from the solid rock of the mountain, still stand. A clear spring bubbles over rose-red rocks. Wild figs grow on the banks. Everything awaits Israel!

C. The pouring out of the last seal judgment (Rev. 8, 9; 11:15-19).

And when he had opened the seventh seal, there was silence in heaven about the space of half an hour (8:1).

This marks the only occasion in recorded history that heaven is silent. There is not the slightest sound or movement.

1. The purpose of the silence.

During the sixth seal mankind seemed to weaken for the first time during the tribulation. A merciful and patient God now awaits further repentance, but all to no

172

avail. God takes no pleasure in the death of the wicked (Ezek. 33:11).

2. The duration of the silence.

It was for thirty minutes. The number thirty in the Bible is often associated with mourning. Israel mourned for thirty days over the death of both Aaron (Num. 20:29) and Moses (Deut. 34:8).

We now examine the contents of the seventh seal, which consists of seven trumpet judgments.

3. The first trumpet (8:7).

The first angel sounded, and there followed hail and fire mingled with blood, and they were cast upon the earth; and the third part of trees was burnt up, and all green grass was burnt up (Rev. 8:7).

It has been observed that plant life was the first to be created, and it is the first to be destroyed (Gen. 1:11, 12).

John Phillips writes:

"Looked upon as a literal occurrence, an ecological disaster without parallel in historic times is described. The planet is denuded of a third of its trees and all of its grass. The consequences of this are bound to be terrible. The United States, for example, has already proceeded with deforestation to such an extent that the country contains only enough vegetation to produce sixty percent of the oxygen it consumes" (*Exploring Revelation*, Moody Press, 1974, p. 129).

4. The second trumpet (8:8, 9).

And the second angel sounded, and as it were a great mountain burning with fire was cast into the sea; and the third part of the sea became blood; and the third part of the creatures which were in the sea, and had life, died; and the third part of the ships were destroyed.

Dr. Herman A. Hoyt writes:

"Here we read of a great mountain burning with fire. This may refer to a meteoric mass from the sky falling headlong into the sea, perhaps the Mediterranean Sea. The result is to turn a third part of the sea a blood-red color and bring about the death of a third part of the life in the sea. Death may be caused by the chemical reaction in the water, such as radioactivity following atomic explosion. The third part of ships may be destroyed by the violence of the waters produced by the falling of the mass" (*Revelation*, BMH Press, 1966, p. 49).

5. The third trumpet (8:10, 11).
And the third angel sounded, and there fell a great star from heaven, burning as it were a lamp, and it fell upon the third part of the rivers, and upon the fountains of waters; and the name of the star is called Wormwood; and the third part of the waters became wormwood; and many men died of the waters, because they were made bitter.

This star could refer to a meteor containing stifling and bitter gases, which fall on the Alps or some other freshwater source. During the second trumpet a third of the salt water was contaminated. Now a third of earth's fresh water suffers a similar fate. Many species of wormwood grow in Palestine. All species have a strong, bitter taste.

6. The fourth trumpet (8:12).
And the fourth angel sounded, and the third part of the sun was smitten, and the third part of the moon, and the third part of the stars; so as the third part of them was darkened, and the day shone not for a third part of it, and the night likewise (Rev. 8:12).

Our Lord may have had this trumpet judgment in mind when he spoke the following words:
And except those days should be shortened, there should no flesh be saved; but for the elect's sake those days shall be shortened (Mt. 24:22).

And there shall be signs in the sun, and in the moon, and in the stars (Lk. 21:25).

The Old Testament prophecy of Amos is also significant here:
And it shall come to pass in that day, saith the Lord God, that I will cause the sun to go down at noon, and I will darken the earth in the clear day (Amos 8:9).

It was on the fourth day that God created the sun,

moon, and stars (Gen 1:14-16). They were to be for "signs, and for seasons, and for days, and for years." After the flood, God promised not to alter this divine arrangement (Gen. 8:22). But in the tribulation, during the fourth trumpet, earth's very light will be limited by judgment.

Between the fourth and fifth trumpets John reports: *And I beheld, and heard an angel flying through the midst of heaven, saying with a loud voice, Woe, woe, woe, to the inhabiters of the earth by reason of the other voices of the trumpet of the three angels, which are yet to sound!* (8:13).

The word angel here should be translated "eagle." An eagle is sometimes pictured as God's method of judgment (Deut. 28:49; Hosea 8:1). Thus, even the brute creation will be used by God during the tribulation. This marks the last of three occasions where a creature speaks in the Bible. (For the other two, see Gen. 3:1-5—a serpent; and Num. 22:28-30—an ass.)

7. The fifth trumpet (9:1-12).
J. Vernon McGee writes:

"The last three trumpets are marked off from the other four by identification with the three woes (8:13; 9:12; 11:14). These woes mark the deepest darkness and most painful intensity of the Great Tribulation. This is generally associated with the last part (three and a half years), the blackest days in human history" (*Reveling Through in Revelation*, p. 73).

The ninth chapter of Revelation, which contains both fifth and sixth trumpet judgments, may be the most revealing section in all the Bible concerning the subject of demonology. Prior to this God has already made it known that there are two kinds of unfallen angels. These are the cherubim (Gen. 3:24; Ex. 25:8; Ezek. 10:1-20), and the seraphim (Isa. 6:1-8). Here he may be describing for us the two kinds of fallen angels. We now note the first type as revealed in the fifth trumpet judgment.

a. The location of these demons.
The bottomless pit (9:1). Literally this phrase is "shaft

of the abyss." The word shaft here indicates that there
is an entrance from the surface of the earth to the
heart of our planet. In this chapter we learn for the
first time of a place called the bottomless pit. God
mentions it no less than seven times in the book of
Revelation (9:1, 2, 11; 11:7; 17:8; 20:1–3).
  b. The identity of these demons.
    Some have identified these with the sons of God in
    Genesis 6:1, 2. Here the theory is that these demons
    attempted sexual relations with women, resulting in
    immediate confinement in the bottomless pit. We do
    know that some demons are already chained and
    others at present have access to the bodies of men.
      (1) Unchained demons (Mt. 8:29; Lk. 4:34;
          8:27–31).
      (2) Chained demons (Jude 1:6, 7; 2 Pet. 2:4; 1 Pet.
          3:18–20). Thus another name for this bottomless
          pit may be the *tartarus* mentioned in the
          Greek text of 2 Peter 2:4. Here Satan will be
          later confined during the millennium (Rev.
          20:3).
  c. The one who releases these demons.
    This "fallen star," mentioned in 9:1, seems to be
    Satan himself. (See also Isa. 14:12; Lk. 10:18; 2 Cor.
    11:14.) Prior to this time Christ has held the key to
    the pit (Rev. 1:18), but he now allows the devil to
    use it for a specific purpose.
  d. The torment of these demons (9:3, 4).
    *And there came out of the smoke locusts upon the earth: and
    unto them was given power, as the scorpions of the earth
    have power. And it was commanded them that they should
    not hurt the grass of the earth, neither any green thing,
    neither any tree; but only those men which have not the
    seal of God in their foreheads.*
    J. A. Seiss writes:

    "The pain from the sting of a scorpion, though not
    generally fatal, is, perhaps, the most intense that any
    animal can inflict upon the human body. The insect
    itself is the most . . . malignant that lives and its

poison is like itself. Of a boy stung in the foot by a scorpion (it was related that) . . . he rolled on the ground, grinding his teeth, and foaming at the mouth. It was a long time before his complainings moderated, and even then he could make no use of his foot, which was greatly inflamed. And such is the nature of the torment which these locusts from the pit inflict. They are also difficult to be guarded against, if they can be warded off at all, because they fly where they please, dart through the air, and dwell in darkness" (*The Apocalypse*, p. 83).

e. The duration of these demons.
Charles Ryrie writes:

"Horrible as the torment will be, God will place certain limitations on the activity of these demons. They will be limited as to what they may strike and as to how far they may go and as to how long they may do what they will do. They will not attack the vegetation of the earth (as common locusts do); they may only attack certain men, that is, those who have not the seal of God in their foreheads (the 144,000; cf. 7:3). The wicked will persecute God's servants, the 144,000; but in turn they will be tormented by this plague which God allows. The demon-locusts will also be limited in that they may not kill men, just torment them.

Further, the duration of this plague will be five months. The effect of this torment is to drive men to suicide, but they will not be able to die. Although men will prefer death to the agony of living, death will not be possible. Bodies will not sink and drown; poisons and pills will have no effect; and somehow even bullets and knives will not do their intended job" (*Revelation*, Moody Press, 1968, p. 62).

The reason men cannot die is probably because Satan has the key to the shaft and will not allow his followers to leave the earth scene where the battle of light and darkness is being fought.

f. The description of these demons (9:7–10).
The shapes of these creatures are absolutely hideous.
They are like horses prepared for battle. Crowns of
gold seem to be upon their heads. Their faces are like
men, their hair like women, their teeth like lions.
They have on breastplates as of iron. Their tails are
like those of a scorpion. The sound of their wings is
like that of many chariots rushing toward battle.

g. The king of these demons (9:11).
His name is Apollyon, which means "destroyer." Here
is Satan's hellish "Michael the Archangel."

h. The horrible reality of these demons.
John Phillips writes:

"Modern man professes not to believe in demons, but
they exist just the same. Moreover, they are clever
with a diabolical cunning. Man's attitude toward the
demon world may well be likened to man's attitude in
the dark ages toward bacteria. If we could be
transported back to London in the year 1666, we
would find ourselves in a nightmare world. The great
bubonic plague is at its height. The sights and sounds
of the city are like the terrible climax of a horror
movie. It is generally believed that fresh air is the
culprit. The College of Physicians recomends the
frequent firing of guns to blow away the deadly air.
People seal themselves into their rooms and burn
foul-smelling messes to ward off the fresh air.
Chimneys are sealed, rooms are gray with smoke, and
people choke in the suffocating stench. Outside, palls
of black smoke hang over the city. People sit in the
tightly sealed chambers, grimly determined to endure
the smarting smoke, convinced they are thus immune
to the plague. We tell them they are wrong, that the
plague is not caused by fresh air but by germs,
microscopic organisms spread by fleas—and they
laugh us to scorn.

Modern man has adopted a similar attitude toward
the demon world. We tell them that the world is in
the grip of Satan and that he has countless hosts of

invisible demons to aid him in his dark designs against mankind. We say that these unseen beings are intelligent, and that before long, they are to be joined by countless more of their kind worse even than themselves. People look at us with pitying scorn and suggest we peddle our theories to the publishers of science fiction. But it is true all the same. Once the pit is opened, the world of men will be invaded by a virus far more dreadful than the bubonic plague, a virus all the more deadly because it is able to think and because it directs its attack against the soul rather than the body" (*Exploring Revelation*, Moody Press, 1974, p. 137).

8. The sixth trumpet (9:13–21).
   As we have already noted, it would seem John describes two kinds of demons which will invade earth during the tribulation. The sixth trumpet now ushers in the second invasion.
   a. The leaders of this invasion.
      Four special satanic angels. These may function to Satan as the four living creatures do to God (Rev. 4:6–8).
   b. The armies of this invasion.
      (1) They number two hundred million. By normal standards this mighty army would occupy a territory one mile wide and eighty-seven miles long.
      (2) The description. These demons, unlike the first invasion, seem to be mounted upon some type of hellish horse. The horses' heads looked much like lions', with smoke, fire, and flaming sulphur billowing from their mouths. The riders wore fiery-red breastplates.
   c. The source of this invasion.
      The Euphrates River: This is where evil began on earth (Zech. 5:8–11; Gen. 3), where false religion began (Gen. 4:3; 10:9, 10; 11:4), and where it will come to its end (Rev. 17–18).
   d. The duration of this invasion.

Thirteen months.

e. The damage wrought by this invasion.

One third of humanity is killed through fire, smoke, and brimstone. One fourth had already been slain by the fourth seal (6:8). This would be approximately one billion. Now one third is killed, meaning another billion die. This invasion is therefore the opposite of the fifth trumpet judgment during which no man was able to die.

f. The results of this invasion (9:20, 21).

And the rest of the men which were not killed by these plagues yet repented not of the works of their hands, that they should not worship devils, and idols of gold, and silver, and brass, and stone, and of wood: which neither can see, nor hear, nor walk: Neither repented they of their murders, nor of their sorceries, nor of their fornication, nor of their thefts.

At this point over one half of the world's population has been wiped out. And what is the response of the survivors? Total unrepentance and intensified rebellion. That very year the F.B.I. reports will probably show a thousand percent increase in idolatry, murder, drug-related crimes (the word sorceries is the Greek *pharmakeion*, from which we get our "pharmacy"; it is the Greek word for drugs), sex, felonies, and robbery.

9. Interlude (10:1—11:2).

We have already noted a previous time-out period between the sixth and seventh seal judgments. At this time a similar interlude occurs between the sixth and seventh trumpet judgments. During this pause two significant events take place.

a. The message of the angel of God (10:1-11).

(1) Who is he? He apparently is not Jesus, for he "sware by him that liveth for ever and ever" (10:6). If this were Christ he would have sworn by himself. (See Heb. 6:13.) He may well be Michael the Archangel (see Dan. 12:1). He is probably the same angel referred to in 5:2; 7:2; 8:3; and 18:2.

(2) What does he have? A little open book. This is probably the seven-sealed book of Revelation 5:1.

(3) What does he say? He announces no further delay would transpire before earth felt the total and terrifying hammer of God's angry judgment. He also orders John to consume his little black book, predicting that it would be sweet in his mouth, but bitter in his stomach. Up to this point John had seen the first part of the tribulation and it had been sweet indeed to witness ungodly Gentiles receiving their just punishment. But now he will be allowed to preview the last three and a half years of the tribulation, which period will begin with the wholesale slaughter of Israel's people by the antichrist. This was indeed bitter medicine to him.

b. The measuring of the Temple of God (11:1, 2).
Here John is put to work with a nine-foot ruler (see Ezek. 40:5), measuring the tribulation Temple. He is also to record the identity of its worshipers. God is always interested in who worships him. However, the outer court was to be left out, "for it is given unto the Gentiles: and the holy city shall they tread under foot forty and two months" (11:2).

See also Luke 21:24 where Jesus predicted this. The forty-two-month final tribulational period is referred to in Daniel 7:25; 12:7; Revelation 12:6, 14; 13:5.

10. The seventh trumpet (11:15–19).
And the seventh angel sounded; and there were great voices in heaven, saying, The kingdoms of this world are become the kingdoms of our Lord, and of his Christ; and he shall reign for ever and ever (11:15).

This seventh angel proclaims the glorious news that very soon now the Lord Jesus Christ will take over the nations of this world as their rightful ruler. The announcement produces a twofold reaction:

(1) The citizens of heaven rejoice.

(2) The nations of the earth become angry.

The seventh angel prepares us not only for the consummation of the ages, but also for the explanation of all things.

But in the days of the voice of the seventh angel, when he shall begin to sound, the mystery of God should be finished (10:7).

Dr. W. A. Criswell writes:

"The mystery of God is the long delay of our Lord in taking the kingdom unto Himself and in establishing righteousness in the earth. The mystery of God is seen in these thousands of years in which sin and death run riot. There is no village and there is no hamlet without its raging, and there is no human heart without its dark, black drop. There is no life without its tears, and its sorrows. There is no home that ultimately does not break up, and there is no family that does not see the circle of the home dissolve in the depths of the grave.

There is no life that does not end in death. The pages of history, from the time of the first murder until this present hour, are written in blood, tears, and death. The mystery is the delay of God in taking the kingdom unto Himself. That is the most inexplicable mystery that mind could dream of, the mystery of the presence of evil. For these thousands of years, God has allowed Satan to wrap his vicious slimy, filthy, cruel tentacles around this earth. Does God know it? Is He indifferent to it? Is He not able to cope with it? Oh, the mystery of the delay of God! That mystery has brought more stumbling to the faith of God's people than any other experience in all life. The infidel, the atheist, the agnostic and the unbeliever laugh and mock us, and God lets them mock and laugh. The enemies of righteousness and the enemies of all that we hold dear rise, increase in power and spread blood and darkness over the face of the earth, and we wonder where God is. Our missionaries are slain, our churches are burned to the ground, people in this earth by uncounted millions and millions are oppressed, living in despair, and God just looks. He seemingly does not intervene; He does not say anything, and He does not move. Sin just develops. It goes on and on. Oh, the mystery of the delay of the Lord God! But somewhere beyond the starry sky there stands a herald angel with a trumpet in his hand, and by the decree of the Lord God Almighty, there is a day, there is an hour, there is a moment, there is an elected time when the angel shall sound and the kingdoms of this world shall become the kingdoms of our God and of His Christ" (*Sermons on Revelation*, Zondervan, 1969, pp. 199, 200).

Note: At the sounding of this trumpet, "the temple of God was opened in heaven, and there was seen in this temple the ark of his testament" (11:19). It would appear an actual tabernacle exists in heaven from this and other verses. (See Isa. 6:1–8; Ex. 25:9, 20; Heb. 8:2, 5; 9:24; Rev. 14:15, 17; 15:5, 6, 8; 16:1, 17.)

D. The pouring out of the seven vial (bowl) judgments (Rev. 14–16).

1. Those events preceding the vial judgments (14–15).

We have already seen that two chapters (4–5) are given over to describing some heavenly action just prior to the fearful seal judgments which began in Revelation 6. Here John introduces the vial judgments in a similar way. Chapters 14 and 15 record some heavenly action before the vial judgments in 16.

a. The song of the 144,000 (14:1–5).

Here we note:

(1) This group is the same as mentioned in chapter 7. There they are redeemed. Here they are raptured. And note—not one is missing. J Vernon McGee writes:

"It is clear from Chapter 13 that this is the darkest day and the most horrible hour in history. It is truly hell's holiday. Every thoughtful mind must inevitably ask the question—How did God's people fare during this period? Could they make it through to the end with overwhelming odds against them? The Shepherd who began with 144,000 sheep is now identified with them as a Lamb with 144,000 sheep. He did not lose one" (*Reveling Through Revelation*, p. 21).

(2) This group makes up the greatest numbered choir of all time!

(3) They sing a new song, accompanied by heavenly harps (Ps. 57).

(4) They are undefiled women (14:4; cf. 9:21).

(5) There is no guile in their mouth (14:5; cf. 13:3 and 2 Thess. 2:9–12).

b. The messages from three special angels (14:6–12).

(1) The first message.

And I saw another angel fly in the midst of heaven, having the everlasting gospel to preach unto them that dwell on the earth, and to every nation, and kindred, and tongue, and people, saying with a loud voice, Fear God, and give glory to him; for the hour of his judgment is come: and worship him that made heaven, and earth, and the sea, and the fountains of waters (Rev. 14:6, 7).

We see in this verse something absolutely unique—an angel of God preaching the gospel to sinners! Up to this point God has used only men to reach other men (Acts 1:8; 2 Cor. 4:7; 2 Pet. 1:21). But now, due to the severity of the tribulation, angels will be used. Thus, God, like Paul, becomes all things to all men, that by all means he might save some (1 Cor. 9:22).

(2) The second message.

And there followed another angel, saying, Babylon is fallen, is fallen, that great city, because she made all nations drunk of the wine of the wrath of her fornication (Rev. 14:8).

This second message is to announce the imminent destruction of political and economic Babylon (see Rev. 18).

(3) The third message.

And the third angel followed them, saying with a loud voice, If any man worship the beast and his

184

image, and receive his mark in his forehead, or in his hand, the same shall drink of the wine of the wrath of God, which is poured out without mixture into the cup of his indignation; and he shall be tormented with fire and brimstone in the presence of the holy angels, and in the presence of the Lamb: And the smoke of their torment ascendeth up forever and ever: and they have no rest day nor night, who worship the beast and his image, and whosoever receiveth the mark of his name (Rev. 14:9–11).

Here is the last hellfire-and-brimstone message that will ever be preached to the unsaved, and it is delivered not by a Jonathan Edwards or a Billy Sunday, but by an angel. Apparently no one responds to the invitation. Here God will pour out his undiluted wrath, something he has done once before upon Christ at Calvary. How tragic that Christ once drank this same cup for the very unrepentant sinners who are now forced to drink it again.

c. The message from the Holy Spirit (14:13).

And I heard a voice from heaven saying unto me, Write, Blessed are the dead which die in the Lord from henceforth: Yea, saith the Spirit, that they may rest from their labours; and their works do follow them.

Up to this point in history the general rule is, Blessed are the living. (See Eccl. 9:4; Phil. 1:23, 24.) But now it is better for believers to die. John Phillips writes:

"In happy contrast with the doom of those who deify the beast is the destiny of those who defy the beast. Two things are said of these as well. They will resist. John says, 'Here is the patience of the saints: here are they that keep the commandments of God, and the faith of Jesus. And I heard a voice from heaven saying unto me, Write, Blessed are the dead which die in the Lord from henceforth: Yea, saith the Spirit, that they may rest from their labours; and their works do follow them.' Except for the hundred and forty-four

185

thousand, those who defy the beast can anticipate death in a thousand fiendish ways, but it is death instantly transformed by God into blessing! 'I'll make you suffer!' screams the beast. 'You'll make us saints!' reply the overcomers. 'I'll persecute you to the grave,' roars the beast! 'You'll promote us to glory!' reply the overcomers. 'I'll blast you!' snarls the beast. 'You'll bless us!' reply the overcomers. The beast's rage against these noble martyrs will all in vain. He will utterly fail at last.

They will be rewarded. 'Yes, saith the Spirit, that they may rest from their labours; and their works do follow them.' Their troubles will be over. They will enter into reward on the shining banks of the crystal sea" (*Exploring Revelation*, Moody Press, 1974, p. 193).

d. The first announcement of Armageddon (14:14-20).
And I looked, and behold a white cloud, and upon the cloud one sat like unto the Son of man, having on his head a golden crown, and in his hand a sharp sickle. And another angel came out of the temple, crying with a loud voice to him that sat on the cloud, Thrust in thy sickle, and reap: for the time is come for thee to reap; for the harvest of the earth is ripe. And he that sat on the cloud thrust in his sickle on the earth; and the earth was reaped. And another angel came out of the temple which is in heaven, he also having a sharp sickle. And another angel came out from the altar, which had power over fire; and cried with a loud cry to him that had the sharp sickle, saying, Thrust in thy sharp sickle, and gather the clusters of the vine of the earth; for her grapes are fully ripe. And the angel thrust in his sickle into the earth, and gathered the vine of the earth, and cast it into the great winepress of the wrath of God. And the winepress was trodden without the city, and blood came out of the winepress, even unto the horse bridles, by the space of a thousand and six hundred furlongs.

The full implications of these verses will be more fully discussed in Revelation 19.

e. The sights and sounds of the temple in heaven (15:2–4).
   (1) John hears the songs of the triumphal (15:2–4).
      (a) What they sing. They sing the song of Moses and the song of the Lamb (15:3). Note the contrast between these songs:
         The song of Moses was sung beside the Red Sea (Ex. 15); the song of the Lamb will be sung beside the crystal sea.
         The song of Moses was sung over Egypt; the song of the Lamb will be sung over Babylon.
         The song of Moses described how God brought his people out; the song of the Lamb will describe how God brings his people in.
         The song of Moses was Scripture's first song; the song of the Lamb will be Scripture's last song.
      (b) Why they sing. ". . . For thou only art holy . . . for thy judgments are made manifest" (15:4).
   (2) John sees the smoke of the temple (15:5–8). (See also Isa. 6:1–8; Ex. 25:9, 40; Heb. 8:2, 5; 9:24; Rev. 14:15, 17; 16:1, 17.)
And one of the four beasts gave unto the seven angels seven golden vials full of the wrath of God, who liveth for ever and ever. And the temple was filled with smoke from the glory of God, and from his power; and no man was able to enter into the temple, till the seven plagues of the seven angels were fulfilled (15:7, 8).
    John Phillips writes:

"Since Calvary, the way into the holiest in heaven has been opened to all, because the blood of Christ has blazed a highway to the heart of God. But now, for a brief spell, that royal road is barred. God's wrath, once poured out upon His Son on man's behalf, is to be out-poured again.

187

The world which crucified the Lamb and which now has crowned its rebellions with the worship of the beast, is to be judged to the full. So bright glory burns within the temple, filling it with smoke and standing guard at the door. The way into the holiest is barred again for a while" (*Exploring Revelation*, Moody Press, 1974, p. 198).

2. Those events accompanying the vial judgments (Rev. 16).
    a. The first vial judgment.
    And the first went, and poured out his vial upon the earth; and there fell a noisome and grievous sore upon the men which had the mark of the beast, and upon them which worshipped his image (16:2).
    J. Vernon McGee writes:

    "God is engaged in germ warfare upon the followers of antichrist . . . . These putrefying sores are worse than leprosy or cancer. This compares to the sixth plague in Egypt, and is the same type of sore or boil (Ex. 9:8–12)" (*Reveling Through Revelation*, p. 36).

    b. The second vial judgment.
    And the second angel poured out his vial upon the sea; and it became as the blood of a dead man; and every living soul died in the sea (16:3).
    Dr. Charles Ryrie writes the following concerning this plague:

    "The second bowl is poured on the sea, with the result that the waters became blood and every living thing in the sea dies. The 'as' is misplaced in the Authorized Version, the correct reading being 'became blood as of a dead man.' The vivid image is of a dead person wallowing in his own blood. The seas will wallow in blood. Under the second trumpet, one-third of the sea creatures died (8:9); now the destruction is complete. The stench and disease that this will cause along the shores of the seas of the earth are unimaginable"

(*Revelation*, Moody Press, 1968, p. 97).

c. The third vial judgment.

And the third angel poured out his vial upon the rivers and fountains of waters; and they became blood. And I heard the angel of the waters say, Thou art righteous, O Lord, which art and wast and shall be, because thou hast judged thus. For they have shed the blood of saints and prophets, and thou hast given them blood to drink; for they are worthy. And I heard another out of the altar say, Even so, Lord God Almighty, true and righteous are thy judgments (Rev. 16:4–7).

Two significant things may be noted in these verses:

(1) This third vial judgment is, among other things, an answer to the cry of the martyrs under the altar at the beginning of the tribulation. Their prayer at that time was, "How long, O Lord, holy and true, dost thou not judge and avenge our blood on them that dwell on the earth?" (Rev. 6:10).

(2) These verses indicate that God has assigned a special angel as superintendent on earth's waterworks. When we compare this with Revelation 7:1, where we are told that four other angels control the world's winds, we realize that even during the hellishness of the tribulation this world is still controlled by God.

d. The fourth vial judgment.

And the fourth angel poured out his vial upon the sun; and power was given unto him to scorch men with fire. And men were scorched with great heat, and blasphemed the name of God, which hath power over these plagues; and they repented not to give him glory (Rev. 8–9).

See also Deut. 32:24; Isa. 24:6; 42:25; Mal. 4:1; Lk. 21:25.)

Perhaps the two most illuminating passages in Scripture about man's total depravity can be found in Revelation 9:20, 21 and 16:9. Both sections deal with the world's attitude toward God during the tribulation.

And the rest of the men which were not killed by these

plagues yet repented not of the works of their hands, that they should not worship devils, and idols of gold, and silver, and brass, and stone, and of wood, which neither can see, nor hear, nor walk; neither repented they of their murders, nor of their sorceries, nor of their fornication, nor of their thefts (Rev. 9:20, 21).

. . . and they repented not to give him glory (Rev. 16:9). What do these verses prove? They prove that in spite of horrible wars, of terrible famines, of darkened skies, of raging fires, of bloody seas, of stinging locusts, of demonic persecutions, of mighty earthquakes, of falling stars, and of cancerous sores, sinful mankind still will not repent.

e. The fifth vial judgment.

And the fifth angel poured out his vial upon the seat of the beast; and his kingdom was full of darkness; and they gnawed their tongues for pain, and blasphemed the God of heaven because of their pains and their sores, and repented not of their deeds (Rev. 16:10, 11).

(See also Isa. 60:2; Joel 2:1, 2, 31; Amos 5:18; Nahum 1:6, 8; Zeph. 1:15.)

This plague, poured out upon "the seat of the beast" (literally, his "throne"), will apparently concentrate itself upon the ten nations of the revived Roman Empire. Again we read those tragic words "and repented not of their deeds."

f. The sixth vial judgment.

And the sixth angel poured out his vial upon the great river Euphrates; and the water thereof was dried up, that the way of the kings of the east might be prepared. And I saw three unclean spirits like frogs come out of the mouth of the dragon, and out of the mouth of the beast, and out of the mouth of the false prophet. For they are the spirits of devils, working miracles, which go forth unto the kings of the earth and of the whole world, to gather them to the battle of that great day of God Almighty (Rev. 16:12-14).

Here the God of heaven employs psychological warfare upon his enemies, conditioning them to gather themselves together in the near future at Armageddon.

The Euphrates River is 1800 miles long and in some places 3600 feet wide. It is thirty feet deep. This river has been the dividing line between Western and Eastern civilization since the dawn of history. It served as the eastern border of the old Roman Empire. Thus, the Euphrates becomes both the cradle and grave of man's civilization. Here the first godless city (Enoch, built by Cain; see Gen. 4:16, 17) went up, and here the last rebellious city will be constructed (Babylon, built by the antichrist; see Rev. 18).

g. The seventh vial judgment.

And the seventh angel poured out his vial into the air; and there came a great voice out of the temple of heaven, from the throne, saying, It is done. And there were voices, and thunders, and lightnings; and there was a great earthquake, such as was not since men were upon the earth, so mighty an earthquake, and so great. And the great city was divided into three parts, and the cities of the nations fell; and great Babylon came in remembrance before God, to give unto her the cup of wine of the fierceness of his wrath. And every island fled away, and the mountains were not found. And there fell upon men a great hail out of heaven, every stone about the weight of a talent and men blasphemed God because of the plague of the hail, for the plague thereof was exceeding great (16:17-21).

Thus end the seal, trumpet, and vial judgments.

Three items in this last vial are worthy of observation:

The statement, "It is done," is the second of three biblical occurrences in which this phrase is connected with some great event. The first event was Calvary and the last will be the threshold of eternity.

When Jesus therefore had received the vinegar, he said, It is finished; and he bowed his head, and gave up the ghost (Jn. 19:30).

And he said unto me, It is done. I am Alpha and Omega, the beginning and the end. I will give unto him that is athirst of the fountain of the water of life freely (Rev. 21:6).

The world's greatest earthquake takes place. The intensity of an earthquake is measured on an instru-

191

ment called a Richter scale. The greatest magnitude ever recorded so far has been 8.9. The greatest loss of life due to an earthquake occurred on January 23, 1556, in Shensi Province, China, and killed some 830,000 people. However, that earthquake will be but a mild tremor compared to the tribulation earthquake, which, we are told, will level all the great cities of the world!

The world's greatest shower of hailstones comes crashing down on mankind. These gigantic icy chunks will weigh up to 125 pounds apiece.

E. The destruction of economic and political Babylon (Rev. 18).
And there followed another angel, saying, Babylon is fallen, is fallen, that great city, because she made all nations drunk of the wine of the wrath of her fornication (Rev. 14:8).

. . . and great Babylon came in remembrance before God, to give unto her the cup of the wine of the fierceness of his wrath (Rev. 16:19).

And after these things I saw another angel come down from heaven, having great power; and the earth was lightened with his glory. And he cried mightily with a strong voice, saying, Babylon the great is fallen. . . (Rev. 18:1, 2).

It seems likely that literal Babylon will be rebuilt during the tribulation. The Old Testament city of Babylon is mentioned more times in the Bible than any other city with the exception of Jerusalem. It is mentioned no less than 260 times.

1. Old Testament history of the city of Babylon.
And the whole earth was of one language, and of one speech. And it came to pass, as they journeyed from the east, that they found a plain in the land of Shinar; and they dwelt there. And they said one to another, Go to, let us make brick, and burn them thoroughly. And they had brick for stone, and slime had they for mortar. And they said, Go to, let us build us a city and a tower, whose top may reach unto heaven; and let us make us a name, lest we be scattered abroad upon the face of the whole earth. And the Lord came down to see the city and the tower, which the children of men builded. And the Lord said, Behold, the people is one, and they have all one language; and this they begin to do; and now

nothing will be restrained from them, which they have imagined to do. Go to, let us go down, and there confound their language, that they may not understand one another's speech. So the Lord scattered them abroad from thence upon the face of all the earth: and they left off to build the city. Therefore is the name of it called Babel; because the Lord did there confound the language of all the earth: and from thence did the Lord scatter them abroad upon the face of all the earth (Gen. 11:1-9).

These verses describe for us the first ecumenical meeting in history and the official beginning of religion. All this took place in the city of Babylon. Archaeological evidence suggests the Tower of Babel was in reality a temple given over to astrology. Among the ruins of ancient Babylon is a building 153 feet high with a 400-foot base. It was constructed of dried bricks in seven stages to correspond with the known planets to which they were dedicated.

The lowermost was black, the color of Saturn, the next orange, for Jupiter, the third red, for Mars, and so on. These stages were surmounted by a lofty tower, on the summit of which were the signs of the Zodiac. An apostate great-grandson of Noah (through Ham) named Nimrod (Gen. 10:8-10) was probably the instigator of this ancient city and satanic church. He may have even served as its first pastor.

Years later this city once built by Nimrod would reach the summit of its glory under King Nebuchadnezzar. This arrogant monarch once boasted as he overlooked his glittering metropolis:

Is not this great Babylon, that I have built for the house of the kingdom by the might of my power, and for the honor of my majesty? (Dan. 4:30).

Ancient Babylon was indeed a sight to behold. Lehman Strauss writes:

"Babylon was founded by Nimrod, the great-grandson of Noah (Gen. 10:8-10). Surviving a series of conflicts, it became one of the most magnificent and luxurious cities in the known world. Superbly constructed, it spread over

193

an area of fifteen square miles, the Euphrates River flowing diagonally across the city. The famous historian Herodotus said the city was surrounded by a wall 350 feet high and 87 feet thick—wide enough for six chariots to drive abreast. Around the top of the wall were 250 watchtowers placed in strategic locations. Outside the huge wall was a large ditch, or moat, which surrounded the city and was kept filled with water from the Euphrates River. The large ditch was meant to serve as an additional protection against attacking enemies, for any attacking enemy would have to cross this body of water first before approaching the great wall. The cost of constructing this military defense was estimated to be in excess of one billion dollars. When we consider the value of a billion dollars in those days, plus the fact that it was all built with slave labor, one can imagine something of the wonder and magnificence of this famous city.

But in addition to being a bastion for protection, Babylon was a place of beauty. The famous hanging gardens of Babylon are on record yet today as one of the seven wonders of the world. Arranged in an area 400 feet square, and raised in perfectly-cut terraces one above the other, they soared to a height of 350 feet. Viewers could make their way to the top by means of stairways, which were 10 feet wide. Each terrace was covered with a large stone slab topped with a thick layer of asphalt, two courses of brick cemented together, and, finally, plates of lead to prevent any leakage of water. On top of all this was an abundance of rich, fertile earth planted with vines, flowers, shrubs, and trees. From a distance these hanging gardens gave the appearance of a beautiful mountainside, when viewed from the level plains of the valley. The estimated cost to build this thing of beauty ran into hundreds of millions of dollars. The tower of Babel with its temples of worship presented an imposing sight. The tower itself sat on a base 300 feet in breadth and rose to a height of 300 feet. The one chapel on the top contained an image alone reported to be worth $17,500,000 and sacred vessels, used in worshipping

Babylonian gods, estimated at a value of $200,000,000. In addition to this wealth and grandeur the temple contained the most elaborate and expensive furniture ever to adorn any place of worship" (*The Prophecies of Daniel*, Neptune, N.J.: Loizeaux, 1969, pp. 147, 148).

But after an extended rule (612-562 B.C.), Nebuchadnezzar died. On October 13, 539 B.C., the city of Babylon was captured by the Medes and Persians (Dan. 5). Shortly after this time the city began its decline.

2. New Testament prophecies concerning the city. We have already seen the important role assigned to Babylon in Genesis, the original biblical book. This is even more so in Scriptures' final book, the book of Revelation. Note:

And there followed another angel, saying, Babylon is fallen, is fallen, that great city, because she made all nations drink of the wine of the wrath of her fornication (Rev. 14:8).

. . . and great Babylon came in remembrance before God, to give unto her the cup of the wine of the fierceness of his wrath (Rev. 16:19).

One of the seven angels who had poured out the plagues came over and talked with me. "Come with me," he said, "and I will show you what is going to happen to the Notorious Prostitute, who sits upon the many waters of the world. The kings of the world have had immoral relations with her, and the people of the earth have been made drunk by the wine of her immorality." So the angel took me in spirit into the wilderness. There I saw a woman sitting on a scarlet animal that had seven heads and ten horns, written all over with blasphemies against God. The woman wore purple and scarlet clothing and beautiful jewelry made of gold and precious gems and pearls, and held in her hand a golden goblet full of obscenities. A mysterious caption was written on her forehead: "Babylon the Great, Mother of Prostitutes and Idol Worship Everywhere around the World." I could see that she was drunk—drunk with the blood of the martyrs of Jesus

195

she had killed. I stared at her in horror (Rev. 17:1–6, The
Living Bible).

*After all this I saw another angel come down from heaven
with great authority, and the earth grew bright with his
splendor. He gave a mighty shout, "Babylon the Great is
fallen, is fallen; she has become a den of demons, a haunt of
devils and every kind of evil spirit. For all the nations have
drunk the fatal wine of her intense immorality. The rulers of
earth have enjoyed themselves with her, and businessmen
throughout the world have grown rich from all her luxurious
living." Then I heard another voice calling from heaven,
"Come away from her, my people; do not take part in her
sins, or you will be punished with her. For her sins are piled
as high as heaven and God is ready to judge her for her
crimes. Do to her as she has done to you, and more—give
double penalty for all her evil deeds. She brewed many a cup
of woe for others—give twice as much to her. She has lived in
luxury and pleasure—match it now with torments and with
sorrows. She boasts, 'I am queen upon my throne. I am no
helpless widow. I will not experience sorrow'"* (Rev. 18:1–7,
TLB).

3. Reasons for rebuilding the city.
   Will ancient Babylon actually be rebuilt on the
   Euphrates, as in Daniel's time? Some believe it will, for
   the following reasons:
   a. Ancient Babylon was never suddenly destroyed, as
      prophesied in Isaiah 13:19.
   b. The description of literal Babylon by Jeremiah in
      chapter 51 is very similar to the one given by John in
      Revelation 18.
   c. Babylon is said to be destroyed during the day of the
      Lord, which is an Old Testament term referring to
      the tribulation. See Isaiah 13:6.
   d. According to Isaiah 14 Israel will enter into God's
      rest after Babylon is destroyed. Since this has not yet
      happened, the event must be still future.
   e. Archaeological discoveries have shown that bricks and
      stones from ancient Babylon have been reused for
      building purposes, contrary to the prophecy of

Jeremiah 51:26. Jeremiah predicts (25:17-26) that Babylon will drink of the cup of the wrath of God *last* among all the kingdoms of the earth.
f. The vision of the woman in the ephah (Zech. 5:5-11) indicates a return of wickedness and commerce to Babylon.
g. The description in Revelation 18 is best understood if taken literally.
(This list is derived from *Bible Prophecy Notes*, by R. Ludwigson.)
Dr. J. Vernon McGee suggests:

"In this day Babylon will dominate and rule the world; she will have the first total dictatorship. The stock market will be read from Babylon; Babylon will set the styles for the world; a play to be successful will have to be a success in Babylon. And everything in the city is in rebellion against Almighty God and centers in Antichrist" (*Reveling Through Revelation*, p. 6).

But what purpose or purposes might be served by the rebuilding of Babylon? Several could be listed. As God has placed his name and associated his presence upon a certain location, the city of Jerusalem (1 Ki. 8:29, 11:36; 15:4), it seems not unreasonable that Satan may do the same—upon the city of Babylon.

Also, this city could serve as a natural geographical location for the antichrist's capital headquarters. Babylon is located on the Euphrates River. This mighty body of water has always marked the boundary between eastern and western empires in ancient days. From this city the antichrist may attempt to unite the powers of the East (China, Japan, India, etc.) with his ten-nation western empire.

Does there exist any present-day desire to rebuild Babylon? Note the following articles:

"Japanese Scholars to Rebuild Babylon"

Japanese scholars plan to rebuild the ruined city of

Babylon in what now is Iraq into an academic research center and tourist site. "Our task is to draw up a comprehensive design of a new city with all monuments restored as faithfully as possible," said Kohi Nishikawa, professor of architecture at Kyoto University and leader of the team. Nishikawa said he was approached on the restoration project by Dr. Juayad Said Damerji, leader of Iraq's Babylon restoration group, when he visited the Iraqi capital of Baghdad last year for an international seminar on Babylon.

The Iraqi government already has begun to restore the legendary city, one of the leading centers of the ancient world.

But Babylon today is one of the most dilapidated archaeological sites in the region," Nishikawa said. The Japanese plan includes restoration of the legendary Tower of Babel.

"There has so far been no established theory on what the tower looked like, how high it was and what shape it had because only its foundation now exists," Nishikawa said.

"Archaeologists have their own versions of the tower. We propose the complete restoration of portions which have been established in research and to use our imagination to the fullest extent for the remainder."

The Iraqi government plans to turn the location along the Euphrates River, 55 miles south of Baghdad, into a tourist site and museum city. It will feature such monuments as a colosseum theater built by Alexander the Great after he captured the city in 350 B.C. and the palace of Nebuchadnezzar, where Alexander died in 323 B.C. The Japanese design also will include reconstruction of the Ishtar Gate which led to the main temple of Maruk, the Sumerian deity worshipped in Babylon. The city was partially rebuilt by Kings Nabopolassar and Nebuchadnezzar in the 6th and 7th centuries, the remains of which survive. (*The Ventura County* [Calif.] *Star-Free Press*, 10 May 1980).

"Iraqi Archaeologists Try to Save
Once-Glorious Babylon"

Two grizzled workers bent under a heavy sun to pick
at a mound of bricks with their trowels. They
scraped the dirt loose and took a broom to whisk it
away, then sought an archaeologist's map for a look
at what lay underneath.

"Where is the map?" shouted one to the other. "The
map is more important than my blood, and even
the blood of my mother."

The two had bared what may have been another
little protrusion of the southern palace of Babylon
built during the reign of Nebuchadnezzar II in the
6th century B.C., when this dusty evacuation site was
a magnificent city that historians called the most
beautiful and prosperous of its time.

About 750 Iraqi workers are digging, picking and
sweeping through the ancient ruins here in a massive
project to save from the ravages of time, water, salt,
bugs and plunderers what little remains of their
splendor.

A visitor to Babylon, about 60 miles south or
Baghdad, finds it zig-zagged with conveyor belts
carrying away to trucks and carts the saline earth
that surrounds the ruins and has corroded much of
them away during the centuries.

Some carts get pulled away to dumps by tractors.
Others run along narrow-gauge rails, pushed from
behind by turbaned laborers. The work goes on at
17 sites, 16 hours a day, seven days a week, across
the flat expanse where Babylon was once one of the
Seven Wonders of the World, according to the
ancient Greeks.

The place looks more like an open-pit mine than
the glorious city guarded by statues of lions that
historians say it was. Only one of the lions remains,
and its head was knocked off and carted away by
Germans at the turn of the century.

The Procession Street where New Year's parades

199

were the occasion for pomp and feast more than 2,500 years ago looks like the overgrown driveway of an untended European castle.

The tower of Babel recorded in the Bible—experts say it actually was a sort of tiered pyramid called a ziggurat—has left only impressions in the ground. Like much of the rest of Babylon, the tower fell victim to a harsh climate, salty soil and the greed of nearby residents who pillaged the mud and clay bricks to build surrounding cities in more recent centuries.

Babylon has known hard times before. It first flourished as the capital of Hammurabi, who ruled a vast empire from 1792 to 1750 B.C., and entered history as the first to issue a legal code to govern his subjects.

About a thousand years later, the Assyrians destroyed Babylon and founded their own empire. But Nebuchadnezzar rebuilt it even more grandly during his reign. The ruins being excavated are what remains of his epoch, little brick walls and stone walkways scraped out of the hard, dry earth. Archaeologists also have discovered a few traces of Hammurabi's Babylon. But they lie much deeper under the soil and below a table of water that has done much to erode the later ruins.

Since Nebuchadnezzar's day, the Greeks under Alexander the Great, the Romans, several Moslem dynasties from Baghdad, the Ottoman Turks and European powers all came here. Babylon remained, sinking deeper into the wind-blown dust as the centuries went by. Ali Mohammed Medhi, an archaeologist who is field engineer for the Iraqi government's Babylon restoration project, is resolved to change that. For the last 19 months, he has been running the excavation from a little office where he studies charts and sleeps most nights on an iron cot.

"We are trying to restore Babylon to the way it

was, one of the Seven Wonders of the World," he said. "Babylon is a special place. World civilization springs from Babylon. It's worth all the attention we give it."

The Iraqi government is spending about $6 million a year for the 10-year project to explore the ruins scientifically, preserve as many as possible and restore them artificially when necessary with building materials similar to those used millennia ago. The effort flows from increased Iraqi nationalism fostered by President Saddam Hussein's Arab Baath Socialist Party rule and fueled by an estimated $14 billion this year in oil revenues.

"Anything we want, we get," said Medhi, smiling from behind his thick glasses. "Not a million or two but whatever we want, without limits."

In another reflection of Iraqi pride, the project has an entirely Iraqi staff—the 750 workers along with more than 50 archaeologists and other specialists.

The organized sifting marks the first complete scientific study of the entire site. German archaeologists, particularly Robert Goldway, dug in the ruins at the turn of the century. But they based most of their conclusions on extrapolations from small sample findings, some of which have turned out to be misleading.

The traditionally accepted site of Babylon's hanging gardens, for example, has been thrown into doubt. Indeed, Iraqi experts now believe the gardens were terraced rather than hanging in any case.

"The spot (identified by early archaeologists) actually was a granary," said Dr. Behnam Abu Suf, head of the government's General Antiquities Establishment in Baghdad. "We don't have any written or archaeological proof it really was there."

In addition, Medhi's team has found what he called a "library" with more than 3,000 oblong cuneiform tablets including the ancient equivalent of textbooks, language studies and descriptions of

ancient Babylonian religious observances following
annual cycles (Edward Cody, *The Washington Post*,
6 October 1979).

David Webber writes:

"On March 29, 1971, a news release from Beirut,
Lebanon, announced a plan by the government of
Iraq to rebuild Babylon with its great walls and
hanging gardens according to its 'original architectural
designs.' The news item stated: 'Iraq says it plans to
rebuild the ancient city of Babylon, whose hanging
gardens were among the Seven Wonders of the World.
The project will cost about $30 million. . . .' Such an
undertaking by the government of Iraq would not have
been even remotely possible thirty years ago. Before
1950, all the Arab countries combined could not have
restored Nebuchadnezzar's footstool without foreign aid.
The event that has changed the poorest of nations into the
richest and made possible the rebuilding of Babylon, was
the discovery of oil in the Middle East. However, it was
readily apparent from the beginning of the restoration
that the initial $30 million would only be a drop in the
Euphrates River. The United Nations Educational,
Scientific, and Cultural Organization (UNESCO) later
appropriated $35 million for the project, and other
contributions have come from individual oil-rich Arabs"
(*Is This the Last Century?*, Nashville: Thomas Nelson
Publishers, 1979, pp. 105, 106).

Dr. J. Vernon McGee says:

"In chapters 17 and 18 two Babylons are brought
before us. The Babylon of chapter 17 is ecclesiastical. The
Babylon of chapter 18 is economic. The first is religious—
the apostate church. The second is political and commercial. The apostate church is hated by the kings of the
earth (Rev. 17:16); the commercial center is loved by the
kings of the earth (Rev. 18:9). The apostate church
is destroyed by the kings of the earth; political Babylon
is destroyed by the judgment of God (verses 5, 8).

Obviously, mystery Babylon is destroyed first—in the midst of the Great Tribulation; while commercial Babylon is destroyed at the Second Coming of Christ. These two Babylons are not one and the same city" (*Reveling Through Revelation*, p. 58).

Dr. Charles Ryrie writes:

"Whether the city will be rebuilt once again on the Euphrates is a matter of debate. Nevertheless, the name is used for more than a city in these chapters (17–18); it also stands for a system. This is much the same as the way Americans speak of Wall Street or Madison Avenue. They are actual streets, but they also stand for the financial or advertising purposes" (*Revelation*, Moody Press, 1968, p. 100).

Let us now observe the description and destruction of this city. The first explains the second.
4. The description of the city.
   a. It had become the habitation of demons and false doctrines (Rev. 18:2; Mt. 13:32).
   b. Both rulers and merchants had worshiped at her shrine of silver (Rev. 18:3).
   c. Her sins had reached into the heavens (Rev. 18:5).
   d. She had lived in sinful pleasure and luxury (Rev. 18:7).
   e. Her prosperity had blinded her to the judgment of God (Rev. 18:7).
   There is in this chapter a list (Rev. 18:11–17) of no less than twenty-five of the world's most expensive luxury items. Again the words of J. Vernon McGee are revealing:

"Everything listed here is a luxury item. Babylon will make these luxury items necessities. You will not find a cotton dress or a pair of overalls anywhere in this list. First there is the jewelry department—
   '. . . the merchandise of gold, and silver and precious stones, and of pearls.'

Then we move from the jewelry department to the ladies' ready-to-wear '. . . and fine linen, and purple, and silk, and scarlet.'

Then to the luxury gift department '. . . and all thyine wood, and every vessel of ivory, and every vessel made of most precious wood, and of brass, and marble.'

We move on to the spice and cosmetic department '. . . and cinnamon, and spice, and odors, and ointments, and frankincense.'

To the liquor department and the pastry center '. . . and wine, and oil, and fine flour, and wheat.'

On to the meat department for T-bone steaks and lamb chops '. . . and cattle, and sheep.' "

f. She had deceived all nations with her sorceries (Rev. 18:23).

g. She was covered with the blood of many of God's saints (Rev. 18:24).

5. The destruction of the city.

a. The source of her destruction.

God himself (see Rev. 18:8, 20). The means of her destruction: It would almost seem that atomic power of some sort is used to accomplish this. This is strongly suggested by the swiftness of the judgment, the raging fires, and the distance kept by those who watch her burn—possibly due to fear of radioactive fallout. (See Rev. 18:9, 10, 15, 17, 19.)

b. The reaction to her destruction.

(1) By those on earth.

And they cast dust on their heads, and cried, weeping and wailing, saying, Alas, alas, that great city, wherein were made rich all that had ships in the sea by reason of her costliness! For in one hour is she made desolate (Rev. 18:19).

There are three classes of people who weep over Babylon. They are the monarchs (18:9), the merchants (18:11), and the mariners (18:17).

(2) By those in heaven.

*Rejoice over her, thou heaven, and ye holy apostles
and prophets; for God hath avenged you on her*
(Rev. 18:20).

There are three events in the tribulation which
cause all of heaven to rejoice:

When Satan is cast out (Rev. 12:12).
When Babylon is destroyed (Rev. 18:20).
When the Lamb is married to the church (Rev.
19:7).

c. The reasons for her destruction.
  (1) The city will become the headquarters of all
      demonic activity during the tribulation (Rev.
      18:2).
  (2) Her devilish pride (Rev. 18:7).
  (3) Her gross materialism. This wicked city will
      import and export twenty-eight principal items
      of merchandise, beginning with gold and ending
      with the bodies of men (Rev. 18:12, 13).
  (4) Her drug activities (Rev. 18:23).
  (5) Her bloodshedding (Rev. 18:24).
d. The Old Testament foreshadows her destruction.
On the night of October 13, 539 B.C., the Babylon of
the Old Testament was captured by the Medes and
Persians. Just prior to this, Daniel the prophet had
read the fearful words of God to a frightened
Belshazzar:
*God hath numbered thy kingdom, and finished it. . . .
Thou art weighed in the balances, and art found
wanting. . . . Thy kingdom is divided* (Dan. 5:26–28).

Someday God himself will once again write these
fearsome words across the skies of Babylon. J. Vernon
McGee's words aptly summarize this chapter. He
writes:

"This is Satan's city. He is a murderer—this city
murdered. The final crime was the slaying of God's
people. As we contemplate the destruction of
Babylon, we think of other great cities and
civilizations of the past that have fallen. One of the

most widely read books of all time is *The Decline and Fall of the Roman Empire*. Written in 1788 by Edward Gibbon, it sets forth five basic reasons why that great civilization withered and died. These were:

The undermining of the dignity and sanctity of the home, which is the basis of human society.

Higher and higher taxes; the spending of public money for free bread and circuses for the populace.

The mad craze for pleasure; sports becoming every year more exciting, more brutal, more immoral.

The building of great armaments when the real enemy was within the decay of individual responsibility.

The decay of religion; faith fading into mere form, losing touch with life, losing power to guide the people.

The oft-heard warning that 'history repeats itself' has an ominous meaning in the light of the above.

The average age of the world's great civilizations has been 200 years. These nations progressed through this sequence:

From Bondage to Spiritual Faith
From Spiritual Faith to Great Courage
From Courage to Liberty
From Liberty to Abundance
From Abundance to Selfishness
From Selfishness to Complacency
From Complacency to Apathy
From Apathy to Dependence
From Dependence Back Again to Bondage"
(*Reveling Through Revelation*, p. 65).

F. The bloodbath at Armageddon (Rev. 19).
　　1. The glory feast in heaven.
　　　Introducing a bride (19:1-10).
　　　This glorious event is celebrated by the use of heaven's greatest praise word. That word is *Alleluia* (Hallelujah)! Nowhere else in the New Testament can it be found. The Holy Spirit has reserved it for this occasion. In the Old

Testament it appears some twenty-four times in the Psalms. Heaven now celebrates the Lamb's victory over the harlot, and his marriage to the bride. We are told that "to her was granted that she should be arrayed in fine linen, clean and white: for the fine linen is the righteousness of saints" (19:8). Dr. Charles Ryrie writes:

"The bride's array, fine linen, which is explained as 'the righteousness,' requires the translation 'righteous deeds.' In other words, the wedding garment of the bride will be made up of the righteous deeds done in life. The bride is the bride because of the righteousness of Christ; the bride is clothed for the wedding because of her acts" (*Revelation*, Moody Press, 1968, p. 111).

Dr. Lehman Strauss writes: "Has it ever occurred to you . . . that at the marriage of the Bride to the Lamb, each of us will be wearing the wedding garment of our own making?"

2. The glory feast on earth.
   Introducing a battle (Rev. 19:11–21).
   The Holy Spirit of God has chosen five capable authors to describe for us in clear and chilling language that culmination of all battles—Armageddon! These five authors include David, Isaiah, Joel, Zechariah, and John.
   Why do the nations rage, and the people imagine a vain thing? The kings of the earth set themselves, and the rulers take counsel together, against the Lord, and against his anointed, saying, Let us break their bands asunder, and cast away their cords from us. He that sitteth in the heavens shall laugh: the Lord shall have them in derision. Then shall he speak unto them in his wrath, and vex them in his great displeasure. Thou shalt break them with a rod of iron; thou shalt dash them in pieces like a potter's vessel (Ps. 2:1–5, 9).
   Come near, ye nations, to hear; and hearken, ye peoples: let the earth hear, and all that is therein; the world, and all things that come forth of it. For the indignation of the Lord is upon all nations, and his fury upon all their armies: he hath utterly destroyed them, he hath delivered them to the slaughter. Their slain also shall be cast out, and their stench shall come

*up out of their carcasses, and the mountains shall be melted
with their blood. And all the host of heaven shall be
dissolved, and the heavens shall be rolled together as a scroll:
and all their host shall fall down, as the leaf falleth off from
the vine, and as a falling fig from the fig tree. For my sword
shall be bathed in heaven; behold, it shall come down upon
Edom, and upon the people of my curse, to judgment. The
sword of the Lord is filled with blood; it is made fat with
fatness, and with the blood of lambs and goats, with the fat
of the kidneys of rams; for the Lord hath a sacrifice in
Bozrah, and a great slaughter in the land of Edom*
(Isa. 34:1-6).

*I have trodden the winepress alone; and of the people there
was none with me; for I will tread them in mine anger, and
trample them in my fury; and their blood shall be sprinkled
upon my garments, and I will stain all my raiment. For the
day of vengeance is in mine heart, and the year of my
redeemed is come. And I will tread down the people in mine
anger, and make them drunk in my fury, and I will bring
down their strength to the earth* (Isa. 63:3, 4, 6).

*I will also gather all nations, and will bring them down
into the valley of Jehoshaphat, and will plead with them
there for my people and for my heritage Israel, whom they
have scattered among the nations, and parted my land . . . .
Proclaim this among the Gentiles; Prepare war, wake up the
mighty men, let all the men of war draw near; let them come
up: beat your plowshares into swords, and your pruninghooks
into spears: let the weak say, I am strong. Assemble
yourselves, and come, all ye nations, and gather yourselves
together round about: thither cause thy mighty ones to come
down, O Lord. Let the nations be wakened, and come up to
the valley of Jehoshaphat: for there will I sit to judge all the
nations round about. Put ye in the sickle, for the harvest is
ripe; come, get you down; for the press is full, the vats
overflow; for their wickedness is great. Multitudes, multitudes
in the valley of decision: for the day of the Lord is near in the
valley of decision. The sun and the moon shall be darkened,
and the stars shall withdraw their shining. The Lord also
shall roar out of Zion, and utter his voice from Jerusalem, and
the heavens and the earth shall shake: but the Lord will be*

the hope of his people, and the strength of the children of Israel (Joel 3:2, 9–16).

Behold I will make Jerusalem a cup of trembling unto all the people round about, when they shall be in the siege both against Judah and against Jerusalem (Zech. 12:2).

For I will gather all nations against Jerusalem to battle; and the city shall be taken, and the houses rifled, and the women ravished; and half the city shall go forth into captivity, and the residue of the people shall not be cut off from the city. Then shall the Lord go forth, and fight against those nations, as when he fought in the day of battle. . . . And this shall be the plague with which the Lord will smite all the people that have fought against Jerusalem: their flesh shall consume away while they stand upon their feet, and their eyes shall consume away in their holes, and their tongue shall consume away in their mouth (Zech. 14:2, 3, 12).

And I looked and behold, a white cloud, and upon the cloud one sat like the Son of man, having on his head a golden crown, and in his hand a sharp sickle. And another angel came out of the temple, crying with a loud voice to him that sat on the cloud, Thrust in thy sickle, and reap: for the time is come for thee to reap; for the harvest of the earth is ripe. And he that sat on the cloud thrust in his sickle on the earth; and the earth was reaped. . . . And another angel came out from the altar, which had power over fire; and cried with a loud cry to him that had the sharp sickle, saying, Thrust in thy sharp sickle, and gather the clusters of the vine of the earth, for her grapes are fully ripe. And the angel thrust his sickle into the earth, and gathered the vine of the earth, and cast it into the great winepress of the wrath of God. And the winepress was trodden without the city, and blood came out of the winepress, even unto the horse bridles, by the space of a thousand and six hundred furlongs (Rev. 14:14–20).

And he gathered them together into a place called in the Hebrew tongue Armageddon (Rev. 16:16).

And I saw heaven opened, and behold a white horse; and he that sat upon him was called Faithful and True, and in righteousness he doth judge and make war. His eyes were as a flame of fire, and on his head were many crowns; and he had a name written, that no man knew, but he himself. And he *was clothed with a vesture dipped in blood; and his name is called The Word of God. And the armies which were in heaven followed him upon white horses, clothed in fine linen, white and clean. And out of his mouth goeth a sharp sword, that with it he should smite the nations: and he shall rule them with a rod of iron: and he treadeth the winepress of the fierceness and wrath of Almighty God. And he hath on his vesture and on his thigh a name written, KING OF KINGS AND LORD OF LORDS. And I saw an angel standing in the sun; and he cried with a loud voice, saying to all the fowls that fly in the midst of heaven, Come and gather yourselves together unto the supper of the great God; that ye may eat the flesh of kings, and the flesh of captains, and the flesh of mighty men, and the flesh of horses and of them that sit on them, and the flesh of all men, both free and bond, both small and great. And I saw the beast, and the kings of the earth, and their armies, gathered together to make war against him that sat on the horse, and against his army. And the beast was taken, and with him the false prophet that wrought miracles before him, with which he deceived them that had received the mark of the beast, and them that worshipped his image. These both were cast alive into a lake of fire burning with brimstone. And the remnant were slain with the sword of him that sat upon the horse, which sword proceeded out of his mouth: and all the fowls were filled with their flesh* (Rev. 19:11–21).

This coming war of Armageddon will be by far the biggest, boldest, bloodiest, most brazen, and most blasphemous of all times. We shall now consider the negative and positive elements of this war.

3. Negative.
   a. Armageddon is not the same as the Russian invasion of Ezekiel 38. Note the differences:
      Russia invades from the north, but at Armageddon the nations come from all directions.
      Russia invades to capture Israel's wealth, but this invasion is to destroy the Lamb and his people.
      Gog leads the Russian invasion, but the antichrist leads this one.
   b. Armageddon is not the final war in the Bible—the

final war occurs after the millennium (Rev. 20:7-9). Armageddon takes place at the end of the tribulation.
4. Positive.
   a. The location of the battle.
     Dr. Herman A. Hoyt aptly describes the location:

"The staggering dimensions of this conflict can scarcely be conceived by man. The battlefield will stretch from Megiddo on the north (Zech. 12:11; Rev. 1:16) to Edom on the South (Isa. 34:5, 6; 63:1), a distance of sixteen hundred furlongs—approximately two hundred miles. It will reach from the Mediterranean Sea on the west to the hills of Moab on the east, a distance of almost one hundred miles. It will include the Valley of Jehoshaphat (Joel 3:2, 12) and the Plains of Esdraelon. At the center of the entire area will be the city of Jerusalem (Zech. 14:1, 2).

Into this area the multiplied millions of men, doubtless approaching 400 million, will be crowded for the final holocaust of humanity. The kings with their armies will come from the north and the south, from the east and from the west. . . . In the most dramatic sense this will be the 'Valley of decision' for humanity (Joel 3:14) and the great winepress into which will be poured the fierceness of the wrath of Almighty God (Rev. 19:15)" (*The End Times*, p. 163).

Thus there would seem to be at least four important names involved in Armageddon:
  (1) The Valley of Jehoshaphat—a valley just east of Jerusalem, between the Holy City and the Mount of Olives (Joel 3:2, 12). This valley, known in the New Testament as the Kidron Valley, plays an important role in the Bible.
    (a) David crossed over this valley, weeping as he fled from his rebellious son Absalom (2 Sam. 15:23).
    (b) King Asa burned the idols of his own mother here (1 Ki. 15:13).
    (c) Hezekiah destroyed some idols here also (2 Chron. 30:14).

(d) Josiah destroyed the idols previously placed in the Temple by Ahaz and Manasseh (2 Ki. 23:4, 6, 12).

(e) Jesus crossed over this valley en route to the Garden of Gethsemane (Jn. 18:1).

The Valley of Jehoshaphat has been a favorite burial ground for Jews for thousands of years. They believed the final resurrection trumpet would sound from here. Some even taught that the bodies of the righteous, regardless of where they were originally buried on earth, would roll back underground to the Valley of Jehoshaphat on that glad day.

As we have already seen, the ground area involved at Armageddon is unbelievably massive—running some 200 miles north and south, and 100 miles east and west, for a total of 20,000 square miles. But the climax will happen in the Valley of Jehoshaphat.

(2) The Valley of Esdraelon—a valley twenty miles long and fourteen miles wide, north and west of Jerusalem between the Holy City and the Mediterranean Sea.

(3) Megiddo—a flat plain in the Valley of Esdraelon (Zech. 12:11).

(4) Bozrah—a city in Edom, east of the Jordan River and near Petra, the capital city of Edom. These two cities will play an important role during the Second Coming of our Lord (Isa. 34:6 and 63:1).

Marvin Vincent writes concerning Armageddon and its location:

"Megiddo was in the plain of Esdraelon, which has been the chosen place for encampment in every contest carried on in Palestine from the days of . . . Assyria unto the disastrous march of Napoleon Bonaparte from Egypt into Syria. Jews, Gentiles, Saracens, Christian Crusaders, and anti-Christian Frenchmen; Egyptians, Persians, Druses, Turks, and Arabs, warriors of every nation that is under heaven, have pitched their tents on the plains of Esdraelon, and have beheld the banners of their nation wet with the dews of Mt. Tabor and Mt. Hermon" *(Word Studies in the New Testament,* p. 542).

(5) In addition to this, a number of battles in the Old Testament took place in this area:
   (a) Deborah and Barak defeated the Canaanites (Jdg. 4, 5).
   (b) Gideon defeated the Midianites (Jdg. 7).
   (c) The Philistines defeated and killed Saul (1 Sam. 31).
   (d) David defeated Goliath (1 Sam. 17).
   (e) An Egyptian king killed Josiah (2 Ki. 23). Two authors aptly describe this battle for us:

   "Palestine is to be given a blood bath of unprecedented proportions which will flow from Armageddon at the north down through the valley of Jehoshaphat, will cover the land of Edom, and will wash over all Judea and the city of Jerusalem. John looks at this scene of carnage and he describes it as blood flowing to the depths of the horses' bridles. It is beyond human imagination to see a lake that size that has been drained from the veins of those who have followed the purpose of Satan to try to exterminate God's chosen people in order to prevent Jesus Christ from coming to reign" (J. D. Pentecost, *Prophecy for Today,* p. 118).

   "The Battle of Armageddon will result in wholesale carnage among the legions of the beast. The brilliance of Christ's appearing will produce a trembling and demoralization

in the soldiers (Zech. 12:2; 14:13). The
result of this demoralization and trembling
will be the desertion from the antichrist and
the rendering of him inoperative (2 Thess.
2:8). This tremendous light from heaven
will produce astonishment and blindness in
animals and madness in men (Zech. 12:4).
A plague will sweep through the armies
from this light and men will not fight where
they stand (Zech. 14:12, 15). The blood of
animals and men will form a lake two
hundred miles long and bridle deep (Rev.
14:19, 20). The stench of this rotting mass
of flesh and blood will fill the entire region
(Isa. 34:1-3). The mangled forms of men
and beasts will provide a feast for the
carrion birds (Rev. 19:17, 18, 21). The
beast and the false prophet will then be cast
alive into the lake of fire forever (Rev. 19:20)"
(*The End Times*, p. 165).

b. The reasons for the battle.
What will draw all the nations of the world into the
area of Armageddon? They will gather themselves
there for various reasons. It would seem that the
following are three of the more important reasons:
(1) Because of the sovereignty of God. In at least
five distinct passages we are told that God
himself will gather the nations here:
He hath delivered them to the slaughter (Isa. 34:2).
*I will also gather all nations, and will bring them
down into the Valley of Jehoshaphat* (Joel 3:2).
*For I will gather all nations against Jerusalem to
battle* (Zech. 14:2).
*For my determination is to gather the nations . . .
to pour upon them mine indignation, even all my
fierce anger* (Zech. 3:8).
*And he gathered them together into a place called
in the Hebrew tongue Armageddon* (Rev. 16:16).

214

(2) Because of the deception of Satan (Rev. 16:13, 14). In this passage we are told that three special unclean spirits will trick the nations into gathering at Armageddon.

(3) Because of the hatred of the nations for Christ. A number of passages tell us of this devilish hatred (Ps. 2:1-3; Rev. 11:18). The nations, led by the antichrist, will doubtless realize the imminent return of Christ (Rev. 11:15; 12:12). They will also be aware of his touching down on the Mount of Olives (Zech. 14:4; Acts 1:9-12). Thus it is not unreasonable to assume they will gather in that area to try to destroy Christ at the moment of his return to earth.

c. The chronology of the battle.

(1) The drying up of the Euphrates River (Rev. 16:12).

Dr. Donald Barnhouse quotes Seiss in describing this:

"From time immemorial the Euphrates with its tributaries has been a great and formidable boundary between the peoples east of it and west of it. It runs a distance of 1800 miles, and is scarcely fordable anywhere or any time. It is from three to twelve hundred yards wide, and from ten to thirty feet in depth; and most of the time it is still deeper and wider. It was the boundary of the dominion of Solomon, and is repeatedly spoken of as the northeast limit of the lands promised to Israel. . . . History frequently refers to the great hindrance the Euphrates has been to military movements; and it has always been a line of separation between the peoples living east of it and those living west of it" (*Revelation*, p. 301).

Thus when this watery barrier is removed, tens of millions of soldiers from China, India, and other Asian powers will march straight for Armageddon and destruction.

(2) The destruction of Jerusalem.

Perhaps the saddest event during the tribulation will be the siege and destruction of the Holy City. This will be the forty-seventh and last takeover of the beloved city of David. The following passages bear this out:

Behold, I will make Jerusalem a cup of trembling unto all people around about, when they shall be in the siege (Zech. 12:2).

For I will gather all nations against Jerusalem to battle; and the city shall be taken, and the houses rifled, and the women ravished; and half the city shall go forth into captivity (Zech. 14:2).

And when we shall see Jerusalem compassed with armies, then know that the desolation thereof is nigh (Lk. 21:20).

When these two events transpire, both the angels in paradise and the demons in perdition will surely hold their breath.

TEN
THE SECOND
COMING OF
CHRIST

The greatest day in history occurred during an April Sunday morning some 2,000 years ago, when the crucified Savior rose from the dead! But God is preparing an even greater, grander, and more glorious day than the resurrection of his beloved Son—and that event is his return to earth again!

A. The chronology of the Second Coming of Christ.
    1. It begins with fearful manifestations in the skies.
        Immediately after the tribulation of those days shall the sun be darkened, and the moon shall not give her light, and the stars shall fall from heaven, and the powers of the heavens shall be shaken (Mt. 24:29).

        And there shall be signs in the sun, and in the moon, and in the stars; and upon the earth distress of nations, with perplexity; the sea and the waves roaring; men's hearts failing them for fear . . . for the powers of heaven shall be shaken (Lk. 21:25, 26).

    2. In the midst of this, the heavens open and Jesus comes forth.
        And then shall appear the sign of the Son of man in heaven: and then shall all the tribes of the earth mourn, and they shall see the Son of man coming in the clouds of heaven with power and great glory (Mt. 24:30).

        . . . the Lord Jesus shall be revealed from heaven with his mighty angels (2 Thess. 1:7).

*Behold, he cometh with clouds; and every eye shall see him
. . .* (Rev. 1:7).

*And I saw heaven opened, and behold a white horse; and
he that sat upon him was called Faithful and True . . .* (Rev.
19:11).

3. The returning Savior touches down upon the Mount of
   Olives, causing a great earthquake (Zech. 14:4, 8). The
   Mount of Olives is one of the most important mountains
   in both biblical history and prophecy.
   a. It towers over Mt. Moriah by 318 feet.
   b. It rises to a height of 2743 feet above sea level.
   c. Its name derives from the olives grown there.
   d. Sometimes it was called the Mount of Lights (desig-
      nating the beginning of a new month, year, etc.).
   e. David paused here, wept, and worshiped God after
      being driven from Jerusalem by Absalom his son
      (2 Sam. 15:30, 32).
   f. Tradition says that Christ first spoke the Lord's
      Prayer on this mountain.
   g. The Church of the Lord's Prayer, built in 1868, has
      the prayer engraved in thirty-two languages on thirty-
      two marble slabs, each three feet wide and six feet
      long. The Bible says Jesus often visited here.
      *And he came out, and went, as he was accustomed, to the
      Mount of Olives; and his disciples also followed him* (Lk.
      22:39).
   h. From here he sent for a colt to ride during the
      triumphal entry of Palm Sunday (Mt. 21:1).
   i. Here he delivered the Mt. Olivet Discourse (Mt.
      24–25).
   j. He visited here after leaving the upper room and may
      have uttered his high priestly prayer (Jn. 17) from this
      spot (Mt. 26:30).
   k. He slept here on occasion during the passion week
      (Lk. 21:37).
   l. He ascended from here (Acts 1).
   m. He will touch down here at the Second Coming
      (Zech. 14).
4. After touching down on the Mount of Olives, Christ
   proceeds to Petra and Bozrah, two chief cities in Edom.

While it is impossible to be dogmatic here, it would seem that he goes to Edom to gather the hiding Israelite remnant. Accompanied by the holy angels, the church, and the remnant, Christ marches toward Armageddon (Isa. 34:6; 63:1).

We have already referred to William Hull's novel, *Israel, Key to Prophecy*. Hull offers the following account of our Lord's visit to Petra.

"Then into the heart of Petra the Lord advanced with His great host of saints. The Jews could be heard praying and crying on every hand, but a blast on a silver trumpet brought them running. From every part of the great enclosure, from temple, house and cave they poured forth. Young and old, men and women, children of all ages, all gathered to greet the mighty host. One glimpse of the Lord Himself, and they fell on their knees. Then began a wailing and mounting which filled the air, echoing back from wall to wall. 'And they shall mourn for him, as one mourneth for his only son, and shall be in bitterness for him. . . .'

Soon a great shout arose—'Lo, this is our God; we have waited for him, and he will save us: this is the Lord.' Then once more they fell on their faces and wept as they realized the enormity of the sin of their fathers and of theirs, too. To have rejected such a holy, lovely, compassionate Saviour was more than mind could think on. Tears coursed down their cheeks, they beat their breasts, they cast dust on their heads and mourned and cried without stopping. But the Lord had promised, '. . . to comfort all that mourn; to appoint unto them that mourn in Zion, to give unto them beauty for ashes, the oil of joy for mourning, the garment of praise for the spirit of heaviness.'

His tender sweet smile encouraged them. He spoke words of endearment and love to them. Soon they were on their feet, faces shining, hands raised to heaven and praises on their lips, until the volume of praise equaled and exceeded their former mourning. The shouts of the Jews were joined by those of the accompanying saints and soon the volume of praise became as thunder, as the sound of mighty waters. There was an ecstasy of rejoicing which welled up in one majestic organ chord of heavenly music, beautiful beyond words.

The saints moved among the enraptured Jews. They were preparing them for the triumphant return to Jerusalem. The controversy of Zion was to be completely settled and Israel was to be permanently restored. The Lord had come—'to bind up the brokenhearted, to proclaim liberty to the captives, and the opening of the prison to them that are bound; to proclaim the acceptable year of the Lord, and the day of vengeance of our God.'

A grand procession began to form, the Lord leading the way, the Jews and saints intermingled following Him. The Song of Solomon revealed the picture. 'Who is this that cometh up from the wilderness, leaning upon her beloved?' But Isaiah gives us the clearest picture of all as he gazes from Jerusalem through the prophetic telescope. 'Who is this that cometh from Edom, with dyed garments from Bozrah? this that is glorious in his apparel, travelling in the greatness of his strength?' Then the answer of the Lord echoing back, as the vast procession slowly approaches Zion, 'I that speak in righteousness, mighty to save!'

Onward swept the mighty throng. The ground seemed to smooth itself before the feet of the Creator. The stones crumbled to powder and fertilized the soil. The grass sprang up on every hand and flowers burst into bloom as the procession passed by. The birds sang and their song seemed to echo Isaiah's question, 'Who is this? Who is this?' Who indeed? Who but the King of Kings and Lord of Lords!" (*Israel, Key to Prophecy*, Zondervan, pp. 93, 94).

B. The purpose of the Second Coming of Christ.
    1. To defeat the antichrist and the world's nations assembled at Armageddon. John Phillips writes the following, describing the events mentioned in Revelation 19:17–21.

"In a few graphic sentences we are told how Satan's rickety empire collapses like a house of cards when the Lord appears. We are told how Satan's forces are to be doomed at Armageddon. John says, 'And I saw an angel standing in the sun; and he cried with a loud voice saying to all the fowls that fly in the midst of heaven, Come and gather yourselves together unto the supper of the great God; that ye may eat the flesh of kings, and the flesh of captains, and the flesh of mighty men, and the flesh of horses, and of them that sit on them, and the flesh of all men, both free and bond, both small and great.' As the armies, assembled at the cockpit of the earth, stare in amazement at the appearing of the King of glory, their gaze is momentarily directed to the sun. There, standing in its glare, is an angel; at his summons, enormous flocks of birds appear, circling and wheeling around the armies of earth, croaking to one another in anticipation of the coming feast, dipping low over the horrified troops, and climbing again to the skies. The battle has not yet been fought, but the omens are dreadful. With each passing moment, the sky grows darker with these birds of prey. There cannot be a vulture, an eagle, a raven, left on earth that has not obeyed the summons and come to the supper of God. Satan's armies are doomed; the fierce fowls know it and have come to bury the dead in the name of the living God.

We are next told how Satan's forces are to be drawn to Armageddon. John says, 'And I saw the beast, and the kings of the earth, and their armies gathered together to make war against him that sat on the horse and against his army.' Thus, tersely, is the mobilization of the world described. Whatever may have been their original motives in converging on Armageddon, all animosities are forgotten, and the men are united by the challenge from on high.

In recent times, science fiction writers have made much of imagined plots against our planet. They have told of invasions from Venus and Mars and from the deep recesses of space. They have depicted a terrified

221

world suddenly united in a common cause in the face of a threat from the far reaches of the sky. This is what happens here, but this is no fantasy of fiction; this is the real thing. The planet is invaded at last from outer space, not by horrible insect-like monsters, but by the Lord Himself and His glorious hosts. The devil knows his hour has come but, careless of human life, he fights to the bitter end. What the beast will say to his armies, his allies, and his antagonists can well be imagined:

'Gentlemen, we are at war and have been at war one with another. The time has come for us to unite in a common cause. The things which unite us now are far more important than the things which divide us. It is no longer a question of which of us will rule the world; it is a question of common survival. The time has come for us to take final counsel together against the Lord and against His anointed. He has put Himself in our power. He has dared to appear on earth. The last time He came, we crucified Him; this time we shall cast His bands asunder and cast away His cords from us forever. We have tried uniting for peace; it has not proved a durable bond. Now let us unite for war. Let us deal with this invasion of our planet once and for all. Let us deal with this invasion of white-robed psalm singers. Let us show them how men, freed of all religious opiates, can fight. Let us hurl our defiance in their teeth. Time and again I have given you proofs of my mighty and supernatural powers. That dread lord of darkness whom we serve has defied these heavenly hosts for countless ages and is more than a match for them all. Come, let us rid the world and its atmosphere forever of these unwanted chanters of hymns.'

The nations unite, as Psalm 2 foretells. Yet, as the great conference of kings disbands and the heralds proclaim the new resolutions, peal after peal of mocking laughter sound down from the sky for 'He that sitteth in the heavens shall laugh; the Lord shall have them in derision' (Ps. 2:4).

It is the same old story. The nations in their folly were united against Christ at His first advent. The early church proclaimed it so: 'Lord, thou art God, which hast made heaven, and earth, and the sea, and all that in them is: Who by the mouth of thy servant David hast said, Why did the heathen rage, and the people imagine vain things? The kings of the earth stood up, and the rulers were gathered together against the Lord, and against his Christ. For of a truth against thy holy child Jesus, whom thou hast anointed, both Herod, and Pontius Pilate, with the Gentiles, and the people of Israel, were gathered together, for to do whatsoever thy hand and thy counsel determined before to be done. And now, Lord, behold their threatenings' (Acts 4:24-29). The nations united against Christ at His first coming, and they will do so again. They did their worst when they crucified Him but only succeeded in accomplishing God's will. They will do the same when they unite against the Lord to oppose His return. The nations will imagine that they are working out their own schemes and plans as they march toward Esdraelon, but they are simply marching in step with God's will. They are drawn to Armageddon.

Finally, we are told how Satan's forces are to be destroyed at Armageddon. We read, 'And the beast was taken, and with him the false prophet that wrought miracles before him, with which he deceived them that had received the mark of the beast, and them that worshipped his image. These both were cast alive into the lake of fire burning with brimstone. And the remnant were slain with the sword of him that sat upon the horse, which sword proceeded out of his mouth: and all the fowls were filled with their flesh.' With what panoply and pomp the armies march across the plains of Galilee, file through the passes and deploy on the fertile fields of Megiddo! What masses of military equipment are stockpiled in the hills! What fleets ride at anchor in the Red Sea, the Persian Gulf, and along the shorelines of the eastern Mediterranean! What stirring strains of martial music are heard. The ground shakes to the beat of marching feet; the skies darken with aircraft drawn from the ends of the earth. Amazing new weapons, given to men by the beast, are brought into place. Miracles are wrought by the false prophet to encourage the troops. The final commands are given.

Then suddenly it will all be over. In fact, there will be no war at all, in the sense that we think of war. There will be just a word spoken from Him who sits astride the great white horse. Once He spoke a word to a fig tree, and it withered away. Once He spoke a word to howling winds and heaving waves, and the storm clouds vanished and the waves fell still. Once He spoke to a legion of demons bursting at the seams of a poor man's soul, and instantly they fled. Now He speaks a word, and the war is over. The blasphemous, loud-mouthed beast is stricken where he stands. The false prophet, the miracle-working windbag from the pit is punctured and still. The pair of them are bundled up and hurled head-long into the everlasting flames. Another word, and the panic-stricken armies reel and stagger and fall down dead. Field marshals and generals, admirals and air commanders, soldiers and sailors, rank and file, one and all—they fall. And the vultures descend and cover the scene. Thus ends the battle of Armageddon! For a thousand years there will be peace on earth after that. Men will beat their swords into plowshares and their spears into pruning hooks, their tanks into tractors and their missiles into silos for grain. The ages will roll by, and the words for war in human speech will become archaic fragments of a language dead to mankind. One can picture a school-boy reading an ancient book sometime during the second half of the Millennium. 'Say, Dad,' he says, 'what is an intercontinental ballistic missile?' To which the father replies, 'Go and ask your mother!' The mother, being questioned, answers, 'Some kind of cabbage, I expect. Go and ask your dad.' What a day that will be!"
(*Exploring Revelation*, Moody Press, 1974, pp. 247–250).

2. To regather, regenerate, and restore faithful Israel. Perhaps the most frequent promise in all the Old Testament concerns God's eventual restoration of Israel. The prophets repeat this so often that it becomes a refrain—a chorus of confidence.

Note the following:
Fear not: for I am with thee: I will bring thy seed from the east, and gather thee from the west; I will say to the north, Give up; and to the south, Keep not back: bring my sons from far, and my daughters from the ends of the earth (Isa. 43:5, 6).

For I will set mine eyes upon them for good, and I will bring them again to this land: and I will build them, and not pull them down . . . (Jer. 24:6).

. . . Thus saith the Lord God, I will even gather you from the people, and assemble you out of the countries where ye have been scattered, and I will give you the land of Israel (Ezek. 11:17).

And ye shall dwell in the land that I gave to your fathers; and ye shall be my people, and I will be your God (Ezek. 36:28).

And I will bring again the captivity of my people of Israel, and they shall build the waste cities, and inhabit them; and they shall plant vineyards, and drink the wine thereof; they shall also make gardens, and eat the fruit of them. And I will plant them upon their land, and they shall no more be pulled up out of their land which I have given them, saith the Lord thy God (Amos 9:14, 15).

Perhaps the most sublime song of praise concerning Israel's restoration is sung by the prophet Micah:
Who is a God like unto thee, that pardoneth iniquity, and passeth by the transgression of the remnant of his heritage? He retaineth not his anger for ever, because he delighteth in mercy. He will turn again, he will have compassion upon us; he will subdue our iniquities; and thou wilt cast all their sins into the depths of the sea (Micah 7:18, 19).

In the New Testament our Lord also speaks about this during one of his last sermons:
And he shall send his angels with a great sound of a trumpet, and they shall gather together his elect from the four winds, from one end of heaven to the other (Mt. 24:31).

Thus will our Lord gather Israel when he comes again and, as we have already observed, he will begin by appearing to the remnant hiding in Petra. Here we note:
a. Their temporary sorrow.

*And I will pour upon the house of David, and upon the
inhabitants of Jerusalem, the spirit of grace and of
supplications: and they shall look upon me whom they
have pierced, and they shall mourn for him, as one
mourneth for his only son, and shall be in bitterness for
him, as one that is in bitterness for his firstborn. In that
day shall there be a great mourning in Jerusalem . . . in
the valley of Megiddon. And the land shall mourn, every
family apart; the family of the house of David apart, and
their wives apart* . . . (Zech. 12:10–12).

*And one shall say unto him, What are these wounds in
thine hands? Then he shall answer, Those with which I
was wounded in the house of my friends* (Zech. 13:6).

*Behold, he cometh with clouds; and every eye shall see
him, and they also which pierced him; and all kindreds of
the earth shall wail because of him* (Rev. 1:7).

b. Their ultimate joy.

*He will swallow up death in victory; and the Lord God
will wipe away tears from off all faces; and the rebuke of
his people shall he take away from off all the earth: for
the Lord hath spoken it. And it shall be said in that day,
Lo, this is our God; we have waited for him, and he will
save us: this is the Lord . . . we will be glad and rejoice in
his salvation* (Isa. 25: 8, 9).

*Moreover, the light of the moon shall be as the light of
the sun, and the light of the sun shall be sevenfold, as the
light of seven days, in the day that the Lord bindeth up the
breach of his people, and healeth the stroke of their wound*
(Isa. 30:26).

*He shall feed his flock like a shepherd: he shall gather
the lambs with his arm, and carry them in his bosom, and
shall gently lead those that are with young* (Isa. 40:11).

*I, even I, am he that blotteth out thy transgressions for
mine own sake, and will not remember thy sins* (Isa.
43:25).

*Can a woman forget her sucking child, that she should
not have compassion on the son of her womb? Yea, they
may forget, yet will I not forget thee* (Isa. 49:15).

*For the Lord shall comfort Zion: he will comfort all her
waste places; and will make her wilderness like Eden, and*

*her desert like the garden of the Lord; joy and gladness
shall be found therein; thanksgiving, and the voice of
melody* (Isa. 51:3).

*For ye shall go out with joy, and be led forth with peace:
the mountains and the hills shall break forth before you
into singing, and all the trees of the field shall clap their
hands* (Isa. 55:12).

3. To judge and punish faithless Israel.

In the book of Romans the great Apostle Paul makes
two significant statements concerning his beloved nation
Israel. He writes,

For they are not all Israel, which are of Israel (Rom. 9:6).

*And so all Israel shall be saved: as it is written, There
shall come out of Sion the Deliverer, and shall turn away
ungodliness from Jacob* (Rom. 11:26).

By the first statement Paul of course meant that all
faithful Israel would be saved. As we have previously
seen, this blessed event will occur during the tribulation.

By the second statement Paul writes concerning
faithless Israel. In other words, all that glitters is not
gold! From the very moment God began working
through Abraham (the first Hebrew), Satan also began
working through members of that same race. Thus, as
the Bible has been advanced by faithful Israel throughout
history, it has likewise been opposed by faithless Israel.

Therefore, when the master of all Israel returns, he will
be especially gracious to true Israel but especially harsh
with false Israel. Note the tragic record of false Israel.

a. Her sins against the Father.

    (1) Rebelling (Num. 14:22, 23).

    (2) Rejecting (1 Sam. 8:7).

    (3) Robbing (Mal. 3:2-5).

b. Her sins against the Son.

    (1) She refused him (Jn. 1:11).

    (2) She crucified him (Acts 2:22, 23; 3:14, 15;
        4:10; 5:30; 1 Thess. 2:14-16).

c. Her sins against the Holy Spirit—stubborn resistance.
See Acts 7:51.

d. Her sins against the kingdom.

    (1) She refused to use her God-given abilities to

promote it (Mt. 25:24–30; Lk. 19:20–24).
   (2) She made light of the marriage feast (Mt. 22:5).
   (3) She refused to wear the proper wedding
       garments (Mt. 22:11–13).
e. Her sins against her own people.
   (1) She stole from widows (Mt. 23:14).
   (2) She killed her own prophets (Mt. 23:31, 34, 35;
       Acts 7:58).
f. Her sins against the world.
   (1) She led others into her own wretched blindness
       (Mt. 23:16, 24).
   (2) She was filled with hypocrisy (Mt. 16:6, 12;
       Rom. 2:17–23).
   (3) She had blasphemed the name of God among
       the Gentiles (Rom. 2:24).
g. Her sins against the gospel.
   (1) She opposed it in Jerusalem (Acts 4:2; 5:28;
       9:29; 21:28; 23:2, 12).
   (2) She opposed it in Damascus (Acts 9:22–25).
   (3) She opposed it in Antioch of Pisidia (Acts
       13:45, 50).
   (4) She opposed it in Iconium (Acts 14:2).
   (5) She opposed it in Lystra (Acts 14:19).
   (6) She opposed it in Thessalonica (Acts 17:5).
   (7) She opposed it in Berea (Acts 17:13).
   (8) She opposed it in Corinth (Acts 18:6, 12).
   (9) She opposed it in Caesarea (Acts 25:6, 7).
The Apostle Paul dearly loved his nation, and doubtless
wrote the following description of faithless Israel and her
future judgment with a heavy and weeping heart:
*Who both killed the Lord Jesus, and their own prophets, and
have persecuted us; and they please not God, and are contrary
to all men: Forbidding us to speak to the Gentiles that they
might be saved, to fill up their sins alway: for the wrath is
come upon them to the uttermost* (1 Thess. 2:15, 16).
Thus the tragic prophecy of Ezekiel will someday be fulfilled upon faithless Israel:
*But as for them whose heart walketh after the heart of their
detestable things and their abominations, I will recompense*

228

their way upon their own heads, saith the Lord God (Ezek. 11:21).

And I will purge out from among you the rebels, and them that transgress against me . . . (Ezek. 20:38).

4. To separate the sheep from the goats.

When the Son of man shall come in his glory, and all the holy angels with him, then shall he sit upon the throne of his glory: And before him shall be gathered all nations: and he shall separate them one from another, as a shepherd divideth his sheep from the goats: And he shall set the sheep on his right hand, but the goats on the left. Then shall the King say unto them on his right hand, Come, ye blessed of my Father, inherit the kingdom prepared for you from the foundation of the world: For I was an hungered, and ye gave me meat: I was thirsty, and ye gave me drink: I was a stranger, and ye took me in: Naked, and ye clothed me: I was sick, and ye visited me: I was in prison, and ye came unto me.

Then shall the righteous answer him, saying, Lord, when saw we thee an hungered, and fed thee? or thirsty, and gave thee drink? When saw we thee a stranger, and took thee in? or naked, and clothed thee? Or when saw we thee sick, or in prison, and came unto thee?

And the King shall answer and say unto them, Verily I say unto you, Inasmuch as ye have done it unto one of the least of these my brethren, ye have done it unto me.

Then shall he say also unto them on the left hand, Depart from me, ye cursed, into everlasting fire, prepared for the devil and his angels: For I was an hungered, and ye gave me no meat: I was thirsty, and ye gave me no drink: I was a stranger, and ye took me not in: naked, and ye clothed me not: sick, and in prison, and ye visited me not.

Then shall they also answer him, saying, Lord, when saw we thee an hungered, or athirst, or a stranger, or naked, or sick, or in prison, and did not minister unto thee?

Then shall he answer them, saying, Verily I say unto you, Inasmuch as ye did it not to one of the least of these, ye did it not to me. And these shall go away into everlasting punishment: but the righteous into life eternal (Mt. 25:31–46).

a. The false views of this judgment.

(1) That this "sheep and goat" judgment is the same as the great white throne judgment of Revelation 20:11-15. They are not the same, for one takes place at the end of the tribulation while the other occurs at the end of the millennium.

(2) That the sheep and goat judgment deals only with entire nations. Some have imagined the nations of the world lined up before God. At his command, Russia steps forward and is judged—then America, then Cuba, etc. This is not the case. The word translated "nations" in Matthew 25:32 should be rendered "Gentiles."

b. The basis of this judgment.

The test in this judgment is how those Gentiles who survive the tribulation have treated faithful Israel (here referred to by Christ as "my brethren"). In Nazi Germany, during the Second World War, escaping Jews were on a number of occasions befriended and protected by various German families who, in spite of their nationality, did not agree with Adolf Hitler. Apparently the same thing will happen during the tribulation. Gentiles from all nations will hear the message of faithful Israel and believe it and, at the risk of their own lives, will protect the messengers. This, then, would seem to be the nature of the sheep and goat judgment. See also Matthew 13:38-43, 47-50; Genesis 12:1-3.

5. To bind Satan.

And the God of peace shall bruise Satan under your feet shortly . . . (Rom. 16:20).

And I saw an angel come down from heaven, having the key of the bottomless pit and a great chain in his hand. And he laid hold on the dragon, that old serpent, which is the Devil, and Satan, and bound him a thousand years, and cast him into the bottomless pit, and shut him up, and set a seal upon him, that he should deceive the nations no more till the thousand years should be fulfilled . . . (Rev. 20:1-3).

A cynic once poked fun at God's eternal plan by composing a limerick which read:

God's plan had a hopeful beginning
But man ruined all this by his sinning
We trust that the story
Will end in God's glory
But at present the other side's winning!

However, as this passage in Revelation 20 demonstrates, while Satan was allowed to win a few battles, God himself has determined to win the war!

6. To resurrect Old Testament and tribulational saints.
   It is the view of this study guide that at the rapture of the church God will raise only those believers who have been saved from Pentecost till the rapture. According to this view, all other believers will be resurrected just prior to the millennium at this time.

   a. The fact of this resurrection.
      At least nine passages bring out this resurrection.
      (1) Job 19:25, 26:
          For I know that my redeemer liveth, and that he
          shall stand at the latter day upon the earth; and
          though after my skin worms destroy this body, yet in
          my flesh shall I see God.
      (2) Psalm 49:15:
          But God will redeem my soul from the power of the
          grave: for he shall receive me.
      (3) Isaiah 25:8:
          He will swallow up death in victory. . . .
      (4) Isaiah 26:19:
          Thy dead men shall live, together with my dead body
          shall they arise. . . .
      (5) Daniel 12:2:
          And many of them that sleep in the dust of the earth
          shall awake, some to everlasting life, and some to
          shame and everlasting contempt.
      (6) Hosea 13:14:
          I will ransom them from the power of the grave; I
          will redeem them from death: O death, I will be thy
          plagues; O grave, I will be thy destruction. . . .
      (7) John 5:28, 29:

> Marvel not at this: for the hour is coming, in the
> which all that are in the graves shall hear his voice,
> and shall come forth; they that have done good, unto
> the resurrection of life; and they that have done evil,
> unto the resurrection of damnation.

(8) Hebrews 11:35:

> . . . and others were tortured, not accepting deliver-
> ance; that they might obtain a better resurrection.

(9) Revelation 20:4, 5:

> . . . and I saw the souls of them that were beheaded
> for the witness of Jesus, and for the word of God,
> and which had not worshipped the beast, neither his
> image, neither had received his mark upon their
> foreheads, or in their hands; and they lived and
> reigned with Christ a thousand years. But the rest of
> the dead lived not again until the thousand years
> were finished. . . .

b. The order of this resurrection.

This is the third of four major biblical resurrections.
These are:

(1) The resurrection of Christ (1 Cor. 15:23).
(2) The resurrection of believers at the rapture
(1 Thess. 4:16; 1 Cor. 15:51–53).
(3) The resurrection of Old Testament and
tribulational saints.
(4) The resurrection of the unsaved (Rev. 20:5,
11–14).

Thus one of the reasons for the Second Coming will be
to resurrect those non-church-related saints. For many
long centuries Father Abraham has been patiently
awaiting that city "which hath foundations, whose
builder and maker is God" (Heb. 11:10); God will not
let him down.

Dr. Clarence Mason has written:

"Resurrection! What a magic word.

It has always been the dream of man. In the artifacts
of the tomb of Queen Shubad, at the University of
Pennsylvania Museum, are the crushed skulls of her

bodyguards and ladies-in-waiting. These servants were by this means presumptively sent along to accompany the queen from Abraham's hometown of Ur into the future life. That was about the third millennium before Christ.

Philosophers have conjectured and yearned. Rationalists have drawn a blank with their nihilism about the future. This is one area in which their writings show poignant depair.

The early church had a unique message. They preached 'Jesus and the resurrection.' Other religions had their salvation schemes, their lofty ethics, their colorful rites and ceremonies. They had their great men, saints, and alleged miracles, even including virgin births. They had their millions of devotees. Their founders were wreathed in extravagant claims.

But none of them claimed to have a resurrected founder who had come forth from the grave. In this, Christianity is unique among religions. It was this message that startled the philosophers on Mars Hill, accustomed though they were to hearing 'some new thing.' This was really new!" (*Prophetic Problems*, Moody Press, 1973, p. 129).

7. To judge fallen angels.
   Know ye not that we shall judge angels? (1 Cor. 6:3).
   All fallen angels are of course included in this judgment. But they fall into two main categories: chained and unchained.
   a. Unchained fallen angels.
      And Jesus asked him, saying, What is thy name? And he said, Legion: because many devils were entered into him. And they besought him that he would not command them to go out into the deep (Lk. 8:30, 31).
      And there was in their synagogue a man with an unclean spirit; and he cried out, saying, Let us alone; what have we to do with thee, thou Jesus of Nazareth? Art thou come to destroy us? I know thee who thou art, the Holy One of God (Mk. 1:23, 24).
      For we wrestle not against flesh and blood, but against

principalities, against powers, against the rulers of the darkness of this world, against spiritual wickedness in high places (Eph. 6:12).

The point of these three passages is simply this—there is a group of fallen angels (demons) who have freedom of movement, and can therefore possess the bodies of both men and animals. Their one sin was that of following Satan in his foul rebellion against God. See Isaiah 14:12-17; Ezekiel 28:12-19.

    b. Chained fallen angels.

Christ also suffered. He died once for the sins of all us guilty sinners, although he himself was innocent of any sin at any time, that he might bring us safely home to God. But though his body died, his spirit lived on, and it was in the spirit that he visited the spirits in prison, and preached to them—spirits of those who, long before in the days of Noah, had refused to listen to God, though he waited patiently for them while Noah was building the ark. Yet only eight persons were saved from drowning in that terrible flood (1 Pet. 3:18-20, TLB).

And the angels which kept not their first estate, but left their own habitation, he hath reserved in everlasting chains under darkness unto the judgment of the great day (Jude 6).

According to the above passages these fallen angels do not have the freedom the previous angels do, but are right now in "solitary confinement" awaiting their judgment at the end of the tribulation. Why the difference? Many Bible scholars believe that this group of angels was guilty of two grievous sins—not only did they join Satan's revolt, but they also committed sexual perversion with "the daughters of men" before the flood. See Genesis 6:2.

C. The time element involved in the Second Coming of Christ.

According to Daniel 12:11, 12, there will be a period of seventy-five days between the Second Coming of Christ and the millennial reign. Dr. S. Franklin Logsdon has written:

"We in the United States have a national analogy. The President is elected in the early part of November, but he is not inaugurated until January 20th. There is an interim of 70-plus days. During this time, he concerns himself with the appointment of Cabinet members, foreign envoys and others who will comprise his government. In the period of 75 days between the termination of the Great Tribulation and the Coronation, the King of glory likewise will attend to certain matters" (*Profiles of Prophecy*, Zondervan, p. 81).

It would therefore appear that the seventy-five days will be spent in accomplishing seven basic things already mentioned under "Purposes of the Second Coming."

ELEVEN
THE
MILLENNIUM —
THE THOUSAND-YEAR
REIGN OF CHRIST

Some 250 years ago, Isaac Watts wrote a hymn based on the truths found in Psalm 98. The name of this world-famous hymn is "Joy to the World"! At Christmas it is sung all across the world by millions of Christians and non-Christians alike. But a close study of the words of this hymn reveal that Watts did not have in mind the Bethlehem coming of Christ, but rather the millennial coming of our Lord! Observe his words:

Joy to the world! The Lord is come!
Let earth receive her King.
Let every heart prepare him room,
And heaven and nature sing.
No more let sins and sorrows grow,
Nor thorns infest the ground;
He comes to make his blessings flow,
Far as the curse is found.
He rules the world with truth and grace,
And makes the nations prove
The glories of his righteousness,
And wonders of his love.

Dr. J. Dwight Pentecost writes:

"A larger body of prophetic Scripture is devoted to the subject of the millennium, developing its character and conditions, than any other one subject. This millennial age, in which the purposes of God are fully realized on the earth, demands considerable attention. An attempt will be made to deduce from the Scriptures themselves the essential facts and features of this theocratic kingdom. While much has been written on the subject of the millennium, that which is clearly revealed in the Word can be our only true guide as to the nature and character of that period" (*Things to Come*, Dunham Press, 1959, p. 476).

A. The fact of the millennium.
   The word itself is a Latin term which signifies "one thousand years."
   . . . *and they lived and reigned with Christ a thousand years* (Rev. 20:4).

   In the first seven verses of Revelation 20, John mentions the thousand-year period no less than six times! In spite of this some have argued that, since this number is found in only one New Testament passage, one cannot insist that the thousand-year period will really come to pass! To emphasize their point, reference is made to 2 Peter 3:8: ". . . One day is with the Lord as a thousand years, and a thousand years as one day."

   It is interesting (and perhaps revealing) to note that the same group which attempts to shorten the thousand-year period of Revelation to one day (and thus do away entirely with the millennium) also attempts to expand the six days of creation in Genesis to thousands of years. One is tempted to ask, "Why can't God mean exactly what he says?"

   Dr. Rene Pache writes the following helpful words:
   "Let us notice again this fact: the teaching of the Old Testament concerning the millennium is so complete that the Jews in the Talmud succeeded in developing it entirely themselves, without possessing the gifts furnished later by the New Testament. For example, they had indeed affirmed before the Apocalypse that the messianic kingdom would last one thousand years. One should not, therefore, claim (as some have done) that without the famous passage of Revelation 20:1–10 the doctrine of the millennium would not exist" (*The Return of Jesus Christ*, Moody Press, 1955, p. 380).

During the history of the Christian church men have held three major views about the millennium.

1. Postmillennialism.

This theory says that through the preaching of the gospel the world will eventually embrace Christianity and become a universal "society of saints." At this point Christ will be invited to assume command and reign over man's peaceful planet. Thus, though postmillennialists believe in a literal thousand-year reign, their position is false, for the Bible clearly teaches that the world situation will become worse and worse prior to Christ's Second Coming—not better and better. (See 1 Tim. 4:1; 2 Tim. 3:1-5.) This position was popularized by a Unitarian minister named Daniel Whitby (1638-1726), and it flourished until the early part of the twentieth century. Then came World War I, and men began to wonder. Finally, the postmillennial theory was quietly laid to rest amid Hitler's gas ovens during the Second World War! Today a postmillennialist is harder to find than a 1940 Wendell Willkie button!

2. Amillennialism.

This view teaches that there will be no thousand-year reign at all, and that the New Testament church inherits all the spiritual promises and prophecies of Old Testament Israel. In this view Isaiah's beautiful prophecy of the bear and the cow lying together and the lion eating straw like the ox (Isa. 11:7) simply doesn't mean what it says at all. However, if the eleventh chapter of Isaiah cannot be taken literally, what proof do we have that the magnificent fifty-third chapter should not likewise be allegorized away?

3. Premillennialism.

This view teaches that Christ will return just prior to the millennium and will personally rule during this glorious thousand-year reign. This position alone is the scriptural one, and is the oldest of these three views. From the apostolic period on, the premillennial position was held by the early church fathers.

a. Theologians who held it during the first century A.D.

   (1) Clement of Rome—40-100.
   (2) Ignatius—50-115.
   (3) Polycarp—70-167.
   b. Theologians who held it during the second century A.D.
      (1) Justin Martyr—100-168.
      (2) Irenaeus—140-202.
      (3) Tertullian—150-200.
   c. Theologians who held it during the third century A.D.
      (1) Cyprian—200-258.
      (2) Commodianus—250-.
          Beginning in the fourth century, however, the Roman Catholic Church began to grow and premillennialism began to wither, for Rome viewed herself as God's instrument to usher in the promised kingdom of glory. For centuries the precious doctrine of premillennialism was lost except to a few groups.
          But in the past few hundred years God has graciously revived premillennialism and restored it to its proper place, using men like Alford, Seiss, Darby, and C. I. Scofield.
B. The purpose of the millennium.
   1. To reward the saints of God.
   Verily there is a reward for the righteous . . . (Ps. 58:11).
   . . . to him that soweth righteousness shall be a sure reward (Prov. 11:18).
   Behold, the Lord God will come with strong hand, and his arm shall rule for him: behold, his reward is with him . . . (Isa. 40:10).
   Rejoice, and be exceeding glad: for great is your reward in heaven . . . (Mt. 5:12).
   For the Son of man shall come in the glory of his Father with his angels; and then he shall reward every man according to his works (Mt. 16:27).
   Then shall the King say . . . Come, ye blessed of my Father, inherit the kingdom prepared for you from the foundation of the world (Mt. 25:34).
   Knowing that of the Lord ye shall receive the reward of the

inheritance . . . (Col. 3:24).
And behold, I come quickly; and my reward is with me . . .
(Rev. 22:12).
2. To answer the oft-prayed model prayer.
In Luke 11:1–4 and Matthew 6:9–13 our Lord, at the request of his disciples, suggested a pattern prayer to aid all believers in their praying. One of the guidelines was this: "Thy kingdom come"! Here the Savior was inviting his followers to pray for the millennium. Someday he will return to fulfill the untold millions of times these three little words have wafted their way to heaven by Christians: "Thy kingdom come."
3. To redeem creation.
In Genesis 3 God cursed nature because of Adam's sin. From that point on, man's paradise became a wilderness. The roses suddenly contained thorns, and the docile tiger became a hungry meat eater. But during the millennium all this will change. Paul describes the transformation for us in his epistle to the Romans:
For all creation is waiting patiently and hopefully for that future day when God will resurrect his children. For on that day thorns and thistles, sin, death, and decay—the things that overcame the world against its will at God's command—will all disappear, and the world around us will share in the glorious freedom from sin which God's children enjoy. For we know that even the things of nature, like animals and plants, suffer in sickness and death as they await this great event (Rom. 8:19–22, TLB).
4. To fulfill three important Old Testament covenants.
a. God promised Abraham two basic things:
(1) That his seed (Israel) would become a mighty nation (Gen. 12:1–3; 13:16; 15:5; 17:7; 22:17, 18).
(2) That his seed (Israel) would someday own Palestine forever (Gen. 12:7; 13:14, 15, 17; 15:7, 18–21; 17:8).
b. The Davidic Covenant (2 Chron. 13:5; 2 Sam. 7:12–16; 23:5).
Here the promise was threefold:

    (1) That from David would come an everlasting throne.

    (2) That from David would come an everlasting kingdom.

    (3) That from David would come an everlasting King.

In a very real sense many of the conditions within these first two covenants have already come to pass. For example, concerning the Abrahamic Covenant, God did form a mighty nation from Abraham and today approximately 25 percent of that nation lives in the Promised Land. Then, in the fullness of time, God sent a babe from the seed of David to rule over the seed of Abraham in the land. (See Lk. 1:30–33.) But a problem soon arose, for when the ruler from David presented himself, he was rejected by Abraham's seed (Lk. 23:18, 21; Jn. 19:15). Thus, a third covenant was needed which would bring to completion the blessings of the first two. This God will wondrously accomplish through the new covenant.

  c. The new covenant (Jer. 31:31–34; Isa. 42:6; Heb. 8:7–12).

This promise was also threefold:

    (1) That he would forgive their iniquity and forget their sin.

    (2) That he would give them new hearts.

    (3) That he would use Israel to reach and teach the Gentiles.

5. To prove a point.

This is the point: regardless of his environment or heredity, mankind apart from God's grace will inevitably fail. For example:

  a. The age of innocence ended with willful disobedience (Gen. 3).

  b. The age of conscience ended with universal corruption (Gen. 6).

  c. The age of human government ended with devil-worshiping at the Tower of Babel (Gen. 11).

d. The age of promise ended with God's people out of the Promised Land and enslaved in Egypt (Ex. 1).

e. The age of the law ended with the creatures killing their Creator (Mt. 27).

f. The age of the church will end with worldwide apostasy (1 Tim. 4).

g. The age of the tribulation will end with the battle of Armageddon (Rev. 19).

h. The age of the millennium will end with an attempt to destroy God himself (Rev. 20).
(Note: Just where and how Satan will gather this unsaved human army at the end of the millennium will be discussed later.)

Dr. J. Dwight Pentecost writes:

"The millennial age is designed by God to be the final test of fallen humanity under the most ideal circumstances, surrounded by every enablement to obey the rule of the king, from whom the outward sources of temptation have been removed, so that man may be found and proved to be a failure in even this last testing of fallen humanity" (*Things to Come*, Dunham Press, 1959, p. 538).

6. To fulfill the main burden of biblical prophecy.
All Bible prophecy concerning the Lord Jesus Christ is summarized in one tiny verse by the Apostle Peter: ". . . the sufferings of Christ, and the glory that should follow" (1 Pet. 1:11).

Here Peter connects Christ's first coming (the sufferings) with his Second Coming (the glory). This in a nutshell is a panorama of the purpose, plan, and program of Almighty Jehovah God. Note this beautiful outline as we trace it through the Word of God:

a. The sufferings—a Baby, wrapped in swaddling clothes (Lk 2:12).
The glory—a King, clothed in majestic apparel (Ps. 93:1).

b. The sufferings—he was the wearied traveler (Jn. 4:6).
The glory—he will be the untiring God (Isa. 40:28, 29).

c. The sufferings—he had nowhere to lay his head (Lk. 9:58).

242

The glory—he will become heir to all things (Heb. 1:2).

d. The sufferings—he was rejected by tiny Israel (Jn. 1:11).

The glory—he will be accepted by all the nations (Isa. 9:6).

e. The sufferings—wicked men took up stones to throw at him (Jn. 8:59).

The glory—wicked men will cry for stones to fall upon them to hide them from him (Rev. 6:16).

f. The sufferings—a lowly Savior, acquainted with grief (Isa. 53:3).

The glory—the mighty God, anointed with the oil of gladness (Heb. 1:9).

g. The sufferings—he was clothed with a scarlet robe in mockery (Lk. 23:11).

The glory—he will be clothed with a vesture dipped in the blood of his enemies (Rev. 19:13).

h. The sufferings—he was smitten with a reed (Mt. 27:30).

The glory—he will rule the nations with a rod of iron (Rev. 19:15).

i. The sufferings—wicked soldiers bowed their knee and mocked (Mk. 15:19).

The glory—every knee shall bow and acknowledge him (Phil. 2:10).

j. The sufferings—he wore a crown of thorns (Jn. 19:5).

The glory—he will wear a crown of gold (Rev. 14:14).

k. The sufferings—his hands were pierced with nails (Jn. 20:25).

The glory—his hands will carry a sharp sickle (Rev. 14:14).

l. The sufferings—his feet were pierced with nails (Ps. 22:16).

The glory—his feet will stand on the Mount of Olives (Zech. 14:4).

m. The sufferings—he had no form or comeliness (Isa. 53:2).

The glory—he will be the fairest of ten thousand (Ps. 27:4).

n. The sufferings—he delivered up his spirit (Jn. 19:30).
The glory—he is alive forevermore (Rev. 1:18).
o. The sufferings—he was laid in the tomb (Mt. 27:59, 60).
The glory—he will sit on his throne (Heb. 8:1).

Here, then, is the "suffering-glory story" of the Savior. Furthermore, when a sinner repents and becomes a part of the body of Christ, he too shares in this destiny. Note the following:

For I reckon that the sufferings of this present time are not worthy to be compared with the glory which shall be revealed in us (Rom. 8:18).

And our hope of you is steadfast, knowing, that as ye are partakers of the sufferings, so shall ye be also of the consolation (2 Cor. 1:7).

If we suffer, we shall also reign with him . . . (2 Tim. 2:12).

Beloved, think it not strange concerning the fiery trial which is to try you, as though some strange thing happened unto you: But rejoice, inasmuch as ye are partakers of Christ's sufferings; that, when his glory shall be revealed, ye may be glad also with exceeding joy (1 Pet. 4:12, 13).

The elders which are among you I exhort, who am also an elder, and a witness of the sufferings of Christ, and also a partaker of the glory that shall be revealed (1 Pet. 5:1).

C. The titles of the millennium.
1. The world to come (Heb. 2:5).
2. The kingdom of heaven (Mt. 5:10).
3. The kingdom of God (Mk. 1:14).
4. The last day (Jn. 6:40).
5. The regeneration (Mt. 19:28).

And Jesus said unto them, Verily I say unto you, That ye which have followed me, in the regeneration when the Son of man shall sit in the throne of his glory, ye also shall sit upon twelve thrones, judging the twelve tribes of Israel (Mt. 19:28).

The word "regeneration" is found only twice in the English Bible, here and in Titus 3:5, where Paul is speaking of the believer's new birth. The word literally means "re-creation." Thus the millennium will be to the earth what salvation is to the sinner.

6. The times of refreshing (Acts 3:19).
7. The restitution of all things (Acts 3:21).
8. The day of Christ. This is by far the most common biblical name for the millennium. See 1 Corinthians 1:8; 5:5; 2 Corinthians 1:14; Philippians 1:6; 2:16.

Thus, during the millennium our blessed Lord will have the opportunity to exercise his rightful and eternal fourfold sonship.

His *racial* sonship—Son of Abraham (Gen. 17:8; Mt. 1:1; Gal. 3:16).

His *royal* sonship—Son of David (Isa. 9:7; Mt. 1:1; Lk. 1:32, 33).

His *human* sonship—Son of Man (Jn. 5:27; Acts 1:11).

His *divine* sonship—Son of God (Isa. 66:15-8, 23; 41:10, 17, 18; Ps. 46:1, 5; 86:9; Zech. 14:16-19).

D. Old Testament examples of the millennium.
  1. The Sabbath.
     This word literally means "rest." In Old Testament times God wisely set aside a Sabbath or rest time after a period of activity.
     A rest was to be observed:
     a. After six workdays (Ex. 20:8-11; Lev. 23:3).
     b. After six work weeks (Lev. 23:15, 16).
     c. After six work months (Lev. 23:24, 25, 27, 34).
     d. After six work years (Lev. 25:2-5).
  2. The jubilee year (Lev. 25:10-12).
  3. The tabernacle—because God's glory dwelt in the Holy of Holies (Ex. 25:8; 29:42-46; 40:34).
  4. The feast of tabernacles (Lev. 23:34-42).
  5. The Promised Land (Deut. 6:3; Heb. 4:8-10).
  6. The reign of Solomon.
     a. Because of the vastness of his kingdom (1 Ki. 4:21).
     b. Because of its security (1 Ki. 4:25).
     c. Because of his great wisdom (1 Ki. 4:29, 34).
     d. Because of the fame of his kingdom (1 Ki. 10:7).
     e. Because of the riches of his kingdom (1 Ki. 10:27).
E. The nature of the millennium.

What will the thousand-year reign of Christ be like? Dr. J. Dwight Pentecost has compiled the following extended and impressive facts:

1. *Peace*. The cessation of war through the unification of the kingdoms of the world under the reign of Christ, together with the resultant economic prosperity (since nations need not devote vast proportions of their expenditure on munitions) is a major theme of the prophets. National and individual peace is the fruit of Messiah's reign (Isa. 2:4; 9:4-7; 11:6-9; 32:17, 18; 33:5, 6; 54:13; 55:12; 60:18; 65:25; 66:12; Ezek. 28:26; 34:25, 28; Hos. 2:18; Micah 4:2, 3; Zech. 9:10).

2. *Joy*. The fullness of joy will be a distinctive mark of the age (Isa. 9:3, 4; 12:3-6; 14:7, 8; 25:8, 9; 30:29; 42:1, 10-12; 52:9; 60:15; 61:7, 10; 65:18, 19; 66:10-14; Jer. 30:18, 19; 31:13, 14; Zeph. 3:14-17; Zech. 8:18, 19; 10:6, 7).

3. *Holiness*. The theocratic kingdom will be a holy kingdom, in which holiness is manifested through the King and the King's subjects. The land will be holy, the city holy, the temple holy, and the subjects holy unto the Lord (Isa. 1:26, 27; 4:3, 4; 29:18-23; 31:6, 7; 35:8, 9; 52:1; 60:21; 61:10; Jer. 31:23; Ezek. 36:24-31; 37:23, 24; 43:7-12; 45:1; Joel 3:21; Zeph. 3:11, 13; Zech. 8:3; 13:1, 2; 14:20, 21).

4. *Glory*. The kingdom will be a glorious kingdom, in which the glory of God will find full manifestation (Isa. 4:2; 24:34; 35:2; 40:5; 60:1-9).

5. *Comfort*. The King will personally minister to every need, so that there will be the fullness of comfort in that day (Isa. 12:1, 2; 29:22, 23; 30:26; 40:1, 2; 49:13; 51:3; 61:3-7; 66:13, 14; Jer. 31:23-25; Zeph. 3:18-20; Zech. 9:11, 12; Rev. 21:4).

6. *Justice*. There will be the administration of perfect justice to every individual (Isa. 9:7; 11:5; 32:16; 42:1-4; 65:21-23; Jer. 23:5; 31:23; 31:29, 30).

7. *Full knowledge*. The ministry of the King will bring the subjects of his kingdom into full knowledge. Doubtless there will be an unparalleled teaching ministry of the

Holy Spirit (Isa. 11:1, 2, 9; 41:19, 20; 54:13; Hab. 2:14).

8. *Instruction.* This knowledge will come about through the instruction that issues from the King (Isa. 2:2, 3; 12:3-6; 25:9; 29:17-24; 30:20, 21; 32:3, 4; 49:10; 52:8; Jer. 3:14, 15; 23:1-4; Micah 4:2).

9. *The removal of the curse.* The original curse placed upon creation (Gen. 3:17-19) will be removed, so that there will be abundant productivity to the earth. Animal creation will be changed so as to lose its venom and ferocity (Isa. 11:6-9; 35:9; 65:25).

10. *Sickness removed.* The ministry of the King as a healer will be seen throughout the age, so that sickness and even death, except as a penal measure in dealing with overt sin, will be removed (Isa. 33:24; Jer. 30:17; Ezek. 34:16).

11. *Healing of the deformed.* Accompanying this ministry will be the healing of all deformity at the inception of the millennium (Isa. 29:17-19; 35:3-6; 61:1, 2; Jer. 31:8; Micah 4:6, 7; Zeph. 3:19).

12. *Protection.* There will be a supernatural work of preservation of life in the millennial age through the King (Isa. 41:8-14; 62:8, 9; Jer. 32:27; 23:6; Ezek. 34:27; Joel 3:16, 17; Amos 9:15; Zech. 8:14, 15; 9:8; 14:10, 11).

13. *Freedom from oppression.* There will be no social, political, or religious oppression in that day (Isa. 14:3-6; 42:6, 7; 49:8, 9; Zech. 9:11, 12).

14. *No immaturity.* The suggestion seems to be that there will not be the tragedies of feeble-mindedness nor of dwarfed bodies in that day (Isa. 65:20). Longevity will be restored.

15. *Reproduction by the living people.* The living saints who go into the millennium in their natural bodies will beget children throughout the age. The earth's population will soar. These born in the age will not be born without a sin nature, so salvation will be required (Jer. 30:20; 31:29; Ezek. 47:22; Zech. 10:8).

16. *Labor.* The period will not be characterized by idleness, but there will be a perfect economic system, in which the needs of men are abundantly provided for by labor in that system, under the guidance of the King. There will

be a fully developed industrialized society, providing for the needs of the King's subjects (Isa. 62:8, 9; 65:21–23; Jer. 31:5; Ezek. 48:18, 19). Agriculture as well as manufacturing will provide employment.

17. *Economic prosperity.* The perfect labor situation will produce economic abundance, so that there will be no want (Isa. 4:1; 35:1, 2, 7; 30:23–25; 62:8, 9; 65:21–23; Jer. 31:5, 12; Ezek. 34:26; 36:29, 30; Joel 2:21–27; Amos 9:13, 14; Micah 4:1, 4; Zech. 8:11, 12; 9:16, 17). Willard Cantelon writes:

"Some who studied the riches of earth estimated the combined value of the gold and silver, the grain and oil and timber, the fish and fruit and minerals, etc., at one decillion dollars! This figure of course, was beyond my comprehension, but slowly I repeated, 'million, billion, trillion, quadrillion, quintillion, sextillion, septillion, octillion, novillion, decillion'! Taking pen and paper, I divided the four billion of earth's population into this figure, and saw that everyone would be a billionaire, if he shared such wealth! The Psalmist said: 'the earth is full of thy riches!' (Ps. 104:24)" (*Money Master of the World*, Logos Press, 1976, p. 137).

18. *Increase of light.* There will be an increase of solar and lunar light in the age. This increased light probably is a major cause in the increased productivity of the earth (Isa. 4:5; 30:26; 60:19, 20; Zech. 2:5).

19. *Unified language.* The language barriers will be removed so that there can be free social interchange (Zeph. 3:9).

20. *Unified worship.* All the world will unite in the worship of God and God's Messiah (Isa. 45:23; 52:1, 7–10; 66:17–23; Zeph. 3:9; Zech. 13:2; 14:16; 8:23; 9:7; Mal. 1:11; Rev. 5:9–14).

21. *The manifest presence of God.* God's presence will be fully recognized and fellowship with God will be experienced to an unprecedented degree (Ezek. 37:27, 28; Zech. 2:2, 10–13; Rev. 21:3).

22. *The fullness of the Spirit.* Divine presence and enablement

will be the experience of all who are in subjection to the authority of the King (Isa. 32:13-15; 41:1; 44:3; 59:19, 21; 61:1; Ezek. 11:19, 20; 36:26, 27; 37:14; 39:29; Joel 2:28, 29).

23. *The perpetuity of the millennial state.* That which characterizes the millennial age is not viewed as temporary, but eternal (Isa. 51:6-8; 55:3, 13; 56:5; 60:19, 20; 61:8; Jer. 32:40; Ezek. 16:60; 37:26-28; 43:7-9; Dan. 9:24; Hos. 2:19-23; Joel 3:20; Amos 9:15) (*Things to Come,* Dunham Press, 1959, pp. 487-490).

F. The citizens of the millennium.
  1. Considered negatively.
     No unsaved persons will enter the millennium (Isa. 35; Jer. 31:33, 34; Ezek. 20:37, 38; Zech. 13:9; Mt. 18:3; 25:30, 46; Jn. 3:3). However millions of babies will evidently be reared in the millennium. They will be born of saved but mortal Israelite and Gentile parents who survived the tribulation and entered the millennium in that state of mortality (thus the possible reason for the tree of life in Rev. 22:2). As they mature, some of these babies will refuse to submit their hearts to the new birth, though their outward acts will be subjected to existing authority. Thus Christ will rule with a rod of iron (Rev. 2:27; 12:5; 19:15; Zech. 14:17-19).

     Dr. Rene Pache writes concerning this:

     "As beautiful as the Millennium is, it will not be heaven. . . . Sin will still be possible during the thousand years (Isa. 11:4; 65:20). Certain families and certain nations will refuse to go up to Jerusalem to worship the Lord (Zech. 14:17-19). Such deeds will be all the more inexcusable because the tempter will be absent and because the revelations of the Lord will be greater. . . . Those who have been thus smitten will serve as examples to all those who would be tempted to imitate them (Isa. 66:24)" (*The Return of Jesus Christ,* Moody Press, 1955, pp. 428, 429).

  2. Considered positively.
     a. Saved Israel.

      (1) Israel will once again be related to God by
           marriage (Isa. 54:1–17; 62:2–5; Hos. 2:14–23).
      (2) Israel will be exalted above the Gentiles (Isa.
           14:1, 2; 49:22, 23; 60:14–17; 61:6, 7).
      (3) Israel will become God's witness during the
           millennium (Isa. 44:8; 61:6; 66:21; Jer.
           16:19–21; Micah 5:7; Zeph. 3:20; Zech. 4:1–7;
           8:3).
    b. Saved Old Testament and tribulation Gentiles (Rev.
      5:9, 10; Isa. 2:4; 11:12).
    c. The church (1 Cor. 6:2; 2 Tim. 2:12; Rev. 1:6; 2:26,
      27; 3:21).
    d. The elect angels (Heb. 12:22).
G. The King of the millennium.

The Lord Jesus Christ will of course be King supreme, but
there are passages which suggest that he will graciously choose
to rule through a vice-regent, and that vice-regent will be
David! Note the following Scripture:
But they shall serve the Lord their God, and David their king,
whom I will raise up unto them (Jer. 30:9).

    Jeremiah wrote these words some 400 years after the death
of David, so he could not have been referring to his earthly
reign here. "And I will set up one shepherd over them, and
he shall feed them, even my servant David; he shall feed
them, and he shall be their shepherd" (Ezek. 34:23). See also
Ezekiel 37:24.
Afterward shall the children of Israel return, and seek the Lord
their God, and David their king; and shall fear the Lord and his
goodness in the latter days (Hos. 3:5).

    If we take these passages literally, David will once again sit
upon the throne of Israel. He will thus be aided in his rule
by:
  1. The church (1 Cor. 6:3).
  2. The apostles (Mt. 19:28).
  3. Nobles (Jer. 30:21).
  4. Princes (Isa. 32:1; Ezek. 45:8, 9).
  5. Judges (Zech. 3:7; Isa. 1:26).
  G. Peters writes:

". . . some writers . . . endeavor to make the Theocracy a
Republic, but the Theocracy, in the nature of the case, is not

a republic. While it is not a monarchy in the sense adverted to by Samuel, viz.: of a purely human origin, yet it is a monarchy in the highest sense. It is not a Republic, for the legislative, executive, and judicial power is not potentially lodged in the people, but in God the King; and yet it embraces in itself the elements both of a Monarchy and of a Republic; a Monarchy in that the absolute Sovereignty is lodged in the person of the One great King, to which all the rest are subordinated, but Republican in this, that it embraces a Republican element in preserving the rights of every individual, from the lowest to the highest. . . . In other words, by a happy combination, Monarchy under divine direction, hence infallible, brings in the blessings that would result from a well-directed ideally Republican form of government, but which the latter can never fully, of itself, realize owing to the depravity and diversity of man" (*Theocratic Kingdom*, Vol. I, p. 221).

H. The geography of the millennium.
　　1. Palestine.
　　　　a. To be greatly enlarged and changed (Isa. 26:15; Obad. 1:17-21). For the first time Israel will possess all the land promised to Abraham in Genesis 15:18-21.
　　　　b. A great fertile plain to replace the mountainous terrain.
　　　　c. A river to flow east-west from the Mount of Olives into both the Mediterranean and the Dead Seas. The following passages from *The Living Bible* bear this out:
　　　　　　. . . *The Mount of Olives will split apart, making a very wide valley running from east to west, for half the mountain will move toward the north and half toward the south. . . . Life-giving waters will flow out from Jerusalem, half toward the Dead Sea and half toward the Mediterranean, flowing continuously both in winter and in summer. . . . All the land from Geba (the northern border of Judah) to Rimmon (the southern border) will become one vast plain . . .*" (Zech. 14:4, 8, 10).
　　　　　　Sweet wine will drip from the mountains, and the hills shall flow with milk. Water will fill the dry stream beds of Judah, and a fountain will burst forth

from the Temple of the Lord to water Acacia Valley
(Joel 3:18).

He told me: *"This river flows east through the desert
and the Jordan Valley to the Dead Sea, where it will heal
the salty waters and make them fresh and pure. Everything
touching the water of this river shall live. Fish will abound
in the Dead Sea, for its waters will be healed. . . . All
kinds of fruit trees will grow along the river banks. The
leaves will never turn brown and fall, and there will
always be fruit. There will be a new crop every month—
without fail! For they are watered by the river flowing from
the Temple. The fruit will be for food and the leaves for
medicine"* (Ezek. 47:8, 9, 12).

2. Jerusalem.
   a. The city will become the worship center of the world.
   *But in the last days Mount Zion will be the most renowned
   of all the mountains of the world, praised by all nations;
   people from all over the world will make pilgrimages there*
   (Micah 4:1, TLB).

   In the last days Jerusalem and the Temple of the Lord
   will become the world's greatest attraction, and people from
   many lands will flow there to worship the Lord. "Come,"
   everyone will say, "let us go up the mountain of the Lord,
   to the Temple of the God of Israel; there he will teach us
   his laws, and we will obey them." For in those days the
   world will be ruled from Jerusalem (Isa. 2:2, 3, TLB).
   b. The city will occupy an elevated site (Zech. 14:10).
   c. The city will be six miles in circumference (Ezek.
   48:35). (In the time of Christ the city was about four
   miles.)
   d. The city will be named "Jehovah-Shammah," meaning
   "the Lord is there" (Ezek. 48:35), and "Jehovah
   Isidkenu," meaning, "the Lord our righteousness"
   (Jer. 23:6; 33:16).
   These two will be the final names for God's beloved
   city. It has been called by many titles in the Bible.

   The city of David (2 Sam. 6:12).
   The city of the Great King (Mt. 5:35).
   The Holy City (Isa. 48:2; 51:1; Mt. 4:5).
   Salem (Gen. 14:18).

The city of God (Ps. 46:4; 48:1; 87:3).
The city of the Lord of Hosts (Ps. 48:8).
The city of righteousness (Isa. 1:26).
The city of truth (Zech. 8:3).
The city of the Lord (Isa. 60:14).
The perfection of beauty (Lam. 2:15).
The joy of the whole earth (Lam. 2:15).

I. The temple in the millennium.
　1. Its biblical order.
　　The millennial temple is the last of seven great scriptural temples. These are:
　　a. The tabernacle of Moses—Exodus 40 (1500–1000 B.C.).
　　b. The Temple of Solomon—1 Kings 8 (1000–586 B.C.).
　　c. The Temple of Zerubbabel (rebuilt later by Herod)—Ezra 6; John 2 (516 B.C. to A.D. 70).
　　d. The temple of the body of Jesus—John 2:21 (4 B.C. to A.D. 30).
　　e. The spiritual temple, the church—Acts 2; 1 Thessalonians 4 (from Pentecost till the rapture).
　　　(1) The whole church (Eph. 2:21).
　　　(2) The local church (1 Cor. 3:16, 17).
　　　(3) The individual Christian (1 Cor. 6:19).
　　f. The tribulational temple—Revelation 11 (from the rapture till Armageddon).
　　g. The millennial temple—Isaiah 2:3; 60:13; Ezekiel 40–48; Daniel 9:24; Joel 3:18, Haggai 2:7, 9.
　2. Its holy oblation.
　　Palestine will be redistributed among the twelve tribes of Israel during the millennium. The land itself will be divided into three areas. Seven tribes will occupy the northern area and five the southern ground. Between these two areas there is a section called "the holy oblation," that is, that portion of ground which is set apart for the Lord. Dr. J. Dwight Pentecost quotes Merrill F. Unger on this:

　　"The holy oblation would be a spacious square, thirty-four miles each way, containing about 1160 square miles. This area would be the center of all the interests of the divine government and worship as set up in

the Millennial earth. . . . The temple itself would be
located in the middle of this square (the holy oblation)
and not in the City of Jerusalem, upon a very high
mountain, which will be miraculously made ready for
that purpose when the temple is to be erected (see
Isa. 2:4; Micah 4:1–4; Ezek. 37:26)" (*Things to Come*,
Dunham Press, 1959, p. 510).

3. Its priesthood.
On four specific occasions we are told that the sons of
Zadok will be assigned the priestly duties (Ezek. 40:46;
43:19; 44:15; 48:11). Zadok was a high priest in David's
time (the eleventh in descent from Aaron). His loyalty to
the king was unwavering. Because of this, he was
promised that his seed would have this glorious
opportunity (1 Sam. 2:35; 1 Ki. 2:27, 35).

4. Its prince.
In his description of the Temple, Ezekiel refers to a
mysterious "prince" some seventeen times. Whoever he
is, he occupies a very important role in the temple itself,
apparently holding an intermediary place between the
people and the priesthood. We are sure that he is not
Christ, since he prepares a sin offering for himself (Ezek.
45:22), and is married and has sons (Ezek. 46:16). Some
suggest that the prince is from the seed of King David,
and that he will be to David what the false prophet was
to the antichrist.

5. Its negative aspects.
Several articles and objects present in the temples of
Moses, Solomon, and Herod will be absent from the
millennial temple.
a. There will be no veil.
This was torn in two from top to bottom (Mt. 27:51)
and will not reappear in this temple. Thus there will
be no barrier to keep man from the glory of God.
b. There will be no table of shewbread.
This will not be needed, for the living Bread himself
will be present.
c. There will be no lampstands.
These will not be needed either, since the Light of the

world himself will personally shine forth.
d. There will be no Ark of the Covenant.
This will also be unnecessary, since the Shekinah
Glory himself will hover over all the world, as the
glory cloud once did over the ark.
e. The east gate will be closed.
Observe the words of Ezekiel: "This gate shall be
shut, and no man shall enter in by it; because the
Lord, the God of Israel, hath entered in by it,
therefore it shall be shut" (Ezek. 44:2). This gate, it
has been suggested, will remain closed for the
following reasons:

(1) This will be the gate by which the Lord Jesus
Christ enters the temple. As a mark of honor to
an eastern king, no person could enter the gate
by which the king entered.

(2) It was from the eastern gate that the glory of
God departed for the last time in the Old
Testament (Ezek. 10:18, 19).

By sealing the gate, God reminds all those within
that his glory will never again depart from his people.
A history of this gate makes interesting reading:
It is both the most famous and important of
Jerusalem's gates. It overlooks the Kidron Valley
and faces the rising sun. The crusaders called it the
Golden Gate. Entrance through this walled gate leads
to the Beautiful Gate of the temple itself; see Acts 3:2.
Tradition says sections of this gate were donated by
the Queen of Sheba. The Arabs call this the Eternal
Gate and, since it is a double gate, they call the
northern portal the Gate of Repentance, and the
southern portal, the Gate of Mercy. It is
mentioned by Nehemiah (3:29).
The glory cloud of God departed through this
gate in Ezekiel's day (Ezek. 10:19). The glory cloud
of God will return through this gate in the millennium
(Ezek. 42:15; 43:4). It will then be forever closed
(Ezek. 44:13). Christ rode through this gate on Palm
Sunday. The present gate was built around A.D. 560.
The "true cross" was recovered from the Persians and

brought through here in A.D. 629. In the year
A.D. 810, for fear that a great Christian conqueror
would enter this way, the Arabs closed the gate and
sealed it with solid masonry. It was reopened again in
1102 by the crusaders. The Arabs resealed it in 1187.
Moslems believe that one day a great Christian
conqueror (perhaps Christ himself) will enter Jerusalem
through this gate and rule the world from here.

6. Its sacrifices.

As we have already seen, several pieces of furniture in
the Old Testament Temple will be missing in the
millennial edifice. However, the brazen altar of sacrifice
will again be present. There are at least four Old
Testament prophecies which speak of animal sacrifices in
the millennial temple: Isaiah 56:6, 7; 60:7; Jeremiah
33:10; Zechariah 14:16–21. But why the need of these
animal blood sacrifices during the golden age of the
millennium?

To answer this, one must attempt to project himself
into this fabulous future period. Here is an age of no sin,
sorrow, sufferings, sickness, Satan, or separation. During
the millennium even the vocabulary will be different. For
example, today respectable and decent society shuns
certain filthy four-letter words, and well they should!

This will doubtless also be practiced during the
millennium, but how the words will change. Below is a
sampling of some four-letter "cuss words" to be shunned
during the thousand-year reign:

fear
pain
jail
hate
dope

These words are so much a part of our sinful society
that it is utterly impossible to avoid or ignore them! The
point is simply this: during the millennium millions of
children will be born and reared by saved Israelite and
Gentile parents who survived the tribulation. In spite of

their perfect environment, however, these "kingdom kids" will need the new birth. As sons and daughters of Adam they, too, as all others, will require eternal salvation (Rom. 3:23; Jn. 3:3). But how can these children be reached? What object lessons can be used? Here is a generation which will grow up without knowing fear, experiencing pain, witnessing hatred, taking dope, or seeing a jail. This is one reason that the sacrificial system will be reinstituted during the millennium. These sacrifices will function as

a. A reminder to all of the necessity of the new birth.
b. An object lesson of the costliness of salvation.
c. An example of the awfulness of sin.
d. An illustration of the holiness of God.

Imagine the following conversation in the millennial temple as a group of school children from Berlin visit the Holy City and witness the slaying of a lamb.

Kurt: Sir, why did you kill that little lamb?

Priest: Because the sin in our hearts must be paid for by innocent blood.

Kurt: Oh, then did that lamb die to pay for my sin?

Priest: No, Kurt, it is simply a reminder that God's Lamb did once die for all our sins!

Kurt: Why, I didn't know God ever had a lamb. Whatever happened to God's lamb?

Priest: Kurt, you've already seen God's Lamb!

Kurt: When did we see God's lamb? I don't remember seeing God's lamb.

Priest: OK, let me ask you a question. What did your group do this morning?

Kurt: Oh, we had a wonderful time! We visited the palace and saw Prince Immanuel, King Jesus himself!

Priest: (Slowly, with great emphasis) then, Kurt, you saw God's Lamb!

Can you imagine the eyes of those German children bulging and their small chins dropping in amazement as they are told this tremendous fact? This is perhaps the Father's most precious secret: that his blessed Son, the mighty Monarch of the millennium, once came as the lowly Lamb of Bethlehem!

TWELVE
THE FINAL REVOLT
OF SATAN

And when the thousand years are expired, Satan shall be loosed out of his prison, and shall go out to deceive the nations which are in the four quarters of the earth, Gog and Magog, to gather them together to battle, the number of whom is as the sand of the sea. And they went up on the breadth of the earth, and compassed the camp of the saints about, and the beloved city . . . (Rev. 20:7–9).

Dr. J. Vernon McGee writes the following words concerning these verses:

"When the late Dr. Chafer (founder of Dallas Theological Seminary) was once asked why God loosed Satan after he once had him bound, he replied, 'If you will tell me why God let him loose in the first place, I will tell you why God lets him loose the second time.' Apparently Satan is released at the end of the Millennium to reveal that the ideal conditions of the kingdom, under the personal reign of Christ, do not change the human heart. This reveals the enormity of the enmity of man against God. Scripture is accurate when it describes the heart as 'desperately wicked' and incurably so. Man is totally depraved. The loosing of Satan at the end of the 1000 years proves it" (*Reveling Through Revelation*, pp. 74, 75).

We have already discussed the purposes accomplished by the sacrifices during the millennium. Apparently millions of maturing children will view these sacrifices and hear the tender salvation plea of the priests, but will stubbornly harden their sinful hearts. The fact that earth's mighty King at Jerusalem once bled as a lowly lamb at Calvary will mean absolutely nothing to them! Outwardly they will conform, but inwardly they will despise.

Finally, at the end of the millennium, the world will be offered for the first time in ten centuries "a choice, and not an echo." Millions will make a foolish and fatal choice.

Dr. J. Dwight Pentecost quotes F. C. Jennings, who writes:

"Has human nature changed, at least apart from sovereign grace? Is the carnal mind at last in friendship with God? Have a thousand years of absolute power and absolute benevolence, both in unchecked activity, done away with all war forever and forever? These questions must be marked by a practical test. Let Satan be loosed once more from his prison. Let him range once more earth's smiling fields that he knew of old. He saw them last soaked with blood and flooded with tears, the evidence and accompaniments of his own reign; he sees them now 'laughing with abundance.' . . . But as he pursues his way further from Jerusalem, the center of this blessedness, these tokens become fainter, until, in the faroff 'corner of the earth,' they cease altogether, for he finds myriads who have instinctively shrunk from close contact with that holy center, and are not unprepared once more to be deceived" (Things to Come, Dunham Press, 1959, p. 549).

However, this insane and immoral insurrection is doomed to utter and complete failure. As a war correspondent, the Apostle John duly records this final battle:
. . . and fire came down from God out of heaven, and devoured them. And the devil that deceived them was cast into the lake of fire and brimstone, where the beast and the false prophet are, and shall be tormented day and night for ever and ever (Rev. 20:9, 10).

Obviously, this battle referred to as Gog and Magog, is not the same as the one in Ezekiel 38 and 39. Dr. J. Vernon McGee writes concerning this:

"Because the rebellion is labeled 'Gog and Magog,' many Bible students identify it with Gog and Magog of Ezekiel 38 and 39. This, of course, is not possible, for the conflicts described are not parallel as to time, place, or participants—only the name is the same. The invasion from the north by Gog and Magog of Ezekiel 38 and 39 breaks the false peace of the Antichrist and causes him to show his hand in the midst of the Great Tribulation. That rebellion of the godless forces from the north will have made such an impression on mankind that after 1000 years the last rebellion of man bears the same label. We have passed through a similar situation in this century. World War I was so devastating that when war again broke out in Europe, it was labeled again 'World War,' but differentiated by the number 2. Now World War III is being predicted! Likewise the war in Ezekiel 38 and 39 is Gog and Magog I, while this reference in verse 8 is Gog and Magog II" (*Reveling Through Revelation*, p. 77).

THIRTEEN
THE GREAT WHITE THRONE JUDGMENT

A. The fact of this throne (Heb. 9:27).

And I saw a great white throne, and him that sat on it, from whose face the earth and the heaven fled away; and there was found no place for them. I saw the dead, small and great, stand before God; and the books were opened: and another book was opened, which is the book of life: and the dead were judged out of those things which were written in the books, according to their works. And the sea gave up the dead which were in it; and death and hell delivered up the dead which were in them: and they were judged every man according to their works. And death and hell were cast into the lake of fire. This is the second death. And whosoever was not found written in the book of life was cast into the lake of fire (Rev. 20:11-15).

I beheld till the thrones were cast down, and the Ancient of days did sit, whose garment was white as snow, and the hair of his head like the pure wool: his throne was like the fiery flame, and his wheels as burning fire. A fiery stream issued and came forth from before him: thousand thousands ministered unto him, and ten thousand times ten thousand stood before him: the judgment was set, and the books were opened (Dan. 7:9, 10).

B. The Judge of this throne—Christ himself!

For the Father judgeth no man, but hath committed all judgment

261

unto the Son . . . and hath given him authority to execute judgment also, because he is the Son of man (Jn. 5:22, 27).

Him God raised up the third day, and showed him openly. . . . And he commanded us to preach unto the people, and to testify that it is he which was ordained of God to be the Judge of quick and dead (Acts 10:40, 42).

I charge thee therefore bre God, and the Lord Jesus Christ, who shall judge the quick and the dead at his appearing and his kingdom . . . (2 Tim. 4:1).

C. The jury at this throne—five sets of books.

    1. The book of conscience (Rom. 2:15).

        Although man's conscience is not an infallible guide, he will nevertheless be condemned by those occasions when he deliberately violated it.

    2. The book of words (Mt. 12:36, 37).

        But I say unto you that every idle word that men shall speak, they shall give account thereof in the day of judgment. For by thy words thou shalt be justified, and by thy words thou shalt be condemned.

        He that rejecteth me, and receiveth not my words, hath one that judgeth him: the word that I have spoken, the same shall judge him in the last day (Jn. 12:48).

    3. The book of secret works.

        God shall judge the secrets of men by Jesus Christ (Rom. 2:16).

        For God shall bring every work into judgment, with every secret thing, whether it be good, or whether it be evil (Eccles. 12:14).

    4. The book of public works.

        For the Son of man shall come in the glory of his Father with his angels; and then he shall reward every man according to his works (Mt. 16:27).

        . . . whose end shall be according to their works (2 Cor. 11:15).

    5. The book of life.

        (See Ex. 32:32, 33; Ps. 69:28; Dan. 12:1; Phil. 4:3; Rev. 3:5; 13:8; 17:8; 20:12, 15; 21:27; 22:19.)

D. The judged at this throne.

As has previously been discussed (see notes under "The

Judgment Seat of Christ"), only unsaved people will stand before this throne.

The wicked shall be turned into hell, and all the nations that forget God (Ps. 9:17).

E. The judgment at this throne.

The eternal lake of fire (Rev. 20:14, 15; Mt. 25:41, 46).

FOURTEEN
THE DESTRUCTION
OF THIS PRESENT
EARTH AND
HEAVENS

A. The fact of this destruction.

Heaven and earth shall pass away, but my words shall not pass away (Mt. 24:35).

Thou, Lord, in the beginning hast laid the foundation of the earth; and the heavens are the works of thine hands: They shall perish; but thou remainest; and they all shall wax old as doth a garment; and as a vesture shalt thou fold them up, and they shall be changed: but thou art the same, and thy years shall not fail (Heb. 1:10–12).

But the day of the Lord will come as a thief in the night; in the which the heavens shall pass away with a great noise, and the elements shall melt with fervent heat, the earth also and the works that are therein shall be burned up (2 Pet. 3:10, 11).

B. The reason for this destruction.

At this stage in the Bible the final rebellion has been put down, the false prophet, the antichrist, and the devil himself are all in the lake of fire forever, and the wicked dead have been judged. In light of this, why the necessity for this awesome destruction?

To help illustrate, consider the following: let us suppose that some crackpot breaks into the money vaults of Fort Knox, Kentucky, and begins pouring filthy crankcase oil on the stacked bars of gold and silver. Upon leaving, however, he is caught, tried, and confined to prison. The authorities thereupon close their books on the Fort Knox case. But the gunk on the gold remains! In this illlustration, the vandal would represent the devil, the crankcase oil would stand for sin, and the gold and silver for God's perfect creation. God will someday arrest the devil, of course, and forever confine him to prison. But what about the oily sin stains that remain on his gold and silver creation? To solve the problem, God does what the Fort Knox authorities might consider doing— he purges the stains in a fiery wash. And it works. For the hotter the flame, the more rapidly the oil evaporates, and the brighter the gold becomes!

God will someday do to creation what he did to his beloved Israel in the Old Testament:

Behold, I have refined thee . . . I have chosen thee in the furnace of affliction (Isa. 48:10).

FIFTEEN
THE NEW
CREATION OF
HEAVEN AND
EARTH

For, behold, I create new heavens and a new earth: and the former shall not be remembered, nor come into mind (Isa. 65:17).

For as the new heavens and the new earth, which I shall make, shall remain before me, saith the Lord, so shall your seed and your name remain (Isa. 66:22).

Nevertheless we, according to his promise, look for new heavens and a new earth, wherein dwelleth righteousness (2 Pet. 3:13).

And I saw a new heaven and a new earth: for the first heaven and the first earth were passed away; and there was no more sea (Rev. 21:1).

SIXTEEN
THE FINAL DESTINY
OF MAN

An epitaph on a gravestone once read:

Remember friend as you pass by,
As you are now, so once was I.
As I am now thus you must be.
So be prepared to follow me.

Found beneath these inscribed words on the grave-marker
were the following two lines, apparently added by a concerned
reader:

to follow you I'm not content,
until I know which way you went!

According to the Word of God, the person that once
inhabited the body in that tomb had only two ways to go. But
before discussing these two places, let us consider some false
views of man's eternal destiny.

A. False views.
   1. Nirvana: An oriental Hindu philosophy (which at certain
      periods in history has wormed its way into Christian
      thought), which teaches that at death a man ceases all
      personal existence and is absorbed by some great life-
      giving principle in the universe. According to this

thought, a man, while he lives, can be pictured as a small ripple, skimming the top of a mighty ocean. But when the wind stops (the moment of death), the wave is then received back into the ocean from whence it came, and forever loses its previous identity. This is refuted by Matthew 17:3; 1 Corinthians 15.

This belief in the transmigration or rebirth of the soul has been fundamental to most religions and philosophies of India. As one sows in the present life, so one shall reap in the next, good deeds resulting in a good state of rebirth, bad deeds in a bad state of rebirth. Thus a man's state of life is seen not as something fortuitous or meaningless but as the working out, for good or ill, of the effects of a previous existence and the predetermining of a future state. This theory is totally without scriptural support.

2. Materialism: Atheistic belief that man, like a weasel in the woods, upon death forever ceases to be and quietly rots into nothingness. This philosophy has been aptly described on an ancient tombstone which read: "I was not, I became, I am not, I care not." This is refuted by 1 Corinthians 15:50-57.

3. Annihilationism: This theory, espoused by the Jehovah's Witnesses, along with various other groups, teaches that all the ungodly will someday literally be "uncreated," or annihilated by God. It is refuted by:
And these shall go away into everlasting punishment: but the righteous into life eternal (Mt. 25:46).

And the third angel followed them, saying with a loud voice, If any man worship the beast and his image, and receive his mark in his forehead, or in his hand, the same shall drink of the wine of the wrath of God, which is poured out without mixture into the cup of his indignation; and he shall be tormented with fire and brimstone in the presence of the holy angels, and in the presence of the Lamb: And the smoke of their torment ascendeth up for ever and ever: and they have no rest day nor night, who worship the beast and his image, and whosoever receiveth the mark of his name (Rev. 14:9-11).

Those believing in annihilationism attempt to under-gird their claims by quoting certain verses in the Psalms:
For evildoers shall be cut off: but those that wait upon the Lord, they shall inherit the earth (Ps. 37:9).
The Lord preserveth all them that love him: but all the wicked will he destroy (Ps. 145:20).
Refuted by: The same Hebrew word *karath*, here translated "cut off" in Psalm 37:9, is also used in reference to the crucifixion of the Messiah as prophesied in Daniel 9:26. Christ was certainly not annihilated at Calvary!

In Psalm 145:20 the identical Hebrew word rendered "Jeshoy" is found in describing the punishment of both Egypt (Ex. 10:7) and Israel (Hosea 13:9), neither of which nation has yet to suffer annihilation!

4. Universalism: The position that says God will eventually save everyone including (probably) the devil himself. Theologian Emil Brunner once wrote:

"That is the revealed will of God . . . a plan of universal salvation, of gathering all things into Christ" (*Eternal Hope*, Westminster Press, 1954, p. 182).

This position is soundly refuted by John 3:17, 18; Matthew 25:31–34, 41, and a host of other scriptural passages.

If these verses teach anything, they strongly and sternly declare that at the moment of death there exists absolutely no chance whatsoever for the salvation of an unsaved person. We may be tempted to argue with God concerning the why of the matter, but not the what of the matter. Origen (second-century church father) was one of the earliest proponents of restorationism. He even taught the possibility of Satan himself being restored to the faith he once rebelled against! Restorationists use the following verses for "proof" of their position.
And he shall send Jesus Christ, which before was preached unto you: Whom the heaven must receive until the times of restitution of all things, which God hath spoken by the mouth of all his holy prophets since the world began (Acts 3:20, 21).

269

For as in Adam all die, even so in Christ shall all be made alive (1 Cor. 15:22).

That in the dispensation of the fulness of times he might gather together in one all things in Christ, both which are in heaven, and which are on earth; even in him (Eph. 1:10).

For this is good and acceptable in the sight of God our Saviour; Who will have all men to be saved, and to come unto the knowledge of the truth (1 Tim. 2:3, 4).

For therefore we both labour and suffer reproach, because we trust in the living God, who is the Saviour of all men, specially of those that believe (1 Tim. 4:10).

For Christ also hath once suffered for sins, the just for the unjust, that he might bring us to God, being put to death in the flesh, but quickened by the Spirit: by which also he went and preached unto the spirits in prison (1 Pet. 3:18, 19).

However, a quick glance at the context of the above verses shows that all the "restored" here are limited to those who have accepted Christ as Savior! The passage in 1 Peter has been the subject of some controversy, but whatever else, it does not teach restorationism. The verb "preached" in verse 19 in the original Greek does not refer to gospel preaching.

5. Soul sleep: The view that the soul sleeps between death and the resurrection. This is refuted by 2 Corinthians 5:6–9; Philippians 1:23, 24; Revelation 6:9–12. This passage in Revelation not only refutes soul sleep, but teaches that departed believers can both ask questions and receive answers in heaven. It also seems to suggest the possibilities of a temporary body given them prior to their future resurrected bodies.

6. Purgatory: The belief of Roman Catholics that all those who die at peace with the church but are not perfect must undergo penal and purifying sufferings. However, this is only for those who die in venial (lesser) sin, for all dying in mortal sin are forever condemned to hell. Roman doctrine teaches that a person's stay in purgatory may be shortened by the gifts or services rendered by living people in behalf of the beloved dead one through the Roman Catholic Church. This is refuted by Hebrews 9:11–14, 24–28; 10:12, 16, 17.

7. Limbo: Another aspect of Roman Catholic theology which teaches that all unbaptized children and the mentally incompetent, upon death, proceed to a permanent place of "natural happiness," but not heaven. This is refuted by Matthew 18:1–10.

These then are but seven of the many prevalent pseudo and (to the human soul) poisonous philosophies in regard to man's destiny.

B. Scriptural facts.
   1. Before the cross. Where was the abode of the dead prior to Calvary? It is held by a number of Bible students that before Jesus died, the souls of all men descended into an abode located somewhere in the earth known as Hades in the New Testament and Sheol in the Old Testament. Originally, there were two sections of Hades, one for the saved and one for the lost. The saved section is sometimes called "paradise," and is at other times referred to as "Abraham's bosom."

   And Jesus said unto him, Verily I say unto thee, To day shalt thou be with me in paradise (Lk. 23:43).

   And it came to pass, that the beggar died, and was carried by the angels into Abraham's bosom: the rich man also died, and was buried (Lk. 16:22).

   There is no name given for the unsaved section apart from the general designation of Hades. In the Luke 16 chapter the Savior relates the account of a poor believer who died and went to the saved part of Hades and of a rich unbeliever who died and went to the unsaved section.

   A number of extremely interesting conclusions may be derived from this historical account as related by Christ.
   a. The activities of angels in carrying believers to their reward.
   b. The possibilities of an intermediate, preresurrection body for the lost as well as the saved.
   c. The irony of an occupant in hell desiring to become a soul-winner.
   d. The nature of the rich man's request to send Lazarus to testify to his five lost brothers, reasoning that "if one went unto them from the dead, they will repent." This pathetic request was of course denied, simply

because it would not have worked. The fact of the matter is that Christ did actually raise a man with the same name as Lazarus a few months later. What were the results of this? Did it cause the unbelieving Jews to come to the Savior? Hardly. In fact, just the opposite occurred, for the wicked Pharisees not only decided to kill Jesus for his action (Jn. 11:53), but actually planned (if necessary) to murder the resurrected Lazarus also (Jn. 12:10, 11).

However, many believe that all this changed after Christ had made full payment for the believer's sin on Calvary. The Scofield Bible suggests that during the time of his death and resurrection our Lord descended into Hades, depopulated paradise, and led a spiritual triumphal entry into the heavenlies with all the saved up to that time. The following is offered as proof of this:

Wherefore he saith, When he ascended up on high, he led captivity captive, and gave gifts unto men. (Now that he ascended, what is it but that he also descended first into the lower parts of the earth? He that descended is the same also that ascended up far above all heavens, that he might fill all things) (Eph. 4:8–10).

In his book *Revelation*, the late Dr. Donald Barnhouse writes:

"When He ascended on High He emptied Hell of Paradise and took it straight to the presence of God. Captivity was taken captive . . . From that moment onward there was to be no separation whatsoever for those who believe in Christ. The gates of Hell would never more prevail against any believer."

This means the lost rich man is still in Hades, there having since been joined by Judas, Herod, Nero, Hitler, etc., and will remain until after the millennium and the resurrection of the unjust. "But the rest of the dead lived not again until the thousand years were finished . . ." (Rev. 20:5).

2. After the cross. The state of the unsaved dead remained

272

(and remains) unchanged after the cross. They remain in Hades awaiting the final great white throne judgment. This is clearly brought out in Revelation 20:11–15.

But a glorious change has occurred concerning the state of those who fall asleep in Jesus. Note the following verses:

But he, being full of the Holy Ghost, looked up steadfastly into heaven, and saw the glory of God, and Jesus standing on the right hand of God. . . . And they stoned Stephen, calling upon God, and saying, Lord Jesus, receive my spirit. And he kneeled down, and cried with a loud voice, Lord, lay not this sin to their charge. And when he had said this, he fell asleep (Acts 7:55, 59, 60).

We are confident, I say, and willing rather to be absent from the body, and to be present with the Lord (2 Cor. 5:8).

For me to live is Christ, and to die is gain. For I am in a strait betwixt two, having a desire to depart, and to be with Christ; which is far better (Phil. 1:21, 23).

Thus, according to these verses, both Stephen and Paul, along with all other departed believers, are now in the heavenlies with Christ. In the following verse Paul refers to this place as "the third heaven." He speaks of being "caught up into paradise, and heard unspeakable words, which it is not lawful for a man to utter" (2 Cor. 12:4).

C. Let us now review what has been said.
   1. Man before the cross:
      a. All unsaved went to the lost compartment in the heart of the earth.
      b. All saved went to the saved compartment in the heart of the earth (also known as Abraham's bosom).
   2. Man after the cross.
      a. All unsaved still go to the same place.
      b. All saved now go to the third heaven.
   3. Man after the final resurrection:
      a. All unsaved are taken from the lost compartment in the heart of the earth to a permanent place of outer darkness (also called Gehenna).
      b. All saved will enter the New Jerusalem.

SEVENTEEN
A SCRIPTURAL
SUMMARY OF HELL

A. Denial of the doctrine.

Of all the many doctrines in the Bible, undoubtedly the very first that the unbeliever will deny and the weak believer will question is the doctrine of hell. Satan has successfully accomplished this coveted goal through following three methods:

1. Rationalism. "There is no God, and therefore there can be no hell." This rationalism often disguises itself in the garb of "science." Harold Bryson writes:

"Other people deny the existence of hell on the basis of modern thinking. Some assume that many scientific discoveries of the twentieth century render belief in a future life impossible. Using scientific study of the dissolution of the chemical elements of the body, they deny any possibility of a bodily resurrection. Also, the theory of organic evolution tries to demonstrate man's common origin with lower life forms. Evolution destroys the basis for believing that man has a higher destiny than any other creature. Some naively insist that the penetration of space leaves no place for the biblical teachings on heaven and hell. It has been assumed that if man finds no evidence of heaven in space then there is likewise no hell located in the opposite direction" (Yes, Virginia, There Is a Hell, p. 12).

Charles Darwin rejected the doctrine of hell.

"Disbelief crept over me at a very slow rate, but was at last complete. I can hardly see how anyone ought to wish Christianity to be true; for, if so, the plain language of the text seems to show that the men who do not believe—and this would include my father, brother, and almost all my best friends—will be everlastingly punished. And this is a damnable doctrine" (*The Christian Agnostic*, London: Hodder & Stoughton, 1965, p. 164).

The English agnostic clergyman John A. T. Robinson, bishop of Woolwich, writes:

"There are still a few who would like to bring back hell, as some want to bring back . . . hanging. They are usually the same types who wish to purge Britain of . . . sex and violence" (*But That I Can't Believe*, New York: The New American Library, 1967, p. 69).

2. Ridicule. "There may be a God, but it is silly to speculate about multitudes of disembodied spirits frying in some literal lake of fire somewhere."

Robert G. Ingersoll, one of America's most famous atheists, thus ridiculed the idea of hell. When asked to coin a slogan to help promote a cigar which bore his name, he quipped, "Smoke in this world, and not in the one to come!" Ingersoll loved the writings of the great poet Robert Burns. He often stated that one page of Burns had more literary merit than an entire book by Moses. Upon Ingersoll's death, some wag suggested that an appropriate epitaph for his tombstone would be to simply print the name of his favorite author—"Robert Burns"!

On this subject, Ingersoll said:

"The idea of hell was born of revenge and brutality on the one side, and cowardice on the other. . . . I have no respect for any man who preaches it. . . . I dislike this doctrine, I hate it, I despise it, I defy this doctrine!"

275

The famous news editor Horace Greeley is said to have refused to make a contribution to a religious group who solicited funds to be used in "keeping people out of hell." His reason was that, in his opinion, there were not nearly enough people going to hell at that present time!
3. Religion. "There is a God, but he is a God of love, and therefore he would not and could not send anyone to hell." This of course is the position of liberalism. Recent theologians like Karl Barth, Emil Brunner, Paul Tillich, and others either denied or downplayed the doctrine of hell. All the cults have at least one common ground: the belief that there is no hell.

The Christian Science church defines hell as error of mortal mind.

The Jehovah's Witnesses teach that the wicked will simply be annihilated.

The Mormons believe in hell, but not as an endless existence. They teach that life after death involves three levels: celestial, terrestrial, and telestial. The celestial level includes Mormons in an intermediate state who will eventually become gods. The terrestrial level includes Christians and other persons who rejected the Mormon message. The telestial level is reserved for those currently in hell who await a final resurrection. Mormons teach that these will ultimately be saved and not suffer punishment forever.

The Seventh Day Adventists claim that God will someday blot out all sin and sinners and establish a clean universe again.

The late Bishop James Pike wrote:

"A Heaven of infinite bliss and a Hell of infinite torment is an impossible contradiction. The kind of people who would qualify for heaven would not be in bliss knowing that there were a lot of people in suffering with no chance whatever for change—the have-nots, the underprivileged. These suitable for Heaven would want to go to Hell to be alongside them in their needs. Jesus, as shown by the reports of his ministry on earth, would be there alongside them too. God in his heaven would find himself lonely and might well join everybody there—or change the whole scheme" (*Protestant Power and the Coming Revolution,* p. 173).

Regardless of the doubts and denials of men, however, the Bible dogmatically declares the existence and reality of hell. Here the devout believer would agree with the Apostle Paul:

God forbid: yea, let God be true, but every man a liar; as it is written, That thou mightest be justified in thy sayings, and mightest overcome when thou art judged (Rom. 3:4).

B. The background of Gehenna hell.

We have already seen that, following the tribulation, all the unsaved dead will be resurrected from Hades in the heart of the earth to appear before the great white judgment throne. This is clearly stated in Revelation 20:11–15. They will then be cast into Gehenna hell forever. Gehenna is a New Testament word with an Old Testament background. It is found twelve times in the Greek New Testament, eleven of those instances coming from the mouth of the Savior himself (Mt. 5:22, 29, 30; 10:28; 18:9; 25:15, 33; Mk. 9:43, 45: 9:47; Lk. 12:5; Jas. 3:6). A brief etymology of the word Gehenna will be helpful here. In the Old Testament, a wicked Israelite king named Ahaz forsook the worship of Jehovah and followed the devil-god Molech. In his insane and immoral attempt to please Molech, the king actually sacrificed his own children in the fires as burnt offerings to his abominable idol.

Ahaz was twenty years old when he began to reign, and he reigned sixteen years in Jerusalem: but he did not that which was right in the sight of the Lord, like David his father: For he walked in the ways of the kings of Israel, and made also molten images for Baalim. Moreover he burnt incense in the valley of the son of Hinnom, and burnt his children in the fire, after the abominations of the heathen whom the Lord had cast out before the children of Israel. He sacrificed also and burnt incense in the high places, and on the hills, and under every green tree (2 Chron. 28:1–4).

And he defiled Topheth, which is in the valley of the children of Hinnom, that no man might make his son or his daughter to pass through the fire to Molech (2 Ki. 23:10).

This all took place in a deep and narrow valley to the south of Jerusalem called the Valley of Hinnom.

It was called by this name because of its owners, the sons of Hinnom. Jeremiah the prophet also writes about both the Valley of Hinnom and Topheth.

And they have built the high places of Tophet, which is in the valley of the son of Hinnom, to burn their sons and their daughters in the fire; which I commanded them not, neither came it into my heart. Therefore, behold, the days come, saith the Lord, that it shall no more be called Tophet, nor the valley of the son of Hinnom, but the valley of slaughter: for they shall bury in Tophet, till there be no place. And the carcases of this people shall be meat for the fowls of the heaven, and for the beasts of the earth; and none shall fray them away (Jer. 7:31–33).

Walter Price writes:

"Topheth was probably the point, south of Jerusalem, where three valleys met. The Tyropoeon Valley which runs through the old city and down by the Western Wall of the temple mount, intersects here with the Valley of Hinnom. The Valley of the Sons of Hinnom sweeps around the western side of the city and turns east below the Ophel to meet the Valley of Kidron. All three of these valleys converge at the spot where ancient Israel offered sacrifices to the Ammonite god Molech (2 Chron. 28:3; 33:6). Here also the field of Akeldama is located (Mt. 27:7, 8; Acts 1:18, 19). The Talmud places the mouth of hell in this place. The Arabs also call this lower end of the Hinnom Valley, where it meets Kidron, at Topheth, the Valley of Hell. In Jesus' day the city garbage dump was located there. The fighting between Jews and Romans ended here in A.D. 70. As many as 600,000 bodies of dead Jews, slain in the defense of Jerusalem against the Romans, were carried out through the Dung Gate to be buried in Topheth" (*The Coming Antichrist*, Moody Press, 1974, pp. 202, 203).

As one therefore combines both Old Testament and New Testament meanings, he has described for him a place of filth and sorrow, of smoke and pain, of fire and death. This, then, is the word the Holy Spirit chose to employ in describing the final destiny for the unsaved. With all these things in mind, one is forced to the sobering fact that Gehenna hell is God's final dumping and burning place for all unsaved men and apostate angels.

C. The location of hell.

Where is Gehenna hell located? The Bible definitely indicates that Hades is down in the heart of the earth somewhere.

And the earth opened her mouth, and swallowed them up, and their houses, and all the men that appertained unto Korah, and all their goods. They, and all that appertained to them, went down alive into the pit, and the earth closed upon them: and they perished from among the congregation (Num. 16:32, 33).

It teaches, however, otherwise about Gehenna. We note the following verses:

But the children of the kingdom shall be cast out into outer darkness: there shall be weeping and gnashing of teeth (Mt. 8:12).

Then said the king to the servants, Bind him hand and foot, and take him away, and cast him into outer darkness; there shall be weeping and gnashing of teeth (Mt. 22:13).

And cast ye the unprofitable servant into outer darkness: there shall be weeping and gnashing of teeth (Mt. 25:30).

These are wells without water, clouds that are carried with a tempest: to whom the mist of darkness is reserved for ever (2 Pet. 2:17).

Raging waves of the sea, foaming out their own shame; wandering stars, to whom is reserved the blackness of darkness for ever (Jude 13).

From these five verses it becomes immediately clear that Gehenna hell is located away from this earth, a place of outer darkness, to be found, perhaps, in some remote spot near the edge of God's universe.

D. The nature and characteristics of hell.

What will Gehenna really be like? Consider:

1. Hell is a place of unquenchable fire.

Whose fan is in his hand, and he will thoroughly purge his floor, and gather his wheat into the garner; but he will burn up the chaff with unquenchable fire (Mt. 3:12).

The Son of man shall send forth his angels, and they shall gather out of his kingdom all things that offend, and them which do iniquity; and shall cast them into a furnace of fire: there shall be wailing and gnashing of teeth (Mt. 13:41, 42).

And if thy hand offend thee, cut it off: it is better for thee to enter into life maimed, than having two hands to go into hell, into the fire that never shall be quenched (Mk. 9:43).

Opposing positions have been taken concerning whether the fire here is literal fire. It has been suggested that the fire is not real fire but something far worse. However, the Greek language would indicate otherwise. The same Greek word for fire (*pur*) used in Matthew 13:42 is also found in Matthew 17:15 and Luke 17:29.

Lord, have mercy on my son: for he is lunatick, and sore vexed: for ofttimes he falleth into the fire, and oft into the water (Mt. 17:15).

But the same day that Lot went out of Sodom it rained fire and brimstone from heaven, and destroyed them all (Lk. 17:29).

Clarence Mason writes:

"The body that God will give the unbeliever will be eternal, but suited to its eternal relation to the lake of fire (Mt. 25:46; Rev. 14:10; 20:14), as the believer's body will be suited to his eternal estate. It is interesting that when men developed a material that would not disintegrate in the flame, they selected the Greek word asbestos. This is the word which is used four times in the New Testament of 'unquenchable fire' (Mt. 3:12; Mk. 9:43, 45; Lk. 3:17). From this we are to understand that unquenchable fire does not destroy the body. The body is prepared by God to abide eternal fire. If men can develop a substance that will not disintegrate in flames, cannot God?" (*Prophetic Problems*, Moody Press, 1973, p. 141).

2. Hell is a place of memory and remorse.
   In Luke 16:19–31 the unsaved rich man experienced memory and remorse over his lost condition in Hades. Surely these experiences will not be lessened in Gehenna. As the poet has written:

The saddest words of tongue or pen,
Are these four, it might have been!

3. Hell is a place of thirst.
It would seem difficult indeed to accept this account
literally unless the fire in hell is literal. But what of
Lazarus' finger and the rich man's tongue? Can this be
interpreted literally? It has been speculated that on the
basis of this passage and also the one in 2 Corinthians 5
that temporary bodies of some sort are given to both
unsaved and saved until the final resurrection of all.

4. Hell is a place of misery and pain.
The same shall drink of the wine of the wrath of God, which
is poured out without mixture into the cup of his indignation;
and he shall be tormented with fire and brimstone in the
presence of the holy angels, and in the presence of the Lamb:
And the smoke of their torment ascendeth up for ever and ever:
and they have no rest day nor night, who worship the beast
and his image, and whosoever receiveth the mark of his name
(Rev. 14:10, 11).

5. Hell is a place of frustration and anger.
And shall cast them into a furnace of fire: there shall be
wailing and gnashing of teeth (Mt. 13:42).

And shall cut him asunder, and appoint him his portion
with the hypocrites: there shall be weeping and gnashing of
teeth (Mt. 24:51).

6. Hell is a place of separation.
Often the unsaved man jokes about hell in the following
manner: "Well, if I do go to hell, I won't be lonely, for
all my friends will be there too." But quite the opposite
is true! In at least four separate passages Gehenna hell is
called "the second death."
He that hath an ear, let him hear what the Spirit saith unto
the churches; He that overcometh shall not be hurt of the
second death (Rev. 2:11).

Blessed and holy is he that hath part in the first resurrection:
on such the second death hath no power, but they shall be
priests of God and of Christ, and shall reign with him a
thousand years. . . . And whosoever was not found written

in the book of life was cast into the lake of fire (Rev. 20:6, 14).

But the fearful, and unbelieving, and the abominable, and murderers, and whoremongers, and sorcerers, and idolaters, and all liars, shall have their part in the lake which burneth with fire and brimstone: which is the second death (Rev. 21:8).

As we have already noted, "death" in the Bible refers to separation. Thus hell is literally the second death, for the sinner will be forever separated from God, and, inasmuch as Gehenna is a place of darkness, this separation will doubtless isolate him from the companionship of unsaved friends as well.

Thus, the worst thing about hell is closely connected to the best thing about heaven, and that is the first is a place where Jesus Christ will be conspicuously absent, while the second location is a place where he will be conspicuously present.

7. Hell is a place of undiluted divine wrath.

Man has already experienced some of God's wrath on this earth, but not in its pure state. After the flood there has been the rainbow, for up to this point God has always heard and answered the prophet Habakkuk's prayer,

O Lord, I have heard thy speech, and was afraid: O Lord, revive thy work in the midst of the years, in the midst of the years make known; in wrath remember mercy (Hab. 3:2).

But no more! All living unsaved men should carefully ponder the following frightful words:

The same shall drink of the wine of the wrath of God, which is poured out without mixture into the cup of his indignation; and he shall be tormented with fire and brimstone in the presence of the holy angels, and in the presence of the Lamb (Rev. 14:10).

8. Hell is a place originally prepared for Satan and his hosts.

Perhaps the saddest fact about hell is that unsaved man goes there as an uninvited guest, so to speak. Note Jesus' words:

Then shall he say also unto them on the left hand, Depart

*from me, ye cursed, into everlasting fire, prepared for the devil
and his angels* (Mt. 25:41).

How tragic, therefore, that the sinner will refuse
heaven, the place prepared for all repenting people, only
to eventually descend into hell, a place originally not
created for him!

*In my Father's house are many mansions: if it were not so, I
would have told you. I go to prepare a place for you*
(Jn. 14:2).

9. Hell is a place created for all eternity.

The Greek word for "everlasting" is *aionios*, and is found
seventy-one times in the New Testament. Sixty-four of
these instances are in reference to God, such as his
eternal power, spirit, kingdom, covenant, etc. The
remaining seven instances are directly related to the
duration of hell. In other words, hell will continue as
long as God's works continue, which is forever! Many
passages bring this truth out:

*And many of them that sleep in the dust of the earth shall
awake, some to everlasting life, and some to shame and
everlasting contempt* (Dan. 12:2).

*And these shall go away into everlasting punishment: but
the righteous into life eternal* (Mt. 25:46).

*Even as Sodom and Gomorrah, and the cities about them in
like manner, giving themselves over to fornication, and going
after strange flesh, are set forth for an example, suffering the
vengeance of eternal fire* (Jude 7).

Without doubt the most difficult truth to accept even
by saved minds is the duration of hell. One might
understand a sixty-five-year-old sinner going to hell for
sixty-five years, or 650, or 6500, or even 65 million
years! But why the endless ages? How can a just God
rightfully forever punish in hell those sins which were
committed in a brief period of time on earth?

A full answer to this exists only in the mind of God.
However, hell does vividly demonstrate the heinousness
of sin and the holiness of God. Thus, sins against God'·
eternal holiness can only be punished by God's eternal
justice.

Finally, the following should be noted: As there is no

injustice or partiality with God (Rom. 2:6, 11) it naturally follows that the degrees of suffering in hell will vary greatly, being in direct relationship to the sinner's life on earth. Various verses bear this out.

Then began he to upbraid the cities wherein most of his mighty works were done, because they repented not: Woe unto thee, Chorazin! woe unto thee, Bethsaida! for if the mighty works, which were done in you, had been done in Tyre and Sidon, they would have repented long ago in sackcloth and ashes. But I say unto you, It shall be more tolerable for Tyre and Sidon at the day of judgment, than for you. And thou, Capernaum, which art exalted unto heaven, shalt be brought down to hell: for if the mighty works, which have been done in thee, had been done in Sodom, it would have remained until this day. But I say unto you, That it shall be more tolerable for the land of Sodom, in the day of judgment, than for thee (Mt. 11:20–24).

And that servant, which knew his lord's will, and prepared not himself, neither did according to his will, shall be beaten with many stripes. But he that knew not, and did commit things worthy of stripes, shall be beaten with few stripes. For unto whomsoever much is given, of him shall be much required: and to whom men have committed much, of him they will ask the more (Lk. 12:47, 48).

Then in the audience of all the people he said unto his disciples, Beware of the scribes, which desire to walk in long robes, and love greetings in the markets, and the highest seats in the synagogues, and the chief rooms at feasts; which devour widows' houses, and for a shew make long prayers: the same shall receive greater damnation (Lk. 20:45–47).

Then saith Pilate unto him, Speakest thou not unto me? knowest thou that I have power to crucify thee, and have power to release thee? Jesus answered, Thou couldest have no power at all against me, except it were given thee from above: therefore he that delivered me unto thee hath the greater sin (Jn. 19:10, 11).

One of the most powerful sermons on hell ever delivered was preached by Jonathan Edwards on the afternoon of July 8, 1741, in Enfield, Connecticut. His text was taken from Deuteronomy 32:35, "their foot shall slide in due time."

Probably no other single sermon has ever had the effect of this one. It was interrupted by outcries from the congregation—men and women stood up and rolled on the floor, their cries often drowning out the voice of the preacher. Some are said to have laid hold on the pillars and braces of the church, apparently feeling that at that very moment their feet were sliding into hell. Through the night, Enfield was like a beleaguered city. In almost every house, men and women could be heard crying out for God to save them. Here are some excerpts from this mighty message:

"God has laid Himself under no obligation, by any promise, to keep any natural man out of Hell one moment.

God is under no manner of obligation to keep him a moment from eternal destruction.

So it is that natural men are held in the hand of God over the pit of Hell.

The Devil is waiting for them; Hell is gaping for them; the flames gather and flash about them, and would fain lay hold on them and swallow them up.

This is the case of every one of you who are out of Christ. That world of misery, that lake of burning brimstone, is extended abroad under you. There is the dreadful pit of the glowing flames of the wrath of God. There is Hell's wide gaping mouth open, and you have nothing to stand on, nor anything to take hold of. There is nothing between you and Hell but the air; it is only the power and mere pleasure of God that holds you up.

Your wickedness makes you as it were heavy as lead, and to tend downward with great weight and pressure towards Hell. If God should let you go, you would immediately sink and swiftly descend and plunge into the bottomless gulf, and your healthy constitution, and your own care and prudence, and best contrivance, and all your righteousness, would have no more influence to uphold you and keep you out of Hell than a spider's web would have to stop a falling rock.

There are the black clouds of God's wrath now hanging directly over your heads, full of the dreadful storm, and big with thunder; and were it not for the restraining hand of God it would immediately burst forth upon you.

The wrath of God is like great waters that are dammed for the present. They increase more and more, and rise higher and higher, till an outlet is given. The longer the stream is stopped, the more rapid and mighty is its course, when once it is let loose.

The waters are continually rising, and waxing more and more mighty; and there is nothing but the mere pleasure of God that holds the waters back, that are unwilling to be stopped, and press hard to go forward.

If God should only withdraw His hand from the floodgate, it would immediately fly open, and the fiery floods of the fierceness and wrath of God would rush forth with inconceivable fury, and would come upon you with omnipotent power. If your strength were ten thousand times greater than it is, yea, ten thousand times greater than the strength of the stoutest, sturdiest devil in Hell, it would be nothing to withstand or endure it.

The God that holds you over the pit of Hell, much as one holds a spider or some loathsome insect over the fire, abhors you, and is dreadfully provoked. You have often offended Him infinitely more than ever a stubborn rebel did his prince, and yet it is nothing but His hand that holds you from falling into the fire every moment.

It is ascribed to nothing else, that you did not go to Hell last night; that you were suffered to awake again in this world after you closed your eyes to sleep. There is no other reason to be given why you have not dropped into Hell since you arose in the morning, but that God's hand has held you up. Yes, there is nothing else that is to be given as a reason why you do not this very moment drop down into Hell.

Consider the fearful danger you are in! It is a great

furnace of wrath, a wide and bottomless pit, full of the fire of wrath, that you are held over in the hand of that God whose wrath is provoked and incensed as much against you as against many of the damned in Hell. You hang by a slender thread, with the flames of divine wrath flashing about it, and ready every moment to singe it and burn it asunder."

E. The occupants of hell.
Who shall be someday confined to Gehenna forever?
   1. Satan.
      And the God of peace shall bruise Satan under your feet shortly. The grace of our Lord Jesus Christ be with you. Amen (Rom. 16:20).
      And the devil that deceived them was cast into the lake of fire and brimstone, where the beast and the false prophet are, and shall be tormented day and night for ever and ever (Rev. 20:10).
   2. The antichrist.
      And then shall that Wicked be revealed, whom the Lord shall consume with the spirit of his mouth, and shall destroy with the brightness of his coming (2 Thess. 2:8).
   3. The false prophet.
      And the beast was taken, and with him the false prophet that wrought miracles before him, with which he deceived them that had received the mark of the beast, and them that worshipped his image. These both were cast alive into a lake of fire burning with brimstone (Rev. 19:20).
      As this judgment takes place prior to the millennium, these two foul criminals thus become the first and second unsaved creatures to enter the lake of fire!
   4. Fallen angels.
      For if God spared not the angels that sinned, but cast them down to hell, and delivered them into chains of darkness, to be reserved unto judgment (2 Pet. 2:4).
      The word translated "hell" is *Tartaros* in the Greek New Testament and is found only here. It is possible that *Tartaros* is a special place in Gehenna.
      And the angels which kept not their first estate, but left

their own habitation, he hath reserved in everlasting chains
under darkness unto the judgment of the great day (Jude 6).

According to Paul the believer will take part in the
passing of judgment upon fallen angels. (See 1 Cor. 6:3.)

5. Judas Iscariot.

The betrayer of Jesus Christ is singled out here in
particular because there are those (notably the late
Kenneth S. Wuest of the Moody Bible Institute faculty)
who believe Judas will be consigned to a special place in
Gehenna on the basis of Peter's words concerning him in
the upper room just prior to Pentecost:

That he may take part of this ministry and apostleship,
from which Judas by transgression fell, that he might go to his
own place (Acts 1:25).

6. All unsaved people.

In Revelation 21:8 John classified all sinners into eight
general categories:

But the fearful, and unbelieving, and the abominable,
and murderers, and whoremongers, and sorcerers, and
idolaters, and all liars, shall have their part in the lake
which burneth with fire and brimstone: which is the second
death (Rev. 21:8).

These categories are:

a. The fearful. At first glance it might seem strange to
find the fearful at the atop of this divine "rogues of
Gehenna" listing, but many obviously will wind up in
hell because they fear the cost of claiming the
Savior's name.

The fear of man bringeth a snare: but whoso putteth his
trust in the Lord shall be safe (Prov. 29:25).

These words spake his parents, because they feared the
Jews: for the Jews had agreed already, that if any man did
confess that he was Christ, he should be put out of the
synagogue (Jn. 9:22).

A sad note is introduced here in the otherwise
thrilling account of the healing of a man born blind.
The tragedy concerns the parents of the boy, who,
unlike their son, refused the spiritual eyesight offered
by Christ, and, to our knowledge, died as lost sinners.
Nevertheless among the chief rulers also many believed on

him; but because of the Pharisees they did not confess him, lest they should be put out of the synagogue: For they loved the praise of men more than the praise of God (Jn. 12:42, 43).

These chief rulers who perhaps came so close to confessing him as Lord, will someday (along with all the unsaved), be forced to confess him as Judge!

That at the name of Jesus every knee should bow, of things in heaven, and things in earth, and things under the earth; and that every tongue should confess that Jesus Christ is Lord, to the glory of God the Father (Phil. 2:10, 11).

b. The unbelieving. Literally, the disbelieving. No man ever goes to hell because he can't believe, but rather because he won't believe! There is no such thing as an honest agnostic.

He that believeth on the Son hath everlasting life: and he that believeth not the Son shall not see life; but the wrath of God abideth on him (Jn. 3:36).

With this in mind, it may be said the distance between heaven and hell is a scant eighteen inches! A person can believe there is a God, a Calvary, and a hell. But to keep those facts in his head means to die lost. However, by removing them to his heart (eighteen inches away) results in eternal salvation!

c. The abominable. Literally, those defiled with abomination.

These six things doth the Lord hate: yea, seven are an abomination unto him: A proud look, a lying tongue, and hands that shed innocent blood, a heart that deviseth wicked imaginations, feet that be swift in running to mischief, a false witness that speaketh lies, and he that soweth discord among brethren (Prov. 6:16–19).

d. Murderers. This refers not only to a human-killer, but also to a human-hater as well:

Whosoever hateth his brother is a murderer: and ye know that no murderer hath eternal life abiding in him (1 Jn. 3:15).

e. Whoremongers. Those guilty of sexual sins:

For this ye know, that no whoremonger, nor unclean person, nor covetous man, who is an idolater, hath any inheritance in the kingdom of Christ and of God (Eph. 5:5).

Marriage is honourable in all, and the bed undefiled: but whoremongers and adulters God will judge (Heb. 13:4).

f. Sorcerers. The Greek word is *pharmakos*, which refers to an enchanter with drugs. In a general sense the world also covers those who commune with Satan through fortune-tellers, mediums, and astrology.

Neither repented they of their murders, nor of their sorceries, nor of their fornication, nor of their thefts (Rev. 9:21).

And the light of a candle shall shine no more at all in thee; and the voice of the bridegroom and of the bride shall be heard no more at all in thee: for thy merchants were the great men of the earth; for by thy sorceries were all nations deceived (Rev. 18:23).

g. Idolaters. Those who worship something or someone else in place of the true God.

Professing themselves to be wise, they became fools, and changed the glory of the uncorruptible God into an image made like to corruptible man, and to birds, and four-footed beasts, and creeping things (Rom. 1:22, 23).

h. Liars.

Ye are of your father the devil, and the lusts of your father ye will do. He was a murderer from the beginning, and abode not in the truth, because there is no truth in him. When he speaketh a lie, he speaketh of his own: for he is a liar, and the father of it (Jn. 8:44).

Who is a liar but he that denieth that Jesus is the Christ? He is antichrist, that denieth the Father and the Son (1 Jn. 2:22).

I know thy works, and thy labour, and thy patience, and how they canst not bear them which are evil: and thou has tried them which say they are apostles, and are not, and hast found them liars (Rev. 2:2).

It is sobering to contemplate that all the above passages concern religious liars.

F. The possible present-day existence of Gehenna hell. We know, according to Jesus, that heaven is still being prepared.

Let not your heart be troubled: ye believe in God, believe also in me. In my Father's house are many mansions: if it were not so, I would have told you. I go to prepare a place for you. And if I go and prepare a place for you, I will come again, and receive you unto myself; that where I am, there ye may be also (Jn. 14:1-3).

But what about hell? There are several scriptural and scientific facts that would strongly indicate that Gehenna hell is right now in existence. Consider Jesus' words:

Then shall he say also unto them on the left hand, Depart from me, ye cursed, into everlasting fire, prepared for the devil and his angels (Mt. 25:41).

In his book *Things to Come*, J. Dwight Pentecost writes:

"The word 'prepared' literally is 'having been prepared,' suggesting that the lake of fire is already in existence and awaiting its occupants. It is the thesis of C.T. Schwarze, then of New York University, that such a place as a lake of fire is known to science today. He writes: 'The word lake must connote a body of matter having liquid form. Therefore, if Scripture is truth, this eternal fire must be in liquid form.

. . . The very simple proof of the portions of Scripture we have been discussing lies in the existence of the singular phenomena of the skies known as midget or white dwarf stars! . . . a midget star is one which, because of some things which have happened to it (not quite clear at this time), should be roughly 5,000 or more times as big as it really is! Applying this idea for illustration to such a planet as the earth, you must conceive the earth as having shrunk to such an extent that its diameter would be about 400 miles . . . instead of being 8,000 miles in diameter as it really is.

This enormous density . . . has a great deal to do with our subject. Most people know the sun, our nearest star, is rather hot . . . . There is general agreement that the temperature at or near the center of stars is between 25 million and 30 million degrees Fahrenheit! . . . At such temperatures, much can happen, like the bursting of atoms, which helps to explain the phenomenon of the white dwarf .

. . . A temperature of 30,000,000 degress Fahrenheit could explode atoms. . . . It would cause the atoms to lose their electrons, even though the attraction between nucleus and

291

electrons is an octillion times the attraction of gravity. The separated parts could then be better packed in, particularly under such great pressure. . . . With the constant activity of X-rays, atom walls could not be reformed; therefore enormous densities, such as are found in the midgets, can be attained. Now, please note, at such high temperatures all matter would be in the form of gas . . . in a white dwarf the pressure is so great that gases become compressed to the consistency of a liquid, although they may still respond to the characteristics of a gas . . .

. . . Before such a star would cool off and gradually become dark it would have to expand to normal proportions. That is, it would have to get to be more than 5,000 times its present size. Here is the difficulty. Such expansion would cause enormous heat which, in turn, would absolutely keep the star compressed, so that, insofar as astronomers and physicists know, the midget stars can never cool off! . . . The white dwarf, to all intents, can never burn out.'"

Thus wrote Dr. Schwarze. Pentecost then concludes:

". . . May I summarize to show that the Bible, God's Word, is scientifically accurate? We find, first, an eternal fire which cannot burn out. Being of a liquid consistency it is, secondly, a lake of fire. In the third place, it cannot be quenched, for any quenching material such as water would immediately have its atoms stripped of electrons and be packed in with the rest. In the fourth place, since astronomers have been, and still are, studying this strange phenomenon, it is only too evident that the lake of fire has been prepared and is now ready. Although we cannot say that God will actually use these lakes of fire in fulfilling His Word, the answer to the skeptic is in the heavens where there are lakes of fire" (*Things to Come*, Dunham Press, 1959, pp. 560, 561).

To this can be added a paragraph which appears under the scientific section of the 1972 *Family Almanac*:

"Astronomers have recently added two new objects to the growing list of strange and puzzling objects speculated about or found in the universe. A 'black hole' is the hypothetical result of a runaway or uncontrolled gravitational collapse of a supernova. Eventually a collapsing object, such as a star, will reach a limited size, called the Schwarzschild Radius, which depends upon the mass of the object. For the Sun the Schwarzschild Radius would be about two miles! If the contracting object continues to contract to less than its Schwarzschild Radius it becomes a 'black hole.' The gravitational forces exerted by this object are so strong that no matter or radiation can escape from it. The light emanating from this object is trapped and effectively removed from the 'observable universe.' "

EIGHTEEN
A SCRIPTURAL
SUMMARY OF
HEAVEN

Both heaven and hell are either ignored, ridiculed, or denied by the world today. In his book *The Biblical Doctrine of Heaven*, Dr. Wilbur Smith lists two significant quotes from a world-famous theologian and a scientist about heaven:

"It is unwise for Christians to claim any knowledge of either the furniture of heaven or the temperature of hell" (Dr. Reinhold Niebuhr).

"As for the Christian theology, can you imagine anything more appallingly idiotic than the Christian idea of heaven?" (Dr. Alfred Whitehead).

A common approach of the liberal clergyman is that he does indeed believe in a literal heaven and hell, but limits them both to this earth! In other words, life's good experiences are "heaven," and its bad moments "hell." Without him probably being at all aware of it, his Bible-denying philosophy does contain a very potent truth! The facts are that this world is indeed the only hell the believer will ever experience, and the only heaven the unbeliever shall ever know!

Sometimes a "pious" objection is raised concerning the very study of heaven. The protest goes: "But don't you think we can become so heavenly minded, that we're no earthly good?" This may be, but for every one like this, there are probably ten believers who are so *earthly* minded that they are no *heavenly* good. (See Col. 3:1–3.)

In reality, we are told a surprising number of things about our future home in the Word of God. Contrary to popular opinion, heaven is discussed far more than hell in the Scriptures.

A. The capital of heaven.

In the Bible we read of three heavens. Briefly, these are:

1. The first heaven—home of the birds and clouds.

    I beheld, and, lo, there was no man, and all the birds of the heavens were fled (Jer. 4:25).

    The leaves thereof were fair, and the fruit thereof much, and in it was meat for all: the beasts of the field had shadow under it, and the fowls of the heaven dwelt in the boughs thereof, and all flesh was fed of it (Dan. 4:12).

    Behold the fowls of the air: for they sow not, neither do they reap, nor gather into barns; yet your heavenly Father feedeth them. Are ye not much better than they? (Mt. 6:26).

    And Jesus saith unto him, The foxes have holes, and the birds of the air have nests; but the Son of man hath not where to lay his head (Mt. 8:20).

    It can be readily seen that as beautiful as this heaven may be on occasion, it is *not* the eternal home of the redeemed.

2. The second heaven—home of the sun, moon, and stars.

    That in blessing I will bless thee, and in multiplying I will multiply thy seed as the stars of the heaven, and as the sand which is upon the seashore; and thy seed shall possess the gate of his enemies (Gen. 22:17).

    The heavens declare the glory of God; and the firmament sheweth his handiwork (Ps. 19:1).

    In the sixties (beginning with the Russian orbit in 1961 and climaxing with the U.S. moon landing in 1969) man for the first time in history succeeded in developing a space craft that would transport him out of the first heaven into the second heaven! But as wide and wonderful as it is, the second heaven (like the first) cannot be confused with the heaven of salvation.

3. The third heaven—home of God.

    I knew a man in Christ above fourteen years ago, (whether in the body, I cannot tell; or whether out of the body, I cannot tell: God knoweth;) such an one caught up to the third heaven (2 Cor. 12:2).

But will God indeed dwell on the earth? behold, the heaven and heaven of heavens cannot contain thee; how much less this house that I have builded? And hearken thou to the supplication of thy servant, and of thy people Israel, when they shall pray toward this place: and hear thou in heaven thy dwelling place: and when thou hearest, forgive (1 Ki. 8:27, 30).

This and this alone is the true third heaven. It has already been noted how man's brain power recently transported him from the first to the second heaven. But no space vehicle can ever be devised which will take him from the second to the third heaven! This journey can only be effected by blood, and not by brain. In fact, Jesus once told Nicodemus a man could not even see this heaven, let alone enter it, apart from the new birth. See John 3:3.

In Matthew 6:9 our Lord taught his disciples to pray: *After this manner therefore pray ye: Our Father which art in heaven, Hallowed by thy name.*

Here of course, he was referring to the third heaven, the abode of God. However, the Bible teaches that within this heavenly abode there exists a dazzling, high, and holy city called the New Jerusalem. This beautiful and blessed city is therefore not only the center of God's presence, but will be the permanent home for all the redeemed throughout eternity. Both Old and New Testament believers looked and longed for this celestial city.

For he looked for a city which hath foundations, whose builder and maker is God. But now they desire a better country, that is, a heavenly: wherefore God is not ashamed to be called their God (Heb. 11:10, 16).

But ye are come unto mount Sion, and unto the city of the living God, the heavenly Jerusalem, and to an innumerable company of angels (Heb. 12:22).

Glorious things are spoken of thee, O city of God. Selah (Ps. 87:3).

There is a river, the streams whereof shall make glad the

city of God, the holy place of the tabernacles of the Most High (Ps. 46:4).

In my Father's house are many mansions: if it were not so, I would have told you. I go to prepare a place for you. And if I go and prepare a place for you, I will come again, and receive you unto myself; that where I am, there ye may be also (Jn. 14:2, 3).

And I John saw the holy city, new Jerusalem, coming down from God out of heaven, prepared as a bride adorned for her husband (Rev. 21:2).

B. The characteristics of heaven (facts about the New Jerusalem).
   1. The shape of this city.

   And the city lieth foursquare, and the length is as large as the breadth . . . the length and the breadth and the height of it are equal (Rev. 21:16).

   This description allows for two possibilities, namely that the New Jerusalem is in the shape of a cube or that of a vast pyramid. Both structures meet the necessary qualifications in this verse. Paul Lee Tan writes:

   "Advocates of the triangular-shaped city are many: H. A. Ironside, Charles H. Welch, Alva McClain, Wilbur Smith, John Walvoord, and others. The awkwardness of a ridiculously low wall (Rev. 21:17, 144 cubits on 216 feet) which encloses a tremendously high cubical city is cited for this alternate choice of a triangle. The low wall seems to harmonize better with a pyramid-shaped city.

   On the other hand, advocates of a cube-shaped city see good reasons for their preferences. In Revelation 21:3, the voice which accompanies the descent of the New Jerusalem to the New Earth is clear: 'Behold, the tabernacle of God is with man.' It is interesting to note that the Holy of Holies inside the tabernacle is cubicle-shaped (20 x 20 x 20 cubits). Gary Cohen takes his stand in the Grace Journal: 'The suggestion that the entire city is a huge Holy of Holies, cubical in shape as was the sacred inner sanctuary of the Temple (1 Ki. 6:20), perfectly fits the truth that this city will be the very place where God makes His dwelling'" (The New Jerusalem, pp. 18, 19).

J. Vernon McGee, however, suggests a third possibility.

"The shape of this city is difficult to describe. . . . Some have envisioned it as a cube, others as a pyramid. In view of the fact that it is hanging in space as a planet or star, it seems that it would be a globe. . . . The city is inside the globe. . . . The light would shine through the twelve foundations, giving a fantastic and startling coloring to the new universe. . . . From the outside, the city looks like a diamond. The gold is transparent and the diamond is the setting for the gold on the inside. . . . We live on the outside of the planet called earth, but the Bride will dwell within the planet called the New Jerusalem. The glory of light streaming through this crystal clear prism, will break up into a polychromed rainbow of breathtaking beauty. The sphere will have the circumference of 8164 miles. The diameter of the moon is about 2160 miles and that of the New Jerusalem sphere is about 2600 miles; thus the New Jerusalem will be about the size of the moon. And it will be a sphere, as are the other heavenly bodies.

While the Bible definitely pictures the New Jerusalem as floating in space, it should not be thought of as a satellite city to the earth, but rather the opposite, that is, the earth as a satellite planet encircling the New Jerusalem."

2. The size of this city.
   . . . *and he measured the city with the reed, twelve thousand furlongs* (Rev. 21:16).

   According to our present-day measurements this city would be roughly 1400 miles long, high, and wide. If placed in America, it would reach from New York City to Denver, Colorado, and from Canada to Florida.

   How big is a city this size? Our earth has approximately 120 million square miles of water surface and 60 million square miles of land surface. If one multiplies 1400 by 1400 by 1400 (the dimensions of the New Jerusalem), he arrives at the total cubic miles of the city, a staggering figure of 2 billion, 700 million! This is some fifteen times the combined surface of the entire earth, including both land and water area.

It has been estimated that approximately 40 billion people have lived on our planet since the creation of Adam. Of this number, over 4 billion are living today. Density studies of city populations assure us that every single one of these 40 billion could easily be accomodated upon just the first "foundational floor" of this marvelous 1400-layered metropolis.

3. The inhabitants of this city.

Who will dwell in that shining city of the stars?

a. The holy and elect angels.

But ye are come unto mount Sion, and unto the city of the living God, the heavenly Jerusalem, and to an innumerable company of angels (Heb. 12:22).

And I beheld, and I heard the voice of many angels round about the throne and the beasts and the elders: and the number of them was ten thousand times ten thousand, and thousands of thousands (Rev. 5:11).

God, of course, knows their number, but they are presented to men as uncountable. There may be as many angels as there are stars in the heavens, for angels are often associated with the stars (Job 38:7; Ps. 148:1-3; Rev. 9:1, 2; 12:3, 4, 7-9). If this is so, there exist untold trillions of these heavenly beings. (See Ps. 68:17; Mt. 26:53; Dan. 7:9, 10.)

Angels are ranked as follows:

(1) Archangels.

    (a) Michael (Dan. 10:13, 21; 12:1; Jude 9; Rev. 12:7).

    (b) Gabriel (Dan. 8:16; 9:21; Lk. 1:19, 26).

(2) Cherubim (Gen. 3:24; Ex. 25:18-20; Ezek. 1:4-28; 10:1-22).

(3) Seraphim (Isa. 6:1-7).

(4) Living creatures (Rev. 4:6-9; 5:8; 6:1, 3, 5, 7).

(5) Ruling angels (Eph. 1:21; 3:10; Col. 1:16; 2:10; 1 Pet. 3:22).

(6) Guardian angels (Mt. 18:10; Heb. 1:14).

(7) Angels associated with horses and chariots

(2 Ki. 2:11; 6:17; Ps. 68:17; Zech. 1:8–11; Rev. 19:14).

b. The twenty-four elders (Rev. 4:4).

c. The church.

As the following passages indicate, the New Jerusalem is in reality the Bridegroom's wedding ring to his beloved bride.

But ye are come unto mount Sion, and unto the city of the living God, the heavenly Jerusalem, and to an innumerable company of angels, to the general assembly and church of the firstborn, which are written in heaven, and the God the Judge of all, and to the spirits of just men made perfect (Heb. 12:22, 23).

And after these things, I heard a great voice of much people in heaven, saying, Alleluia; Salvation, and glory, and honour, and power, unto the Lord our God: Let us be glad and rejoice, and give honour to him: for the marriage of the Lamb is come, and his wife hath made herself ready. And to her was granted that she should be arrayed in fine linen, clean and white: for the fine linen is the righteousness of saints (Rev. 19:1, 7, 8).

And I saw a new heaven and a new earth: for the first heaven and the first earth were passed away; and there was no more sea. And there came unto me one of the seven angels which had the seven vials full of the seven last plagues, and talked with me, saying, Come hither, I will show thee the bride, the Lamb's wife. And he carried me away in the spirit to a great and high mountain, and showed me that great city, the holy Jerusalem, descending out of heaven from God, having the glory of God: and her light was like unto a stone most precious, even like a jasper stone, clear as crystal (Rev. 21:1, 9–11).

d. Saved Israel.

Although the New Jerusalem is basically a wedding present from the Bridegroom (Christ) to the bride (the church), Israel nevertheless is also invited to dwell within these jasper walls.

Several passages bear this out:

But now they desire a better country, that is, a heavenly: wherefore God is not ashamed to be called their God: for he hath prepared for them a city (Heb. 11:16).

And while they went to buy, the bridegroom came; and they that were ready went in with him to the marriage: and the door was shut. His lord said unto him, Well done, good and faithful servant; thou hast been faithful over a few things, I will make thee ruler over many things: enter thou into the joy of thy lord (Mt. 25:10, 23).

Our Lord quotes these words during his Mt. Olivet discourse. In relating two parables he likens saved Israel to some prepared wedding guests (parable of the ten virgins), and later as two faithful servants (parable of the talents). He thus pictures saved Israel as joining the bride and bridegroom.

e. The Father.

And immediately I was in the spirit: and, behold, a throne was set in heaven, and one sat on the throne. And he that sat was to look upon like a jasper and a sardine stone: and there was a rainbow round about the throne, in sight like unto an emerald (Rev. 4:2, 3).

There seems no doubt that the One John sees sitting upon this throne is the Father himself.

The only other description of the Father in the Bible is found in Daniel 7:9:

I beheld till the thrones were placed, and the Ancient of days did sit, whose garment was white as snow, and the hair of his head like pure wool; his throne was like the fiery flame, and his wheels as burning fire.

f. The Son.

And I beheld, and, lo, in the midst of the throne and of the four beasts, and in the midst of the elders, stood a Lamb as it had been slain, having seven horns and seven eyes, which are the seven Spirits of God sent forth into all the earth (Rev. 5:6).

Here we learn that not only is the Lamb of God an occupant of heaven, but the very source and strength and center of heaven, without which there could be no heaven! Thus we see:

The light of heaven is the face of Jesus.
The joy of heaven is the presence of Jesus.
The song of heaven is the name of Jesus.
The theme of heaven is the work of Jesus.
The employment of heaven is the work of Jesus.
The fullness of heaven is the Person of Jesus.

In the book of Revelation John refers to Jesus as a Lamb no less than twenty-seven times. From these verses we see that heaven's Hero will be:

(1) A slain Lamb
And I beheld, and, lo, in the midst of the throne and of the four beasts, and in the midst of the elders, stood a Lamb as it had been slain, having seven horns and seven eyes, which are the seven Spirits of God sent forth into all the earth (Rev. 5:6).

(2) A redeeming Lamb
And they sung a new song, saying, Thou art worthy to take the book, and to open the seals thereof: for thou wast slain, and hast redeemed us to God by thy blood out of every kindred, and tongue, and people, and nation (Rev. 5:9).

(3) A worthy Lamb
Saying with a loud voice, Worthy is the Lamb that was slain to receive power, and riches, and wisdom, and strength, and honour, and glory, and blessing (Rev. 5:12).

(4) A comforting Lamb
For the Lamb which is in the midst of the throne shall feed them, and shall lead them unto living fountains of waters: and God shall wipe away all tears from their eyes (Rev. 7:17).

(5) A life-giving Lamb
And all that dwell upon the earth shall worship him, whose names are not written in the book of life of the Lamb slain from the foundation of the world (Rev. 13:8).

(6) An overcoming Lamb
And they overcame him by the blood of the Lamb, and by the word of their testimony; and they loved not their lives unto the death. These shall make war

with the Lamb, and the Lamb shall overcome them;
for he is Lord of lords, and King of kings: and they
that are with him are called, and chosen, and
faithful (Rev. 12:11; 17:14).

(7) An eternal Lamb

And every creature which is in heaven, and on the
earth, and under the earth, and such as are in the
sea, and all that are in them, heard I saying,
Blessing, and honour, and glory, and power, be unto
him that sitteth upon the throne, and unto the Lamb
for ever and ever (Rev. 5:13).

(8) An angry Lamb

And said to the mountains and rocks, Fall on us,
and hide us from the face of him that sitteth on the
throne, and from the wrath of the Lamb (Rev.
6:16).

(9) A loving Lamb

Let us be glad and rejoice, and give honour to him:
for the marriage of the Lamb is come, and his wife
hath made herself ready (Rev. 19:7).

(10) A shining Lamb

And the city had no need of the sun, neither of the
moon, to shine in it: for the glory of God did lighten
it, and the Lamb is the light thereof (Rev. 21:23).

g. The Holy Spirit.

Although the Spirit of God is not as prominent as the
Father or Son, he is unquestionably an occupant of
the New Jerusalem as attested by the following
passages:

And I heard a voice from heaven saying unto me, Write,
Blessed are the dead which die in the Lord from
henceforth: Yea, saith the Spirit, that they may rest from
their labours: and their works do follow them (Rev.
14:13).

And the Spirit and the bride say, Come. And let him
that heareth say, Come. And let him that is athirst come.
And whosoever will, let him take the water of life freely
(Rev. 22:17).

4. The population of this city.

We have already discussed the possibilities of literally
trillions of angels being in heaven. But do we have any

inkling at all concerning the number of human beings to eventually reach heaven? The surprising answer is it may indeed be possible to project a rough percentage number. As previously stated, it has been estimated that approximately 40 billion people have lived on our planet since the creation of Adam. The question then would be how many of this number will we see in heaven?

To help answer this, consider another statistic. Several anthropologists and sociologists have calculated that as many as 70 percent of all humans born never live to celebrate their eighth birthday; they are killed by disease, war, starvation, etc. What happens to the souls of all these little ones? Various verses make it clear that they go to be with Jesus. (See 2 Sam. 12:23; Mt.18: 1–6, 10; 19:14; Lk. 18:15–17.) Now, add to this figure the millions of babies murdered by abortion each year, 40 million worldwide. In our own country we have slaughtered nearly 8 million since 1973. Abortion is now the number one cause of death in the U.S. These victims of abortion, like those children dying outside the womb, also go to be with Christ. Finally, let us suggest that 10 percent of those 40 billion human beings born on the earth accept Christ as Savior sometime after reaching the age of accountability. Put this figure with the rest and total it up. The column would read:

28,000,000,000 (the 70 percent who died before reaching their eighth birthday)
   500,000,000 (those killed by abortion thus far)
 1,200,000,000 (those who accept Christ as Savior)
29,700,000,000 grand total

Thus, it is possible that nearly three fourths of all human beings will eventually enjoy the glories of this wonderful city.

It should be noted that this figure does not take into account those miscarriages and still-birth deaths which could make the final number even higher.

5. The foundation of this city.
   The city rests upon twelve layers of foundation stones with each layer being inlaid with a different precious gem. These are:

First foundation—inlaid with jasper, a crystal-clear diamond, as bright as a transparent icicle in the sunshine.

Second foundation—inlaid with sapphire, a blue opaque stone with gold specks.

Third foundation—inlaid with chalcedony, a sky-blue stone with stripes of other colors running through it.

Fourth foundation—inlaid with emerald, a bright green stone.

Fifth foundation—inlaid with sardonyx, a white stone with layers of red.

Sixth foundation—inlaid with sardius, a fiery red stone.

Seventh foundation—inlaid with chrysolyte, a transparent golden yellow stone.

Eighth foundation—inlaid with beryl, a sea-green stone.

Ninth foundation—inlaid with topaz, a transparent golden-green stone.

Tenth foundation—inlaid with chrysoprasus, a blue-green stone.

Eleventh foundation—inlaid with jacinth, a violet stone.

Twelfth foundation—inlaid with amethyst, a flashing purple stone.

These twelve foundations were not only inlaid with costly gems, but each foundational layer carried the name of one of the twelve apostles in the New Testament. *And the wall of the city had twelve foundations, and in them the names of the twelve apostles of the Lamb* (Rev. 21:14).

6. The walls of this city.

The walls of the New Jerusalem measure some 216 feet high and are made of jasper.

And he measured the wall thereof, a hundred and forty and four cubits, according to the measure of a man, that is, of the angel. And the building of the wall of it was of jasper: and the city was pure gold, like unto clear glass (Rev. 21:17, 18).

The wall is obviously not for protection, but for design and beauty only. In comparison to size, a 216-foot wall around a 1,400-mile-high city would be like a one-inch curb around the Empire State Building.

The walls surrounding Jerusalem are often mentioned in the Bible.

a. David took the walled city of Jerusalem from the Jebusites around 1,000 B.C. (2 Sam. 5); they had enclosed the ophel area with walls about 1800 B.C.

b. Both David and Solomon enlarged these walls (1 Ki. 3:1; 9:15).

c. Jehoash (northern king) later broke down a part of the wall (2 Ki. 14:13).

d. Jotham (Judean king) rebuilt the wall (2 Chron. 27:3).

e. King Manasseh enlarged it (2 Chron. 33:14).

f. Nebuchadnezzar destroyed the wall (2 Chron. 36:19).

g. Daniel predicted the wall would be rebuilt (Dan. 9:25).

h. Nehemiah rebuilt the wall (Neh. 2:17; 6:15) the remnants of this wall have been discovered by Ben Mazar of Hebrew University.

i. Herod enlarged the wall in 20 B.C.

j. Herod Agrippa I built the north wall (third wall) in A.D. 40–44.

k. Titus destroyed the wall in A.D. 70.

l. Hadrian rebuilt it in A.D. 135.

m. The present wall was built by the Moslem Suleiman the Magnificent in A.D. 1538.

n. The average thickness is ten feet and the height thirty-eight feet.

o. The circumference is two and a-half miles and forms a rough square with the four sides facing the cardinal points of the compass.

p. Past and future walls of Jerusalem.

   (1) About one mile in circumference in David's day.

   (2) Three miles in Solomon's time.

   (3) Four miles in Jesus' day.

   (4) Six miles during the millennium (Ezek. 48:35).

   (5) The circumference of the New Jerusalem (5600 miles).

7. The gates of this city.

There are twelve gates to this city, three gates on each side. On each gate is the name of one of the tribes of

Israel. Each gate is composed of a beautiful solid white pearl.

And had a wall great and high, and had twelve gates, and at the gates twelve angels, and names written thereon, which are the names of the twelve tribes of the children of Israel: On the east three gates; on the north three gates; on the south three gates; and on the west three gates (Rev. 21:12, 13).

In Nehemiah's time there were ten.

a. sheep (3:1)
b. fish (3:3)
c. old (3:6)
d. valley (3:13)
e. dung (3:14)
f. fountain (3:15)
g. water (3:26)
h. horse (3:28)
i. east (3:29)
j. Miphkad (3:31)

In the millennial earthly city of Jerusalem there will be twelve gates, three gates on the north, three on the south, three on the east, and three on the west. Each gate will be named after one of the twelve tribes of Israel.

In the heavenly New Jerusalem there will be twelve gates arranged and named as the gates in the millennial city, but in addition (as we have seen) an angel will be assigned to each gate. Furthermore, every gate will be made of solid pearl.

At the present time there are eleven gates in the old City of Jerusalem. Seven are open gates, and four are closed. The seven open gates are (clockwise, beginning at 12 noon):

Damascus Gate.
Herod's Gate.
St. Stephen's Gate.
Dung Gate.
Zion Gate.
Jaffa Gate.
New Gate.

The four closed gates are:

The Eastern Gate.
The Single Gate.
The Double Gate.
The Triple Gate.

8. The main street of this city.
The central boulevard of the New Jerusalem is composed of pure transparent gold.
And the twelve gates were twelve pearls; every several gate was of one pearl: and the street of the city was pure gold, as it were transparent glass (Rev. 21:21).
When one considers the price of gold (nearly $600 an ounce at the beginning of the eighties), the total worth of this city becomes incomprehensible!

9. The throne within this city.
And immediately I was in the spirit: and, behold, a throne was set in heaven, and one sat on the throne. And he that sat was to look upon like a jasper and a sardine stone: and there was a rainbow round about the throne, in sight like unto an emerald. And before the throne there was a sea of glass like unto crystal: and in the midst of the throne, and round about the throne, were four beasts full of eyes before and behind (Rev. 4:2, 3, 6).

10. The river of life in this city.
And he showed me a pure river of water of life, clear as crystal, proceeding out of the throne of God and of the Lamb (Rev. 22:1).
The Holy Spirit doubtless meant to make at least some reference to this river when he inspired David to write:
And he shall be like a tree planted by the rivers of water, that bringeth forth his fruit in his season; his leaf also shall not wither; and whatsoever he doeth shall prosper (Ps. 1:3).
There is a river, the streams whereof shall make glad the city of God, the holy place of the tabernacles of the most High (Ps. 46:4).

11. The tree of life in this city.
In the midst of the street of it, and on either side of the river, was there the tree of life, which bare twelve manner of fruits, and yielded her fruit every month: and the leaves of the tree

were for the healing of the nations (Rev. 22:2).

When God created man and placed him in the Garden of Eden he placed at Adam's disposal (among many other things) the tree of life. But when man sinned, he was driven from Eden and from this tree.

And out of the ground made the Lord God to grow every tree that is pleasant to the sight, and good for food; the tree of life also in the midst of the garden, and the tree of knowledge of good and evil (Gen. 2:9).

So he drove out the man; and he placed at the east of the garden of Eden cherubim, and a flaming sword which turned every way, to keep the way of the tree of life (Gen. 3:24).

At that point in human history the tree of life disappears, but here in the New Jerusalem it will blossom and bloom as never before. In his book *Reveling Through Revelation*, Dr. J. Vernon McGee writes the following words concerning this river and this tree:

"Up to this chapter, the New Jerusalem seems to be all mineral and no vegetable. Its appearance is as the dazzling display of a fabulous jewelry store, but there is no soft grass to sit upon, no green trees to enjoy, and no water to drink or food to eat. However, here introduced are the elements which add a rich softness to this city of elaborate beauty."

Paul Lee Tan writes:

"Because of the location of the tree of life 'on either side of the river,' theologians have understood the 'tree' to be not a single tree, but a single kind of tree . . . a row of trees on either side of the river. Others, however, see one tree planted at the middle of the river, with branches extending to both banks. The tree is large enough to span the river, so that the river is in the midst of the street, and the tree is on both sides of the river" (*The New Jerusalem*, p. 28).

12. The relationship between this city and earthly Jerusalem. We have already seen that there will be two fabulous cities of God in the future. One is located on the earth.

It will be known as Jehovah Tsidkenu, meaning, "the Lord our righteousness" (Jer. 23:6; 33:16), and the other is Jehovah Shammah, meaning "the Lord is there" (Ezek. 48:35). The other city is suspended in space and is called the New Jerusalem (Rev. 21:2). This one of course is thousands of times the size of the earthly city and will endure forever. The question has often been asked whether these two cities will exist at the same time. If so, who will live in each?

Clarence Mason offers the following comments concerning this:

"It is commonly understood by premillennialists that the redeemed of all ages will share in the millennium on earth. This poses a problem which is not often mentioned but which nonetheless has disturbed many earnest Bible students and puzzled expositors. Evidently because devout students of the Word recognize that they must reverently avoid going beyond what God has revealed, they have tended to 'skip' this problem. After all, there are some mysteries we must be willing to leave with God, and they feel this well may be one of them. But is it?

I refer, of course, to the question in the millennium, how will those who enter that period in resurrected bodies relate to those who enter with nonresurrected bodies, that is, those living Jews and Gentiles who come in saved from the tribulation period?

The general supposition is that we will live side by side, as it were, in the same earth areas and environment; but this would make for some strange situations. I have never heard any attempt to discuss the matter explicitly with suggested solutions, so I shall attempt a solution.

My wife and I live at 330 Harrison Avenue in a Philadelphia suburb. We have neighbors on each side of us, and neighbors on the other side of the street corresponding to the three houses on our side. Suppose God, in line with the usual view, placed my wife and me at 330 Harrison Avenue during the millennium, but with neighbors other than the present ones. Look at this hypothetical chart:

Jews from before Christ (resurrected) 327	Gentiles born during the millennium (nonresurrected) 329	Jews martyred in the tribulation (resurrected) 331

HARRISON AVENUE

328 Living Jews from the tribulation (nonresurrected bodies)	330 The Masons from the church age (resurrected bodies)	332 Living Gentiles from the tribulation (nonresurrected bodies)

1. My wife and I reside at 330, two church-age believers in resurrected bodies.
2. In 328, to our left, is a Jewish family who received Christ as Lord during the tribulation period, were rescued by our Lord at His second coming, and entered the millennium in non-resurrected bodies.
3. In 332, to our right, is a Gentile family who came out of the tribulation also. The father, wife, and two children were saved early in the tribulation period.
4. In 331, directly across the street from them, are a Jew and his wife who believed on the Lord Jesus during the tribulation but were martyred for their faith by Satan's monster of iniquity for refusing to bow down to the image of the beast, set up in the holy place (Mt. 24:15; Rev. 13:14, 15). They also have resurrected bodies.
5. In 329, next to them and directly across the street from us, there is a Gentile father and mother, each of whom were born of saved Gentile parents during the early part of the millennium. Their parents entered the millennium, like those in 328 and 332, when Christ came back to set up His kingdom. These second generation parents have a little boy three years

311

old and a baby on the way. (Each of those in 329 will have to be saved like people in any preceding age; for sadly, each would be capable of sinning brazenly and openly, resulting in their being smitten by Christ's 'rod of iron,' or even be guilty of posing as loyal citizens until opportunity is given to show their true inner feelings when Satan is released at the end of the 1,000 years, perishing with him in his abortive rebellion.)

6. In 327, to their right, is a Jewish family who lived before the time of Christ and died looking for a heavenly city which God had prepared for them (Heb. 11:16). They are in resurrected bodies.

To summarize, the people residing in 327, 330, and 331 have glorified bodies. They do not cohabit with their wives and do not produce children. They do not have old natures. They cannot sin. They have never-dying, never-aging bodies. There is no suggestion in Scripture that they will eat food or be sustained by it.

On the other hand, families living in 328, 329, and 332 do NOT have resurrected bodies. They will eat, sleep, play, cohabit with their wives, have children, and probably work in the earth, which, though curse-freed, will have crops that need to be tilled (Amos 9:13–15).

How would this neighborhood get along together? Will we all 'go to church' together? Or, will we all go up to Jerusalem together (Zech. 14:16, 17; Mic. 4:1, 2)? If so, how? Will 'their' kids play in 'our' backyards? Will the nice people in 332 invite all five neighbor families to a barbecue on their spacious lawn? Will I offer to drive the young pregnant wife and her little boy (in 329) to the supermarket in my Zippo Eight, while her husband is tilling the earth outside of town? Will these neighbors play horseshoes together? What will my wife and I, and the people in 327 and 331 do at night while those in 328, 329, and 332 are sleeping, since we have permanent, resurrected bodies that need no sleep?

What sort of community would it be with people who cannot sin living side by side with those who can? To add to the complications, just what would be the relationship between those in 328 and 332, who are saved but can sin, and that young couple in 329, who could not only sin but might reject Christ's claims and remain unsaved? Why would God put mixed-up groups like this in tens of thousands of neighborhoods all over the world?

However, if we accept the solution that the New Jerusalem will be related to time as well as later to eternity, then things begin to unwind in our thinking. Certainly Christ and all resurrected saints will return to earth in resurrected bodies to join in His day of triumph and exaltation. But that Christ, or we in resurrected bodies, will remain on earth all through the thousand years has been assumed and not stated. As previously suggested as far as Christ is concerned, implicit in the titles 'King of Kings' and 'Lord of lords' is the thought that He will heavily delegate authority, and perhaps David will be His earthly regent over Israel.

Suppose that, during the millennium, Christ and those believers of previous ages who have resurrection bodies, live in the New Jerusalem and the people with nonresurrected bodies live on earth. Kings of the earth would 'bring their glory and honor' into the New Jerusalem and earth's inhabitants' longevity would be assured by the provision of the 'leaves of the tree of life for the healing [health] of the nations.' Each kind of people, resurrected and nonresurrected, would be in suitable habitats. There would be full cooperation between the New Jerusalem and province Earth and full submission to King Jesus. But we would have a really viable solution to the puzzling problem of all kinds of people from all kinds of ages living all mixed up together in earth's neighborhoods.

May this be the solution? Think it over!" (*Prophetic Problems*, Moody Press, 1973, pp. 246–249).

13. The nature of the resurrected bodies in this city.
To summarize, all resurrected bodies shall reside in the heavenly city, but will reign upon the earthly city. Having

now examined our future location, what do we know about our transformation and (finally) our vocation? In other words, what will be the nature of these resurrected bodies and what activities will we carry on through them?

In 1 Corinthians 15 Paul answers questions concerning this transformation.

In verse 44 he writes, "There is a natural body and there is a spiritual body." What is the difference? Consider a book with a sheet of plain white paper stuck inside it. In this illustration the book is man's body and the paper sheet is his spirit. Down here the book "bosses" the spirit. It has the final say. This is the natural body, governed by the physical laws of gravity and time.

But now take the white sheet out of the book and wrap it around the book like a cover. Now the sheet (spirit) is on top. It has the final say. This is the spiritual body, unaffected by the physical laws of gravity or time, but enjoys the blessings of eternity.

In verses 39–41 Paul suggests that the new spiritual body is as superior to the old natural body as

a. The human body is to those of animals (15:39).

b. The heavens are to the earth (15:40).

c. The sun is to the moon (15:41).

In his book *The King of the Earth*, author Erich Sauer writes:

"The results and technical application of atomic physics throw a surprising light on this. Today the transmutation of elements is already possible and men can at any time carry it out in atomic laboratories and plants. As success upon success quickly followed upon Rutherford's first achievement in 1919, the transmutation of atoms soon became almost an 'everyday occurrence in the research institutes.' The idea of the unchangeability of elements belongs to the past.

The basic constituents of matter are everywhere the same. Whether it is mercury, gold or sulphur, carbon or oxygen, we are ultimately only concerned with protons,

314

neutrons and electrons. Which element it is depends only on their number.

If an atomic nucleus consists of seven protons and neutrons and is encircled by the same number of electrons, we call it nitrogen. If there are six, then it is carbon. If there are eighty, then it is mercury; if seventy-nine, then it is gold.

If the atomic nucleus gains or loses one or more protons or neutrons, then the element becomes another. So uranium becomes radium with its radiations, and radium becomes lead. Should we therefore succeed in shooting a proton out of the nucleus of a mercury atom, then the transmutation of mercury into gold has been accomplished, and the old dream of the medieval alchemists has been fulfilled. The physicist of today could, in fact, 'make' gold. The 'philosopher's stone,' sought for in vain for centuries by the alchemists, which makes this miracle possible, is electricity at a tension of a few million volts.

This leads us to ask if men in their laboratories, by bombarding atomic nuclei and removing protons and neutrons from them, are able to transmute elements into other elements, e.g., base metals into semi-precious or precious metals, why should God not be able to transform and transmute elements into others? If man can change mercury into gold, why should God not be able to change water into wine?

Admittedly man requires mighty power stations for this transmutation. But does not God, the Almighty, have infinitely greater sources of power at His disposal, than man's greatest power plants? Indeed, did He not from the very outset, as the Creator of matter, Himself call these atomic powers into being and unite them? Hence they are only a part of His power, and He can at any time freely determine their composition" (Eerdmans, 1955, p. 179).

Such then, will be the nature of our transformed bodies.

These bodies will be like his glorious body (Phil. 3:21; 1 Jn. 3:1-3).

They will consist of flesh and bone (Lk. 24:39, 40).

Christ ate in his glorified body (Lk. 24:41–43; Jn. 21:12–15).

These bodies will not be subjected to laws of gravity and time (Jn. 20:19; Lk. 24:31, 36).

They will be recognizable bodies (Mt. 8:11; Lk. 16:23; 1 Cor. 13:12).

They will be eternal bodies (2 Cor. 5:1).

They will be (as we have already seen) bodies in which the spirit predominates (1 Cor. 15:44, 49).

14. The activities of the redeemed in this city.

A popular but totally perverted concept of heaven would describe that future life in the skies in terms of some disembodied spirits piously perched on fleecy clouds and strumming their golden harps. This may be heaven according to Walt Disney, but New Testament it is not. Scripture would indicate that:

a. Heaven will be a place of singing.

Sing, O ye heavens; for the Lord hath done it; shout, ye lower parts of the earth: break forth into singing, ye mountains, O forest, and every tree therein: for the Lord hath redeemed Jacob, and glorified himself in Israel (Isa. 44:23).

Saying, I will declare thy name unto my brethren, in the midst of the church will I sing praise unto thee (Heb. 2:12).

And they sung as it were a new song before the throne, and before the four beasts, and the elders: and no man could learn that song but the hundred and forty and four thousand, which were redeemed from the earth (Rev. 14:3).

And they sing the song of Moses the servant of God, and the song of the Lamb, saying, Great and marvelous are thy works, Lord God Almighty; just and true are thy ways, thou King of saints (Rev. 15:3).

There are of course some songs we sing down here that we won't sing up there. We will not sing, "When We All Get to Heaven," or "Sweet Hour of Prayer." But other earthly hymns will be appropriate to sing up there, such as "Great Is Thy Faithfulness," and "All Hail the Power of Jesus' Name."

Two of heaven's greatest songs will have for their theme God's two great works.

(1) The hymn praising God for his mighty work of creation:

Thou art worthy, O Lord, to receive glory and honour and power: for thou hast created all things, and for thy pleasure they are and were created (Rev. 4:11).

(2) The hymn praising God for his mighty work of redemption:

And they sung a new song, saying, Thou art worthy to take the book, and to open the seals thereof: for thou wast slain, and hast redeemed us to God by thy blood out of every kindred, and tongue, and people, and nation (Rev. 5:9).

b. Heaven will be a place of fellowship.

One of the most beloved gospel songs is entitled, "Leaning On the Everlasting Arms." The first stanza begins: "What a fellowship, what a joy divine. . . ." Sometimes however, as one observes the petty squabbling which goes on in local churches, this verse might be rephrased to read: "What? A fellowship? What? A joy divine?" But in heaven real and eternal fellowship will prevail.

Not only will believers enjoy blessed fellowship with other believers, but, even more important, we shall know and be known by the Savior in a far more intimate way than ever possible here on earth. Note the things this good and great and chief Shepherd will do for his sheep in heaven as listed by John:

He will feed us that hidden heavenly manna; he will give us a new name.

He that hath an ear, let him hear what the Spirit saith unto the churches; To him that overcometh will I give to eat of the hidden manna, and will give him a white stone, and in the stone a new name written, which no man knoweth saving he that receiveth it (Rev. 2:17).

317

He will lead us beside the living waters; he will dry all our tears.

For the Lamb which is in the midst of the throne shall feed them, and shall lead them unto living fountains of waters: and God shall wipe away all tears from their eyes (Rev. 7:17).

He will allow us to sit with him on his throne.

To him that overcometh will I grant to sit with me in my throne, even as I also overcame, and am set down with my Father in his throne (Rev. 3:21).

He will dress us with his own righteousness.

And to her was granted that she should be arrayed in fine linen, clean and white: for the fine linen is the righteousness of saints (Rev. 19:8).

c. Heaven will be a place of testifying.

Let the redeemed of the Lord say so . . . (Ps. 107:2).

Jesus . . . saith . . . Go . . . tell them how great things the Lord hath done for thee, and hath had compassion on thee (Mk. 5:19).

It has already been suggested that heaven's human population may approach (or exceed) 30 billion. Each of this staggering number will have his or her unique and personal testimony. Thus, the first few million centuries might well be spent in the hearing of these redemption reviews. Add to this number the untold trillions of angels, each doubtless desiring to share what their Creator has done for and meant to them.

d. Heaven will be a place of serving.

And there shall be no more curse: but the throne of God and of the Lamb shall be in it; and his servants shall serve him (Rev. 22:3).

Therefore are they before the throne of God, and serve him day and night in his temple: and he that sitteth on the throne shall dwell among them (Rev. 7:15).

While we cannot be dogmatic on the exact nature of this service, we do know from the following passages that a portion of our labor for the Lamb will be that of exercising authority and judgment over men and angels:

Do ye not know that the saints shall judge the world? and

if the world shall be judged by you, are ye unworthy to judge the smallest matters? Know ye not that we shall judge angels? how much more things that pertain to this life? (1 Cor. 6:2, 3).

If we suffer, we shall also reign with him: if we deny him, he also will deny us (2 Tim. 2:12).

And there shall be no night there; and they need no candle, neither light of the sun; for the Lord God giveth them light: and they shall reign for ever and ever (Rev. 22:5).

e. Heaven will be a place of learning.

For we know in part, and we prophesy in part. But when that which is perfect is come, then that which is in part shall be done away (1 Cor. 13:9, 10).

What will we learn about in heaven?

(1) We will learn concerning the *Person* of God. Let us suppose in heaven we are able to double our learning each year concerning the person and attributes of God. This is not at all an unreasonable assumption, for the Christian will possess a sinless and glorified body, along with a holy and tireless desire to know more about Jesus! So here is a believer who begins eternity with X amount of knowledge about God. At the beginning of his second year he has double this, the third year four times as much, the fourth year he knows eight times as much, etc. By the end of his eleventh year he will increase his knowledge concerning God a thousandfold. At the conclusion of year number twenty-one the figure jumps to one million. At the end of the thirty-first year the number leaps to one billion. Following the fourty-first year it reaches one trillion! As he finishes his first century in eternity his knowledge of God (doubling each year) would reach 10^{30} (one followed by 30 zeros).

This figure is thousands of times more than the combined total of all the grains of sand on all the seashores of the earth. But this number

319

simply marks his first one hundred years. How much knowledge doubling will he have experienced at the end of his first one million years? This staggering figure cannot even be comprehended by the mortal mind, but whatever it is, and however many zeros it represents, it will double itself the very next year! The point of all the above is simply this. Throughout the untold and unnumbered trillions and trillions of years in timeless eternity, each child of God can double his or her learning about the Creator each year and yet never even remotely exhaust the awesome height, depth, or length of the Person of God! Our testimony will continuously be: "O the depth of the riches both of the wisdom and knowledge of God! how unsearchable are his judgments, and his ways past finding out!" (Rom. 11:33).

(2) We will learn concerning the *plan* of God. One of the most painful questions asked here on earth by Christians is why a loving and wise God allows certain terrible tragedies to occur. As an example, here is a young, spirit-filled pastor. He has spent a number of years diligently preparing for the ministry. His wife has sacrificed to help put him through school. But now all this is paying off. His church is experiencing an amazing growth. Souls are saved weekly. New converts are baptized each Sunday. Additional Sunday school buses are purchased and a new building is planned. A skeptical community slowly finds itself being profoundly influenced by this vibrant and exciting pastor and his people. Suddenly, without any warning, the minister is killed in a freak accident. Shortly after the funeral the still-confused and stunned congregation extends a call to another man. But the new minister shows little compassion and less leadership ability. Soon the flock is scat-

tered and the once-thrilling testimony of a growing and glowing work is all but stilled!

How many times since Abel's martyrdom at the dawn of human history have similar tragedies like this taken place? One need only change the names, places, and rearrange some of the details. But the searing and searching question remains. Why does God permit such terrible things?

We may rest assured, however, that in heaven. God will take each of us aside and explain fully the reason for all our sufferings and trials. We then will say the words once stated by a Galilean crowd in Jesus' day: "He hath done all things well . . ." (Mk. 7:37).

(3) We will learn concerning the *power* of God. In the beginning God created the heaven and the earth (Gen. 1:1). Just how vast is our universe? It is so huge that it takes a beam of light (which travels some 700 million miles per hour) over ten billion years to cross the known universe! Within this universe are untold trillions of stars, planets, and other heavenly bodies. God made them all to instruct man concerning his power and glory (Ps. 19:1; 147:4; Isa. 40:26). We shall someday therefore visit each star and explore every corner of our Father's universe!

In closing this section and this book consider:

C. Those elements absent in heaven.

    1. No more sea.

And I saw a new heaven and a new earth: for the first heaven and the first earth were passed away; and there was no more sea (Rev. 21:1).

Compare with the following:

But the wicked are like the troubled sea, when it cannot rest, whose waters cast up mire and dirt. There is no peace, saith my God, to the wicked (Isa. 57:20, 21).

    2. No more tears, no more death, no more pain.

And God shall wipe away all tears from their eyes; and there shall be no more death, neither sorrow, nor crying, neither

shall there be any more pain: for the former things are passed
away (Rev. 21:4).

3. No more sun or moon.
   And the city had no need of the sun, neither of the moon, to
   shine in it: for the glory of God did lighten it, and the Lamb
   is the light thereof (Rev. 21:23).

4. No more insecurity, no more night.
   And the gates of it shall not be shut at all by day: for there
   shall be no night there (Rev. 21:25).

5. No more sin.
   And there shall in no wise enter into it any thing that defileth,
   neither whatsoever worketh abomination, or maketh a lie: but
   they which are written in the Lamb's book of life
   (Rev. 21:27).

6. No more sickness, no more curse.
   In the midst of the street of it, and on either side of the river,
   was there the tree of life, which bare twelve manner of fruits,
   and yielded her fruit every month: and the leaves of the tree
   were for the healing of the nations (Rev. 22:2).

7. No more thirst, or more hunger, or more heat.
   They shall hunger no more, neither thirst any more; neither
   shall the sun light on them, nor any heat (Rev. 7:16).

D. Those elements present in heaven.
   1. Glory.
      Father, I will that they also, whom thou hast given me, be
      with me where I am; that they may behold my glory, which
      thou hast given me: for thou lovedst me before the foundation
      of the world (Jn. 17:24).
      For I reckon that the sufferings of this present time are not
      worthy to be compared with the glory which shall be revealed
      in us (Rom. 8:18).
      And the city had no need of the sun, neither of the moon,
      to shine in it: for the glory of God did lighten it, and the
      Lamb is the light thereof (Rev. 21:23).

   2. Holiness.
      And there shall in no wise enter into it any thing that defileth,
      neither whatsoever worketh abomination, or maketh a lie: but
      they which are written in the Lamb's book of life
      (Rev. 21:27).

   3. Beauty.

Out of Zion, the perfection of beauty, God hath shined (Ps. 50:2).

4. Divine light.

Arise, shine; for thy light is come, and the glory of the Lord is risen upon thee. For, behold, the darkness shall cover the earth, and gross darkness the people: but the Lord shall arise upon thee, and his glory shall be seen upon thee. And the Gentiles shall come to thy light, and kings to the brightness of thy rising (Isa. 60:1–3).

The sun shall be no more thy light by day; neither for brightness shall the moon give light unto thee: but the Lord shall be unto thee an everlasting light, and thy God thy glory. Thy sun shall no more go down; neither shall thy moon withdraw itself: for the Lord shall be thine everlasting light, and the days of thy mourning shall be ended (Isa. 60:19, 20).

5. Unity.

That in the dispensation of the fulness of times he might gather together in one all things in Christ, both which are in heaven, and which are on earth; even in him (Eph. 1:10).

6. Perfection.

But when that which is perfect is come, then that which is in part shall be done away (1 Cor. 13:10).

7. Joy.

Thou wilt show me the path of life: in thy presence is fulness of joy; at thy right hand there are pleasures for evermore (Ps. 16:11).

8. Eternity.

That whosoever believeth in him should not perish, but have eternal life (Jn. 3:15).

NINETEEN
THE TESTIMONY
OF THE TREES

*And as he sat upon the mount of Olives, the disciples came unto him
privately, saying, Tell us, when shall these things be? and what shall be
the sign of thy coming, and of the end of the world? (Mt. 24:3).
And he spake to them a parable; Behold the fig tree, and all the trees;
when they now shoot forth, ye see and know of your own selves that
summer is now nigh at hand. So likewise ye, when ye see these things
come to pass, know ye that the kingdom of God is nigh at hand. Verily I
say unto you, this generation shall not pass away, till all be fulfilled
(Lk. 21:29-32).*

John Naisbitt's number one national best-selling book,
Magatrends 2000, may prove to be the most thought-provoking
volume of the 1990s. Certainly, it is one of the most positive in its
outlook. The author presents a very rosy picture indeed for all
mankind during the final decade of the twentieth century. Here are
some excerpts:

"We stand at the dawn of a new era. Before us is the most important
decade in the history of civilization, a period of stunning
technological innovation, unprecedented economic opportunity,
surprising political reform, and great cultural rebirth. It will be a
decade like none that has come before, because it will culminate in
the millennium, the year 2000.

For centuries that monumental, symbolic date has stood for the
future and what we shall make of it. In a few short years that future
will be here.

Already we have fallen under its dominion. The year 2000 is

operating like a powerful magnet on humanity, reaching down into the 1990s and intensifying the decade. It is amplifying emotions, accelerating change, heightening awareness, and compelling us to re-examine ourselves, our values, and our institutions.

The biblical millennium refers to the thousand-year period after Christ's Second Coming and, after an apocalyptic battle, when the kingdom of God is established on earth.

On a secular level the millennium has come to mean a golden age in human history, a time to close the door on the past and embark upon a new era.

As we move toward this extraordinary date, the mythology of the millennium, consciously or not, is re-engaging us.

The most exciting breakthroughs of the 21st century will occur not because of technology, but because of an expanding concept of what it means to be human" (J. Naisbitt, *Megatrends 2000*, New York: Avon Books, 1991, pp. 17, 20, 23).

Naisbitt then lists some specific achievements:
1. Free trade among all nations.

    As we turn to the next century, we will witness the linkup of North America, Europe, and Japan to form a golden triangle of free trade.
2. No limit to growth.

    The global boom of the 1990s will be free of the limits on growth we have known in the past. In fact, there will be virtually no limits to growth. There will be an abundance of natural resources throughout the 1990s from agricultural products and raw materials to oil. Everything that comes out of the ground will be in oversupply for the balance of this century and probably much longer.
3. No energy crisis.

    There will be no energy crisis to impede the 1900s global boom. Quite simply, the world is using less energy while producing more.
4. Containment of inflation.

    Inflation will be contained because there is now worldwide competition for price and quality, a new phenomenon.
5. The advancement of democracy and the spread of free enterprise.

6. Peace, not war.

It has begun to dawn on people everywhere that war is now an obsolete way of solving problems, certainly among developed countries (pp. 5-7, 10-12).

The author concluded his book with the following:

"The meaning of that great symbol the millennium depends entirely on how it is interpreted. It can mark the end of time or the beginning of the new. We believe the decision has already been made to embrace its positive side. Within the hearts and minds of humanity, there has been a commitment to life, to the utopian quest for peace and prosperity for all, which today we can clearly visualize. Humanity is entering a decade-long race to confront the great challenges remaining in hope of making a fresh start in the year 2000.

The 1990s will be an extraordinary time. The countdown—1992, 1993, 1994—is just about to begin. Get ready. You possess a front-row seat to the most challenging yet most exciting decade in the history of civilization" (p. 338).

Do the Scriptures reflect this optimism? In a nutshell: No and yes! No, man the creator will not through his own efforts usher in the Kingdom. Yes, Christ the Creator will return to establish a glorious thousand-year reign of peace! But how does all this come about? What conditions will prevail at the time of his return? When will it occur? Note Jesus' answer concerning that period of time just prior to his return:

Behold the fig tree, and all the trees; when they now shoot forth . . . the kingdom of God is nigh at hand (Lk. 21:29ff.).

What exactly is the Savior saying here? In the Bible, on occasion, a particular nation is symbolized by a tree. For example, the nation Assyria is depicted as a cedar tree (Ezek. 31:3), the Amorite nation as an oak (Amos 2:9), and here in Luke 21 the nation Israel as a fig tree. In light of all this, our Lord seems to indicate here that when certain "trees" (nations) begin to "shoot forth their leaves" (show intense activity), one may know that his coming is at hand!

The following study presents the testimony of various individual trees or cluster of trees. These are:

RUSSIA

A. Considered historically

1. Both Herodotus (fifth century B.C. Greek philosopher) and Josephus (first century A.D. Jewish historian) suggest the land of Russia may have been originally settled by Magog, Tubal, and Meshach, three sons of Japheth, after the Great Flood (see Gen. 10:2).

2. The Slavic tribes began migrating into Russia from the West in the fifth century A.D.

3. Tradition says the Viking Rurik came to Russia in A.D. 862 and founded the first Russian dynasty in Novgorod.

4. The first Russian state was established by the Scandinavian chieftains in the ninth century. The other various tribes were united by the spread of Christianity in the tenth and eleventh centuries.

5. Ivan the Terrible became the first tsar in 1547.

6. Peter the Great (1682–1725) and Catherine the Great (1762–1796) introduced and established Western culture upon the land.

7. Napoleon invaded but failed to conquer Russia in 1812 and 1813.

8. The nation was soundly defeated by Japan in 1905.

9. She found herself on the winning side during World War I.

10. On November 7, 1917, Vladimir Lenin took over Russia and imposed communism upon the people.

11. The Union of Soviet Socialist Republics was established as a federation on December 30, 1922.

12. Joseph Stalin assumed power following the death of Lenin on January 21, 1924.

13. Germany and Russia signed a nonaggression pact in August, 1939.

14. Germany attacked Russia on June 22, 1941.

15. Russia became the second most powerful nation on earth following the end of World War II in 1945.

16. Russia imposed communism upon the Eastern European countries following World War II.

17. Stalin died on March 5, 1953, and was eventually succeeded by Nikita Khrushchev.

18. Russia exploded the hydrogen bomb in 1953.

19. In 1957 Russia sent the first satellite into space (*Sputnik I*).
20. Mikhail Gorbachev came into power in 1985.

B. Considered currently
1. President: Mikhail S. Gorbachev
2. Population: 291 million
3. Land area: 8,649,496 square miles. Russia is the world's largest country, covering one-sixth of the earth's land area. It is nearly two-and-a-half times the size of the United States.
4. Capital: Moscow
5. Gross national product: $2.5 trillion

C. Considered prophetically

And the word of the Lord came unto me, saying, Son of man, set thy face against Gog, the land of Magog, the chief prince of Meshech and Tubal, and prophesy against him, and say, Thus saith the Lord God: Behold, I am against thee, O Gog, the chief prince of Meshech and Tubal. . . . After many days thou shalt be visited: in the latter years thou shalt come into the land that is brought back from the sword, and is gathered out of many people, against the mountains of Israel, which have been always waste: but it is brought forth out of the nations, and they shall dwell safely all of them. Thou shalt ascend and come like a storm, thou shalt be like a cloud to cover the land, thou, and all thy bands, and many people with thee. Thus said the Lord God; It shall also come to pass, that at the same time shall things come into thy mind, and thou shalt think an evil thought: And thou shalt say, I will go up to the land of unwalled villages; I will go to them that are at rest, that dwell safely, all of them dwelling without walls, and having neither bars nor gates, to take a spoil, and to take a prey; to turn thine hand upon the desolate places that are now inhabited, and upon the people that are gathered out of the nations, which have gotten cattle and goods, that dwell in the midst of the land (Ezek. 38:1-3, 8-12).

There is geographical, historical, and linguistic evidence that the "land of Magog" that will invade Israel in the final days is the U.S.S.R. Bible students have held this view for over a century. However, in recent months this position has been challenged by some on the basis of Moscow's growing inability to control her own fifteen union republics that make up the U.S.S.R. Certainly, no informed person can dispute these facts.

"Hence the inability of the Soviet system by 1990 to so much as put enough bread and meat on the tables of its citizens or cigarettes in their pockets exposed the ultimate bankruptcy of applied communism in the smartest way possible. But the travails of the Soviet Union went beyond the paralysis of industrial production and of agricultural planting and harvesting. The country, a jigsaw puzzle of 100 ethnic pieces, was at the point of falling apart. Almost all of the U.S.S.R.'s fifteen constituent republics were demanding full independence or some degree of autonomy" (*The World Almanac*, New York: Pharos Books, 1991, p. 35).

One of the most revealing signs of this dissatisfaction was seen during the 1990 May Day parade (the most sacred of all Communist holidays) when thousands of marchers openly jeered those Russian top officials on the reviewing stand—something totally unthinkable even a few years ago! In light of all this, can it still be held that Russia will someday attack Israel in this weakened condition?

Here a question may be asked: What kind of bear could be considered the most dangerous of all? Is it a black bear, a polar bear, or a grizzly bear? Would it be a male or female bear? Most would probably agree the most fearful and deadly of all bears is a desperate and starving bear! In other words, Russia's present-day near-desperate condition might actually increase rather than decrease the chances for this attack!

GERMANY AND THE EASTERN EUROPEAN NATIONS

A. Considered historically (Germany)
1. Julius Caesar defeated the Germanic tribes in 55 B.C.
2. Charlemagne consolidated the various peoples in A.D. 800.
3. More territory was added to Germany by the Treaty of Verdun in 843.
4. Otto the Great was crowned king in 936.
5. The Thirty Years' War (1618–1648) devastated Germany's many small principalities and kingdoms.
6. Frederick the Great (1740–1786) reorganized the military.
7. Otto von Bismarck, Prussian chancellor, formed the modern German Empire on January 18, 1871, in Versailles.

8. Germany reached its peak prior to 1914 but lost all of its colonies following the crushing defeat in World War I.
9. Adolph Hitler assumed total power in 1933.
10. In September 1939 Hitler's Germany instigated the Second World War. A defeated Hitler killed himself in April 1945.
11. Germany was controlled by the Allied powers until 1951.
12. The Federal Republic of Germany was proclaimed on May 23, 1949. Konrad Adenauer became the first chancellor.
13. After a forty-five-year division into Communist and non-Communist states, the reunification of Germany was formalized on October 3, 1990.

B. Considered currently (Germany)
1. Chancellor: Helmut Kohl
2. Population: 79,500,000
3. Land area: 290,434 square miles
4. Capital: Bonn
5. Gross national product: $1.327 trillion

C. Considered prophetically (Germany and the Eastern European nations)

Nearly six centuries before the Bethlehem event, God revealed to Daniel that in the final days prior to Christ's return the antichrist would succeed in reviving and controlling the old Roman Empire (see Dan. 2 and 7). John the apostle would later receive the same basic information (see Rev. 13 and 17).

The ancient empire of Rome is now (for the most part) occupied by European nations and the USA. In essence, these prophesies stated the antichrist would rule over the Western world. According to Daniel 11 and Ezekiel 39, however, he would not control Russia! However, at the close of the 1980s these predictions seemed highly unlikely to be fulfilled, for practically all of Eastern Europe and half of Germany suffered under the bondage of Russian communism. But then the impossible and incredible occurred! Consider:

1. *Germany* was reunified on October 3, 1990.
2. *Romanian* president Nicolae Ceausescu was executed by his own countrymen on Christmas Day 1989, and a democratic government was instituted.
3. On December 29, 1989, Vaclav Havel, a dissident playwright who had been imprisoned by the Communists, was elected president of *Czechoslovakia*.

4. Lech Walesa, hero of the Solidarity movement, became president of *Poland* in November 1990.
5. In October 1989 *Hungary* proclaimed itself to be a free republic.
6. *Yugoslavia* began exploring paths toward democracy in the fall of 1990.
7. The *Bulgarian* parliament approved free multiparty elections in April 1989.
8. *Albania,* the smallest and most isolated of the Eastern European countries, made at least cosmetic gestures toward democratic reforms in May 1990.

AMERICA

For the majority of readers, it is unnecessary to consider America from a historical or current aspect. But what of the future? Is America mentioned in prophecy? If so, what role will the United States assume in the final days?

Edgar C. James writes:

"Does the Bible say anything about the future of the United States?

Some, in reading the Scripture, believe various passages may allude to the United States. But such conclusions are very remote. For instance, some hold the 'young lions' (Ezekiel 38:13, KJV), and 'islands' (Psalm 72:10) refer to England's colonies; namely, America. But a careful check shows those are villages or islands of Tarshish, the area of southern Spain (cf. Jonah 1:3).

Others find America as the 'great eagle' (Revelation 12:14) or the 'land shadowing with wings' (Isaiah 18:1, KJV). But the Revelation passage is showing the speed with which the woman flees into the wilderness, not a nation. The Isaiah passage refers to a nation with 'whirling wings' (Isaiah 18:1), most likely a reference to the insects of Ethiopia" (*Armageddon*, Chicago: Moody Press, 1981, pp. 102-103).

However, simply because the United States is not mentioned in prophecy does not mean it has no role in the latter days. To the contrary, it would appear tragically possible the United States will function as the most important member of the antichrist's ten-nation Western confederation. In fact, it may well be that the antichrist will be an American citizen! Consider:

1. The antichrist will no doubt hold citizenship from one of the ten nations he eventually controls.
2. Following the rapture of the church, no other nation on earth will suffer the loss of so many key (saved) leaders in the areas of government, business, education, medicine, sports, etc., than America!
3. In light of this above, it is not unreasonable to envision a United States citizen (antichrist) quickly moving in to fill the tremendous power vacuum which will of necessity exist!

IRAN (ancient Persia)

A. Considered historically
1. It became a powerful empire under Cyrus the Great in the mid sixth century B.C.
2. On October 29, 539 B.C., Cyrus conquered the city of Babylon (Dan. 5).
3. In 538 B.C. he issued his Return Decree, allowing the Jews in his kingdom to return to Jerusalem and rebuild their temple (Ezra 1).
4. Persia was later defeated by the Greeks on various occasions. Two of these wars were significant ones:
   a. The Battle of Marathon in 490 B.C.
   b. The Battle of Arbela in 331 B.C. Alexander the Great totally crushed the Persians at this time. Some two centuries prior to this, Daniel the prophet had predicted its outcome (Dan. 8).
5. In A.D. 1921 a military leader, General Reza Khan, seized the government and did much to modernize the country.
6. In 1935 Persia changed its name to Iran.
7. In 1953 Mohammad Reza Pahlavi, commonly known as the Shah of Iran, came into power.
8. The Shah was driven from power and left Iran on January 16, 1979. He later died in Egypt.
9. An exiled fanatic, the Ayatollah Khomeini, returned to Iran from France on February 1, 1980, and became absolute dictator until his death in June 1989.

B. Considered currently

1. President: Hashemi Rafsanjani
2. Land area: 636,293 square miles
3. Population: 55,600,000
4. Capital: Teheran
5. Gross national product: $93.5 billion

C. Considered prophetically

We have already noted the rule of the Shah of Iran. From the moment he assumed power, the Shah became a staunch and steady friend of the Western world, especially the United States. At times during the troublesome postwar years his voice was the only friendly one coming from the Middle East. All this is well known.

But a problem was seen here in prophetical matters, for according to Ezekiel 35:5, in the last days, Persia (Iran) is to join Russia in an all-out attack upon Israel. In other words, the Scriptures predict Iran would become decidedly anti-West and pro-Communist during the tribulation. This, of course, began to be fulfilled with the tragic betrayal of the Shah by his Western friends (especially the U.S.) in 1979.

It is significant to observe that during the 1991 Persian Gulf War Russia and Iran moved a step closer to each other in their joint efforts to become mediators between the Allied armies and Iraq.

IRAQ (ancient Babylon)

A. Considered historically

1. The original home of man and the Garden of Eden was located in Babylon, between the Tigris and Euphrates rivers (see Gen. 2:10, 14).
2. This area witnessed the first human sin (Gen. 3).
3. It was here the first murder occurred (Gen. 4).
4. The first formal rebellion, the Tower of Babel, took place in this area (Gen. 11).
5. In 1760 B.C. Hammurabi conquered the Tigris-Euphrates Valley and made the city of Babylon, on the Euphrates River, his capital. This was the beginning of the old Babylonian kingdom.
6. In 605 B.C. Nebuchadnezzar defeated Egypt at the Battle of Carchemish (see Jer. 46).

7. Nebuchadnezzar laid siege to the city of Jerusalem on three occasions:
   a. In 605 B.C.—At this time he carried away into Babylon thousands of Jewish hostages, including Daniel (2 Chron. 36:6, 7; Dan. 1:1-3).
   b. In 597 B.C.—Again, he removed Jewish captives, including Ezekiel (2 Ki. 24:14-16).
   c. In 586 B.C.—On the third trip he burned the city and destroyed the Temple of Solomon (book of Lamentations).
8. Following his return, Nebuchadnezzar began extensive improvements on the city of Babylon.
   The king spake, and said, Is not this great Babylon, that I have built for the house of the kingdom by the might of my power, and for the honour of my majesty? (Dan. 4:30).
9. Babylon fell to the Persians in October 539 B.C.
10. Peter wrote his first epistle from Babylon around A.D. 65 (1 Pet. 5:13).
11. In 1920 it was placed under the control of the British.
12. It achieved independence in 1932 and became known as Iraq.
13. In 1979 Saddam Hussein became president.
14. On September 22, 1980, Iraq attacked Iran. A cease-fire went into effect in August 1988.
15. On August 2, 1990, Iraq invaded Kuwait, which led to the Persian Gulf War beginning on January 16, 1991.

B. Considered currently
   1. President: Saddam Hussein
   2. Land area: 167,920 square miles
   3. Population: 18,000,000
   4. Capital: Baghdad
   5. Gross national product: $34 billion

C. Considered prophetically
   Here we will ask and (hopefully) answer five basic questions concerning Iraq (ancient Babylon):
   1. Will the ancient city of Babylon be rebuilt? At least six biblical chapters strongly indicate this will indeed occur. These chapters are: Isaiah 13–14; Jeremiah 50–51; Revelation 17–18. The reason for holding this view centers

in various prophecies made concerning the city of Babylon that have yet to be fulfilled. Consider:

a. Ancient Babylon was never suddenly destroyed as predicted in Isaiah 13:19. Nebuchadnezzar's Babylon simply changed hands one night from the Babylonians to the Persians in a bloodless takeover (see Dan. 5).

b. The description of Babylon given by both Isaiah and Jeremiah is very similar to the one given by John in Revelation 18, where the apostle describes the fate of future Babylon. Note the comparisons:

   (1) This Babylon would become the narcotic of the nations (Jer. 51:7; Rev. 18:3, 9).

   (2) It would be abandoned by the righteous just prior to its destruction (Jer. 51:6, 45; Rev. 18:4).

   (3) Babylon would be destroyed by God himself. (Jer. 51:6, 55; Rev. 18:5).

   (4) This destruction would be sudden (Jer. 51:8; Rev. 18:10, 19).

   (5) This destruction would be by fire (Isa. 13:19; Jer. 51:58; Rev. 18:8, 9, 18).

   (6) It would never be inhabited following this destruction (Jer. 51:26; Rev. 18:23).

   Note: None of the above held true concerning Nebuchadnezzar's Babylon. To the contrary (in regards to point 6), archaeological discoveries have shown that bricks and stones from ancient Babylon have been reused for building purposes!

c. Babylon is said to be destroyed during the day of the Lord, an Old Testament term referring to the great tribulation (Isa. 13:9-13).

d. Isaiah 14 predicts the millennium will follow Babylon's destruction (Isa. 14:4-7).

2. Does one of Zechariah's visions relate to the rebuilding of Babylon?

Zechariah, the Old Testament prophet, saw a flying sin-filled bushel basket with a woman inside. An angel told him she represented the ultimate in wickedness. Upon being asked by the prophet concerning its destination, the angel replied:

And he said unto me, To build it an house in the land of Shinar:

and it shall be established, and set there upon her own base
(Zech. 5:11).

Note two significant phrases in this vision:

a. A wicked woman (Zech. 5:7, 8). Compare this with
Revelation 17:

And the woman was arrayed in purple and scarlet colour,
and decked with gold and precious stones and pearls, having
a golden cup in her hand full of abominations and filthiness
of her fornication: And upon her forehead was a name
written, MYSTERY, BABYLON THE GREAT, THE
MOTHER OF HARLOTS AND ABOMINATIONS
OF THE EARTH (Rev. 17:4, 5).

b. The land of Shinar (Zech. 5:11). Compare this with
Genesis 11:

And the whole earth was of one language, and of one speech.
And it came to pass, as they journeyed from the east, that
they found a plain in the land of Shinar; and they dwelt there
(Gen. 11:1, 2).

3. Who will rebuild future Babylon and for what reason? The
antichrist will rebuild it; for this city, which once served as
Satan's headquarters, will again become his capital.

4. How will this incredible project be financed? The
present-day oil resource of the Middle East in billions of
barrels are as follows:

a. Saudi Arabia—225 billion
b. Iraq—100 billion
c. United Arab Emirates—98.1 billion
d. Kuwait—94.5 billion
e. Iran—92.9 billion

This totals 610.5 billion barrels. At the current market
price of approximately $25 a barrel, the combined oil
wealth of the Middle East is about $15.3 trillion!

Note: This figure is more than three times the gross
national product of the United States!

If one assumes the antichrist gains control of the Middle
East (plus the wealth of the Western nations), the
rebuilding of Babylon will present no financial problem
whatsoever!

5. Is there a present-day interest in the rebuilding of Babylon?

"It is a cloudless September summer night, and the moon casts its shining image on the banks of the gentle Euphrates River. Thousands of guests and dignitaries walk by torch light to Babylon's Procession Street and enter the city from the north. Instructed to line the streets along the massive walls, the guests obediently follow orders. When the audience is in place, the dark-eyed man in charge nods, and the procession begins.

Rows and rows of soldiers parade in, dressed in Babylonian tunics and carrying swords, spears, and shields. Interspersed among the ranks of soldiers are groups of musicians playing harps, horns, and drums. Clusters of children carry palm branches, and runners bear bowls of incense. Then come soldiers and still more soldiers in a seemingly endless line of men and weapons. After the procession, the guests attend a ceremony paying tribute to Ishtar, the mother goddess of Babylon.

Have I just described a scene of pagan worship from the time of Daniel? Perhaps, but it is also exactly what I witnessed when I returned to Babylon in 1988 for the second International Babylon Festival held under the patronage of Saddam Hussein" (Charles Dyer, *The Rise of Babylon*, Wheaton, Ill.: Tyndale House, pp. 16-17).

By the end of 1990, Saddam Hussein had spent nearly one-half billion dollars on restoring ancient Babylon. Over 60 million bricks have been laid. Many buildings are now in place; including the Marduk Gate, Greek Theater, Hammurabi Museum, Nebuchadnezzar's Museum, Ishtar Temple, etc.

EGYPT

A. Considered historically
  1. The period from 3100 B.C. to the reign of Alexander the Great (332 B.C.) was divided politically into thirty dynasties.
  2. Egypt was first mentioned by scripture in Genesis 12:10, at which time Abraham and Sarah went there during a famine (2090 B.C.).

3. Joseph was sold into Egyptian slavery (1897 B.C.; see Gen. 37:28).
4. Some twenty-two years later (1875 B.C.), Jacob and his entire family moved into Egypt (Gen. 46:6).
5. Moses was born in Egypt (1525 B.C.; see Ex. 2:2).
6. Moses later led Israel out of Egypt (1445 B.C.; see Ex. 12:36).
7. Babylon defeated Egypt (605 B.C.; see Jer. 46:2).
8. Persia conquered Egypt in 525 B.C.
9. Alexander occupied Egypt in 332 B.C.
10. From A.D. 641–1517 various Arab caliphs ruled Egypt.
11. Napoleon's armies controlled Egypt from 1798 to 1801.
12. Egypt became an independent state on February 28, 1922.
13. Egypt and Israel have fought four wars since 1948:
    a. The War of Independence (May 15, 1948, to Oct. 24, 1949)
    b. The Sinai War (Oct. 29, 1956, to Nov. 5, 1956)
    c. The Six-Day War (June 5, 1967, to June 10, 1967)
    d. The Yom Kippur War (Oct. 6, 1973, to Oct. 25, 1973)

B. Considered currently
   1. President: Hosni Mubarak
   2. Land area: 389,900 square miles
   3. Population: 54,700,000
   4. Capital: Cairo
   5. Gross national product: $26.6 billion

C. Considered prophetically

"Egypt is prominent not only in the history of ancient Israel, but in the end times as well. Of the 750 references to Egypt (*Mizraim* in the Hebrew), more than 50 are prophetic" (S. Maxwell Coder, *The Final Chapter*, Wheaton, Ill.: Tyndale House, 1984, p.26).

There are three significant Old Testament passages that describe the future role Egypt will play. These are: Isaiah 19:16-25; Ezekiel 30:1-19; Daniel 11:40-43. In essence, these verses predict the divine chastening and converting of Egypt.
   1. The chastening of Egypt.
      For the day is near, even the day of the Lord is near, a cloudy day; it shall be the time of the heathen. And the sword shall come upon Egypt (Ezek. 30:3, 4).

338

Note the expression "the day of the Lord." In the Old Testament this is almost always a reference to the coming great tribulation!

a. Egypt will live in fear of the nation Israel.

And the land of Judah shall be a terror unto Egypt, every one that maketh mention thereof shall be afraid in himself, because of the counsel of the Lord of hosts, which he hath determined against it (Isa. 19:17).

This, of course, has never happened historically. Both the Sinai and Six-Day wars may have served as a foreshadow of this future fear. To say the least, Egypt has a healthy respect for Israel's military power today! This prophetical fear may be based on the antichrist's seven-year peace treaty with Israel (Dan. 9:27).

b. Egypt may suffer the drying up of both the Nile River and the Suez Canal (Isa. 19:5, 6; Ezek. 30:12).

c. Egypt will join forces with Russia in a joint attack against both Israel and the Western (antichrist) leader (Dan. 11:40).

d. Egypt will be soundly defeated by the antichrist (Dan. 11:42).

e. Egypt will be occupied and stripped of its riches by the antichrist (Dan. 11:43).

2. The converting of Egypt

Isaiah 19:18-26 presents one of the greatest and most glorious examples of the manifold grace of God in all the Bible; namely, the ultimate salvation of both Egypt and Assyria (modern Iraq and Iran)!

a. Through her sufferings Egypt will come to know the Lord.

And it shall be for a sign and for a witness unto the Lord of hosts in the land of Egypt: for they shall cry unto the Lord because of the oppressors, and he shall send them a saviour, and a great one, and he shall deliver them. . . . And the Lord shall be known to Egypt, and the Egyptians shall know the Lord in that day, and shall do sacrifice and oblation; yea, they shall vow a vow unto the Lord, and perform it (Isa. 19:20, 22).

b. Egypt will "speak the language of Canaan" (Isa. 19:18).

Note: The prophet Zephaniah may have been referring to this when he wrote:

For then will I turn to the people a pure language, that they may all call upon the name of the Lord, to serve him with one consent." (Zeph. 3:9).

The *New Scofield Bible* comments:

"The prophet is not foretelling a universal language, as though to reverse the consequences of Babel, but the conversion of the nations, a spiritual transformation readily discernible in their purified speech" (Oxford University Press, 1967, p. 959).

c. There will be an altar to God in the center of Egypt and a monument to him at its border (Isa. 19:19).

d. Egypt will offer sacrifices to God; the Egyptians will make promises to God and keep them (Isa. 19:21).

e. Egypt and Assyria (Iraq and Iran) will be connected by a highway, allowing all the peoples to move freely back and forth!

In that day shall there be a highway out of Egypt to Assyria, and the Assyrian shall come into Egypt, and the Egyptian into Assyria, and the Egyptians shall serve with the Assyrians. In that day shall Israel be the third with Egypt and with Assyria, even a blessing in the midst of the land: Whom the Lord of hosts shall bless, saying, Blessed be Egypt my people, and Assyria the work of my hands, and Israel mine inheritance (Isa. 19:23-25).

ISRAEL

A. Considered historically
   1. 2090 B.C.—Conversion and call of Abraham (Gen. 12:1-3).
   2. April 1445 B.C.—Moses led Israel out of Egypt (Ex. 12:51).
   3. June 1445 B.C.—The giving of the Law at Sinai (Ex. 20).
   4. April 1444 B.C.—Completion of the Tabernacle (Ex. 40).
   5. August 1444 B.C.—Refusal of Israel to enter the land (Num. 14).
   6. 1444–1405 B.C.—Israel wandered in the Wilderness (Num. 15—Deut. 34).
   7. April 1404 B.C.—Israel crossed Jordan and entered Canaan (Josh. 3).
   8. 1051 B.C.—Beginning of Saul's reign (1 Sam. 10).

9. 1011 B.C.—Beginning of David's reign (2 Sam. 2).
10. 1005 B.C.—Israel made Jerusalem its capital (2 Sam 5:6, 7).
11. 971 B.C.—Beginning of Solomon's reign (1 Ki. 1:39).
12. October 959 B.C.—Completion of the First Temple (1 Ki. 6:38).
13. 931 B.C.—Israel's tragic civil war (1 Ki. 12).
14. 721 B.C.—Capture of northern ten tribes by the Assyrians (2 Ki. 17).
15. 586 B.C.—Capture of the southern two tribes by the Babylonians. Jerusalem is burned and the First Temple is destroyed (2 Ki. 24).
16. 536 B.C.—Return of the Jews from captivity to Jerusalem (Ezra 1).
17. 516 B.C.—Completion of the Second Temple (Ezra 6:15).
18. 430 B.C.—Completion of the Old Testament books (Malachi).
19. A.D. 70—Destruction of Jerusalem and the Second Temple by the Romans (Mt. 24:1, 2).
20. A.D. 500—Completion of the Talmud.
21. 1095—First European Crusade to free Jerusalem.
22. 1517—Beginning of 400-year Turkish reign over Palestine.
23. 1880—Revival of the Hebrew language.
24. 1882—Beginning of the First Aliyah (modern return of the Jews to Palestine).
25. 1897—The Zionist movement founded in Basel, Switzerland, by Theodor Herzl.
26. November 2, 1917—Great Britain issued the Balfour Declaration, advocating a national homeland for the Jews.
27. December 11, 1917—British general Sir Edmund Allenby liberated Jerusalem from the Turks.
28. 1947—Discovery of the Dead Sea Scrolls.
29. May 14, 1948—Israel signed its Declaration of Independence.
30. May 11, 1949—Israel was voted into the United Nations.
31. January 1, 1950—Jerusalem became Israel's capital.
32. 1953—Israel entered the atomic age.
33. June 7, 1967—Israel gained possession of the Temple Mount.

B. Considered currently
   1. Prime Minister: Yitzhak Shamir

2. Land area: 8,020 square miles
3. Population: 4,371,478
4. Capital: Jerusalem
5. Gross national product: $36 billion

C. Considered prophetically

Now learn a parable of the fig tree; When his branch is yet tender, and putteth forth leaves, ye know that summer is nigh: So likewise ye, when ye shall see all these things, know that it is near, even at the doors. Verily I say unto you, This generation shall not pass, till all these things be fulfilled (Mt. 24:32-34).

Jesus related this parable to answer his disciples' question as to when he would come again (see Mt. 24:3). Inasmuch as the fig tree (Israel) began bearing its leaves on May 14, 1948, it may be our Lord was saying here that the final generation prior to the Second Advent would be the one born that very year! Whatever the case, the following represents a brief overview pertaining to Israel and the future:

1. Israel and the great tribulation (Mt. 24:21)
   a. The mass return of the Jews from all over the world to the land of Israel (Deut. 30:3; Isa. 43:6; Ezek. 34:11-13; 37:1-14).

   For I will take you from among the heathen, and gather you out of all countries, and will bring you into your own land (Ezek. 36:24).

   As recently as 125 years ago it would have been difficult to locate even 50,000 Jewish people in the entire land of Palestine. Today, however, there are nearly 4 million Jews who have returned from over 100 nations to the land of their forefathers!

   b. The Western leader's (antichrist's) seven-year peace covenant with Israel (Isa. 28:18; Dan. 9:27).
   c. The rebuilding of the Third Temple (Dan. 9:27; Mt. 24:15; 2 Thess. 2:3, 4; Rev. 11:1).

   Two recent and remarkable news articles illustrate the growing desire among a number of Israelis concerning the rebuilding of the Third Temple:

   "Jerusalem—Rabbi Yisrael Ariel sees himself as a dreamer, but most Israelis would not be so generous.
   Along with a handful of other rigorously observant

Jews, Rabbi Ariel is dedicating himself to the rebuilding of the temple of Herod on the man-made plateau the Jews call the Temple Mount.

The rabbi's organization, called the Temple Institute, has made and displayed a variety of ornaments and furnishings similar to those that once adorned the temple and its priests: a silver menorah, trumpets, goblets, ritual slaughtering knives, priestly garments and so on.

The idea is to be sure all the accessories are ready for use when the new temple is completed. Like many Jews, members of the Temple Institute dream of that day. But they don't have any clear ideas about how it will be brought about.

'We're promised by the prophets of Israel that the temple will be rebuilt,' Ariel said.

During six years of research, the institute has reconstructed 38 of the ritual implements that will be required when Temple sacrifices are restored: it will complete the other 65 items as funds permit. A museum of the completed pieces has drawn 10,000 visitors during the current holy days. In addition to such items as trumpets, lyres and lots, the institute is preparing vestments for the priests-in-waiting. According to Scripture, the clothing must be painstakingly made with flax spun by hand into six-stranded threads.

One difficulty is the requirement (as in Numbers 19:1-10) that priests purify their bodies with the cremated ashes of an unblemished red heifer before they enter the Temple. Following a go-ahead from the Chief Rabbinate, institute operatives spent two weeks in August scouting Europe for heifer embryos that will shortly be implanted into cows at an Israeli cattle ranch.

Two Talmudic schools located near the Western (Wailing) Wall are teaching nearly 200 students the elaborate details of Temple service. Other groups are researching the family lines of Jewish priests who alone may conduct sacrifices. Next year an organizing convention will be held for those who believe themselves to be of priestly descent. Former Chief

Rabbi, Shlomo Goren, who heads another Temple Mount organization, believes his research has fixed the location of the ancient Holy of Holies so that Jews can enter the Mount without sacrilege. He insists, 'I cannot leave this world without assuring that Jews will once again pray on the Mount.'

A 1983 newspaper poll showed that a surprising 18.3% of Israelis thought it was time to rebuild; a mere 3% wanted to wait for the Messiah" (*New York Times*, April 10, 1989; *Time*, October 16, 1989, pp. 64-65).

    d. The conversion and call of 144,000 Jewish evangelists; 12,000 from each tribe (Rev. 7:1-4; Mt. 24:14).

    e. The Russian invasion into Israel (Ezek. 38–39).

    f. The antichrist breaks his covenant with Israel, resulting in a worldwide persecution for that nation (Dan. 9:27; 12:1, 11; Zech. 11:16; Matt. 24:15, 21; Rev. 12:13).

    g. Israel's recognition of Jesus as her Messiah.
And I will pour upon the house of David, and upon the inhabitants of Jerusalem, the spirit of grace and of supplications: and they shall look upon me whom they have pierced, and they shall mourn for him, as one mourneth for his only son, and shall be in bitterness for him, as one that is in bitterness for his firstborn (Zech. 12:10).

    h. The regenerating, restoring, and regathering of Israel.
And I will cleanse them from all their iniquity, whereby they have sinned against me; and I will pardon all their iniquities, whereby they have sinned, and whereby they have transgressed against me (Jer. 33:8).
Therefore say, Thus saith the Lord God; I will even gather you from the people, and assemble you out of the countries where ye have been scattered, and I will give you the land of Israel (Ezek. 11:17).

2. Israel and the glorious millennium
    a. Israel to become God's witnesses (Isa. 44:8; 61:6).
    b. Jesus to rule from Jerusalem with a rod of iron (Isa. 2:3; 11:4).
    c. Palestine to become greatly enlarged and changed (Isa. 26:15).
    d. A river to flow east-west from the Mount of Olives into

     both the Mediterranean and Dead seas (Ezek. 47:8, 9, 12; Zech. 14:4, 8, 10).

  e. Jerusalem to become the worship center of the world (Isa. 2:2, 3; Mic. 4:1).

Closing thought:

Having heard the tale told by the trees, one final question may be asked: Does anything have to happen before the Rapture can take place? (See 1 Thess. 4:13-18.) The amazing answer is . . . *yes!* But it has nothing to do with current events in Russia, Iraq, or even Israel! Rather, it involves the present-day ministry of the Holy Spirit in preparing a body and bride (the church) for the Head and Bridegroom (Christ). (See 1 Cor. 12:12, 13; Eph. 5:25-27; Rev. 19:7.)

Thus the conversion of the last repenting sinner in the church age will serve to complete the body, perfect the bride, and trigger the return of Christ! *This could happen today!*